Blood, Mud, and Oil Paint

FOREIGN MILITARY STUDIES

History is replete with examples of notable military campaigns and exceptional military leaders and theorists. Military professionals and students of the art and science of war cannot afford to ignore these sources of knowledge or limit their studies to the history of the U.S. armed forces. This series features original works, translations, and reprints of classics outside the American canon that promote a deeper understanding of international military theory and practice.

SERIES EDITOR: Joseph Craig

An AUSA Book

Blood, Mud, and Oil Paint

THE REMARKABLE YEAR THAT MADE WINSTON CHURCHILL

J. FURMAN DANIEL III

Copyright © 2024 by The University Press of Kentucky

Scholarly publisher for the Commonwealth, serving Bellarmine University, Berea College, Centre College of Kentucky, Eastern Kentucky University, The Filson Historical Society, Georgetown College, Kentucky Historical Society, Kentucky State University, Morehead State University, Murray State University, Northern Kentucky University, Spalding University, Transylvania University, University of Kentucky, University of Louisville, University of Pikeville, and Western Kentucky University.
All rights reserved.

Editorial and Sales Offices: The University Press of Kentucky
663 South Limestone Street, Lexington, Kentucky 40508-4008
www.kentuckypress.com

For quotes reproduced from the speeches, works, and writings of Winston S. Churchill: Reproduced with permission of Curtis Brown, London on behalf of The Estate of Winston S. Churchill © The Estate of Winston S. Churchill.

Library of Congress Cataloging-in-Publication Data

Names: Daniel, J. Furman, III, author.
Title: Blood, mud, and oil paint : the remarkable year that made Winston Churchill / J. Furman Daniel III.
Other titles: Remarkable year that made Winston Churchill
Description: Lexington, Kentucky : University Press of Kentucky, [2024] | Series: Foreign military studies | Includes bibliographical references and index.
Identifiers: LCCN 2024020294 | ISBN 9781985901100 (hardcover) | ISBN 9781985901117 (paperback) | ISBN 9781985901131 (pdf) | ISBN 9781985901148 (epub)
Subjects: LCSH: Churchill, Winston, 1874-1965—Psychology. | Churchill, Winston, 1874-1965—Military leadership. | Statesmen—Great Britain—Biography. | Prime ministers—Great Britain—Biography. | Painters—Great Britain—Biography. | World War, 1914-1918—Campaigns—Turkey—Gallipoli Peninsula. | Great Britain—Politics and government—1910-1936. | Comebacks.
Classification: LCC DA566.9.C5 D34 2024 | DDC 940.53092 [B]—dc23/eng/20240513
LC record available at https://lccn.loc.gov/2024020294

This book is printed on acid-free paper meeting the requirements of the American National Standard for Permanence in Paper for Printed Library Materials.

Manufactured in the United States of America.

To Claudia for her Churchillian courage.

Contents

Introduction: Churchill's Life of Failure and Redemption   1
1. The Dardanelles Disaster: Churchill Is Finished   9
2. The Political Outcast: Churchill Turns to Painting   50
3. The Hellish Landscape: Churchill Rejoins the Army   101
4. The Passionate Warrior: Churchill Takes Command   131
5. The Uncertain Future: Churchill Returns to Politics   175
Conclusion: Churchill's Greatest Failure   191

Acknowledgments   209
Notes   211
Index   259

Illustrations follow page   130

Introduction

Churchill's Life of Failure and Redemption

In May 1940, Britain faced destruction and darkness, but the weather was glorious. Despite news of defeats in Norway, a surprise German attack on France and the Low Countries, and rumors of political upheaval, almost everybody could agree that the sunshine and bright blue skies were the best in living memory. The beautiful weather would continue throughout summer and into fall and would be an easy source of conversation and comfort in the uncertain weeks ahead.[1]

In this dire moment, a sixty-five-year-old man, who had been dismissed as a failure countless times, rode in a limousine to meet the king. The man who had faced gunfire on four continents, served in numerous government offices, and become famous for his firmness of character and grit, was nervous. Winston Churchill was about to fulfill his lifelong dream of becoming prime minister and leading his nation in the greatest conflict of modern history, yet he feared that it might be too late.[2]

Despite his well-founded fears, Churchill remained calm, even a bit coy, when he met with King George VI. Churchill knew that the king had preferred his rival, Lord Halifax, for the office, but that Halifax had declined. More importantly, the king did not trust Churchill. For most of the past four decades, he had been seen as something of a show-off and a troublemaker, and in 1936, he had backed George's brother Edward's claim to the throne during the Abdication Crisis. Now, Churchill would rely on his gift for humor and flair for the melodramatic to lighten the mood.

2   BLOOD, MUD, AND OIL PAINT

After staring at Churchill for a moment, the king asked, "I suppose you don't know why I have sent for you?" Adopting his tone, Churchill replied, "Sir, I simply couldn't imagine why." This broke the tension and produced a laugh from the monarch, who responded, "I want to ask you to form a government." This was the moment Churchill had worked toward for his entire adult life, and he accepted it simply: "I said I would certainly do so."[3]

Churchill immediately threw himself into his job as prime minister. He traveled back to his office at the Admiralty, contacted key members of his proposed coalition government, spoke with the outgoing prime minister, Neville Chamberlain, and prepared to submit a list of cabinet members to the king for his approval. Keenly aware of the gargantuan task that lay ahead, he worked feverishly until about three o'clock the next morning. Churchill had a gift for quickly falling into deep sleep, and despite his unusual circumstances, this time was no different. As he later described:

> I went to bed at about 3 a.m. I was conscious of a profound sense of relief. At last I had the authority to give directions over the whole scene. I felt as if I was walking with destiny, and that all my past life had been but a preparation for this hour and for this trial. Ten years in the political wilderness had freed me from ordinary party antagonisms. My warnings over the last six years had been so numerous, so detailed, and were now so terribly vindicated, that no one could gainsay me. I could not be reproached for making the war or with want of preparation for it. I thought I knew a great deal about it all, and I was sure I should not fail. Therefore, although impatient for the morning, I slept soundly and had no need for cheering dreams. Facts are better than dreams.[4]

After a few hours of restorative sleep, Churchill rose, ready to face the colossal task ahead of him.

While the dramatic story is typical of Churchill's self-serving braggadocio, this quote from *The Gathering Storm* contains an element of truth.[5] In his own mind, at least, Churchill *had* been preparing for the job his entire life, and it seems likely that he *did* feel a sense of calm to finally be able to conduct the war as he saw fit.[6] Yet, despite Churchill's confidence, it is important to remember that most of the British ruling elite and many of the common people were less certain. In fact, the Churchill of 1940 was better known for his failures and his rhetorical bombast than for his abilities as a leader.[7]

With the benefit of hindsight, Churchill's bravado in the closing paragraphs of *The Gathering Storm*, his claim that he had been preparing to lead Great Britain during World War II for his entire adult life, seems entirely justified. In terms of military qualifications, he had received a solid military education at Sandhurst,[8] fought in and observed conflicts across the globe,[9] developed well-formed views about the character and conduct of modern war, and been a civilian leader of the Admiralty during two global conflicts.[10] His political qualifications were similarly impressive. He had been a public hero, a best-selling author, a diplomat, and a member of Parliament (MP) for two political parties and had served in the majority and in the opposition and held eight major cabinet positions.[11] He had friends across the world in the press, in finance, in the academy and arts, and in each of the major political parties.

Although this résumé was impressive, it only tells part of the story—Churchill's character had been shaped by failure. In fact, before his triumph in World War II, Churchill had failed frequently, publicly, and catastrophically.[12] Indeed, any one of his troubles—including academics, the early death of his father, financial stress and indebtedness, imprisonment by the Boers, political defeats and frustrations with his parties' platforms, the Dardanelles, the Wilderness Years, the Great Depression, the gold standard, India, the Abdication Crisis, and his frustrations over Appeasement—could have destroyed his life or derailed his career.[13] Instead, these challenges developed character, strength of spirit, empathy, and perspective, which he would later apply to great success.

Understanding Winston Churchill's Most Critical Year, May 1915–May 1916

To better understand how Churchill was shaped by failure, this book examines the most difficult period of his entire life: the twelve-month period from May 1915 to May 1916. During this tumultuous year, Churchill faced defeat and despair on almost every front. He was blamed for the British failures at the Dardanelles, his attempts to influence policy were ignored, his finances were strained, and he resigned from office. With his political career in tatters, he served bravely on the western front but was denied a promotion to higher command. In a rash attempt to topple the Asquith government, he made a disastrous speech on naval policy that caused many to question his sanity. For good reason, Winston Churchill was believed to be finished as a major player in British politics.

Before that year, Winston Churchill had never experienced a significant political defeat.[14] Indeed, since 1900 when he had won his first seat in Parliament at the tender age of twenty-five, his rise had been meteoric. Yet Churchill's rapid ascent and strong personality had come at a cost: many were suspicious and jealous of his success. In the words of his lifelong friend Violet Bonham Carter, who was the daughter of Prime Minister H. H. Asquith and privy to many of the inner workings of the British government, the general attitude toward Churchill was, "at best, one of expectant interest, curiosity, and tolerant amusement; at worst, one of mistrust and acid reprobation. . . . To take him down a peg or even several pegs was not only a pleasure but a duty."[15]

While he had offended many of his contemporaries with his seemingly undeserved success, braggadocio, open desire for higher office, and willingness to cross the floor to the Liberals, this failure was different.

Until his dismissal from the Admiralty, he had never failed. He was young and ambitious, bubbling over with ideas and plans, and now his career suddenly came crashing down. According to many of his critics, this failure proved what they had warned about for years—that Winston Churchill was impetuous, unpredictable, and dangerous. Many Tory MPs had not forgotten his switching parties and abandoning them, and now they were glad that this turncoat had gotten what he deserved. Others made comparisons to his father, Lord Randolph Churchill. Randolph had enjoyed a similarly rapid rise but had recklessly thrown his career away and suffered from the debilitating effects of a strange disease (quite possibly syphilis) that destroyed his once-brilliant mind and oratorical powers. For those in search of a useful analogy to explain Winston's demise, the narrative seemed too good to resist, and his immaturity, self-centeredness, and arrogance only seemed to prove the point.[16]

From Churchill's perspective, his dismissal from the Admiralty was made even crueler because he believed that he had been betrayed by his mentor and friend, Prime Minister H. H. Asquith.[17] While there was an element of truth to this, both the political situation and Asquith's motives were incredibly complex. Indeed, frustration over the conduct of the war had been mounting for months. The Dardanelles Campaign's failure to achieve rapid results, the Shell Crisis, and the resignation of Lord Fisher as First Sea Lord combined to make Asquith's political situation increasingly tenuous. The prime minister's political rivals sensed an opportunity to force him to form a coalition government, and as a condition for their support, they insisted that Churchill be removed from the Admiralty.[18] Desperate to remain in power, Asquith quickly cast Churchill aside as First Lord and invited many of his opponents into his newly formed coalition. While Churchill remained in the cabinet as the chancellor of the Duchy of Lancaster, this was a largely ceremonial office with little power. In this much-reduced capacity, he repeatedly attempted to insert himself into the debates regarding the conduct of the war but quickly found that he was almost totally powerless to shape policy. His frustrations grew as he could see the inner workings of the cabinet and argue passionately but do almost nothing to avoid further defeat and death.

During much of that year, Churchill was at a psychological and spiritual low point. His friends and loved ones noted his dark and depressive moods. At times his outlook brightened as he developed new strategies for how the Allies could achieve victory, but the melancholy returned when these plans came to naught. Throughout his life, he struggled with the "Black Dog" of depression, but this was far worse than anything he had experienced before. Decades later, his wife, Clementine, would confide that the period immediately after Churchill's fall from the Admiralty was the hardest period in their entire time together, noting, "I thought he would never get over the Dardanelles; I thought he would die of grief."[19] Churchill's daughter Sarah made a similar assessment: "This remains to this day one of the most controversial of British military decisions. It was to haunt him to the end of his life."[20] For a man who experienced battle, imprisonment, health scares, financial ruin, and a decade of political irrelevance known universally as the Wilderness Years, these are very powerful statements indeed as to how low and depressed he was during this period.

In addition to engendering his deep personal sense of loss and defeat, the Dardanelles Campaign would also cast a long shadow on Churchill's political life. While the failure at the Dardanelles was the product of many hands, the ambitious young First Lord quickly became the scapegoat for one of the greatest disasters in British military history.[21] The criticism about Churchill's role in the Dardanelles was so enduring in large part because it fit into a larger belief that he was a wild schemer, a narrative well established prior to the Great War.²² The failures at the Dardanelles seemed to prove that these fears had been true all along, and for the next two decades, it became a common trope for politicians to dismiss his ideas by simply noting that he was dangerous and unstable.

Unlike many of Churchill's other controversies, the Dardanelles disaster had considerable staying power. Almost a year after his departure from the Admiralty, while giving a speech on the desperate need for conscription, Churchill first heard the taunt, "What about the Dardanelles?" from an Irish Nationalist MP who did not wish for Irishmen to be included in the proposed draft. While Churchill was typically able to accept heckling or respond with a witty counterpunch, he was clearly upset by this taunt.²³ Sensing that it was an effective means to discredit and distract Churchill, his rivals would rely on this quip for decades to come.²⁴ Being attacked in this manner clearly had a powerful effect on him. For example, when giving an election speech in 1923, he responded angrily, "What do you know about the Dardanelles? The Dardanelles might have saved millions of lives. Don't imagine I am running away from the Dardanelles. I glory in it."²⁵

For the remainder of his life, Churchill did his best to cast the Dardanelles not as a defeat but as proof of his military genius.²⁶ In his multivolume *The World Crisis*, Churchill cast the Dardanelles as one of the few original strategic plans of the entire war. It leveraged Britain's sea power and allowed for the restoration of initiative and movement. If properly executed, he argued, it would have knocked the Ottoman Empire out of the war, prevented the collapse of Czarist Russia, shortened the conflict by months, and saved millions of lives.²⁷

Churchill's impassioned arguments did little to persuade his rivals, who continued to invoke the Dardanelles as a political weapon. For example, in 1927, the Conservative prime minister Stanley Baldwin and Churchill clashed over the proposed budget. Fellow Conservative rival Neville Chamberlain went behind his back to warn others that Churchill was plotting to provoke a crisis and become prime minister himself. Knowing that the Dardanelles analogy still had power, Chamberlain warned, "He [Churchill] has nothing worked out but he gets so enamoured with his ideas that he won't listen to difficulties or wait until plans have been made to get over them. It's like Gallipoli again."²⁸ While the budget crisis was resolved precisely because Churchill listened to the advice of others and compromised, his failure at the Dardanelles continued to cast a dark shadow on his legacy.[29] As late as 1939, private citizens wrote letters to newspaper editors claiming that the Dardanelles was proof that Churchill was untrustworthy and should not be included in Chamberlain's war cabinet.[30]

Yet, somehow, Churchill was able to overcome this year of failures, persevere, and emerge stronger.

Five Life-Changing Gifts

During this remarkable year, Churchill benefited from failure in five ways that were crucial for his future success: painting, friendships, personal growth, time and distance, and insights on modern war. Painting gave him a new creative outlet for his frustrations. Friends provided bonhomie, perspective, and political alliances in the years ahead. Personal growth helped transform him from an immature and naive upstart to a wiser and more seasoned public figure. Time and distance allowed him to avoid many of the bitter divisions that led to the collapse of the Asquith government and allowed him to reinvent himself politically. Insights on modern war gave him a new understanding of tanks, artillery, airpower, aircraft carriers, and military leadership. In sum, many of the skills that made him an effective leader in later years were developed as a response to this bitter defeat.

This book argues that this year of failure and frustration was critical for Winston Churchill's later success. The first chapter will set the stage for the narrative by documenting one of Churchill's biggest failures, the Dardanelles Campaign. While not intended to be an authoritative account of the fighting, Churchill's role in planning the operations, or the political fallout from the disaster, this chapter will briefly describe these events and demonstrate how they led to Churchill's spectacular fall. The chapter will end with Churchill accepting the position of the chancellor of the Duchy of Lancaster, a job that he believed was beneath him.[31]

The second chapter chronicles a period of intense political frustration for Churchill spanning from May to November 1915. During this time, Churchill was at a personal and professional low point, and, out of desperation, he began to paint. The chapter will show how that painting quickly became a means for him to find the mental and spiritual balance he needed to face an uncertain future. This chapter concludes with Churchill's decision to depart the comforts of London for the trenches of the western front.

The third and fourth chapters document Churchill's time as a soldier on the western front. Chapter 3 covers his time with the Grenadier Guards, spanning November 1915–January 1916, and chapter 4 examines the period from January 1916 to May 1916 when he commanded the 6th Battalion of the Royal Scots Fusiliers. These chapters describe how he found redemption and new perspectives in the unlikely setting of the trenches. They argue that these intense few months were critical for the "escaped scapegoat" because they allowed him to avoid the politics of London, demonstrate his courage, and gain insight about modern warfare and the plight of common soldiers.

The final chapter focuses on Churchill's return to politics in May 1916. It argues that after a year of painting, thinking, and serving in the trenches, Churchill was ready to reenter the political fray with a renewed energy, perspective, and sense of purpose. While he had many trying days ahead, he now had a means of reviving his tarnished reputation and applying his hard-won lessons of the previous year. This completes the cycle of failure, rebirth, and redemption and shows how Churchill was able to begin his journey back to political relevance.

The conclusion assesses what Churchill gained during that tumultuous year. It reemphasizes the original thesis that Churchill was continually able to reinvent himself in times of failure and discusses how painting, friendships, personal growth, time and distance, and insights on modern war were essential elements for his revival and future triumphs. Ultimately, it concludes where this book began—in 1940.

Churchill could not have succeeded in 1940 had he not failed in 1915.

1

The Dardanelles Disaster
Churchill Is Finished

The Dardanelles Campaign was an unmitigated disaster for Great Britain. Although originally conceived as a minor operation in a secondary theater, it was a massive campaign with profound military and political consequences.[1] It pitted vast empires against each other. It was fought above and under the seas, in salt lakes, on beaches, in gullies, on rocky hills, and in the skies. It resulted in the collapse of Great Britain's last Liberal government, the death and wounding of over a quarter of a million men, the loss of eight capital ships, the straining of relations between the empire and the Commonwealth nations, the creation of modern Turkey, and the meteoric rise of Mustafa Kemal.[2]

The Dardanelles Campaign also very nearly destroyed the career of Winston S. Churchill. It set into motion a series of events that would force him to resign his position as First Lord of the Admiralty, become a politically marginalized scapegoat, break with his mentor H. H. Asquith, seek redemption as an officer in the trenches of the western front, and cause many to question his sanity. Although Churchill would ultimately prevail, at the time it was reasonable to conclude that he was finished as a major political figure. Years later, Churchill's wife, Clementine, would claim that of all his travails, the Dardanelles was the most difficult to endure. She admitted candidly, "The Dardanelles. I thought it would break his heart."[3]

Ironically, the campaign that nearly destroyed Churchill's reputation and career was not originally his idea. While Churchill had dreamed of employing the Royal Navy to win a decisive victory since the opening days of the war, he had been frustrated by the fact that the German High Seas Fleet had largely remained in port and avoided direct conflict with their more powerful British foes. Given this absence of action and the increasing public pressure to act, Churchill and his staff had considered multiple options for amphibious operations against Germany but rejected each as impractical. Despite the challenges of amphibious operations and the resistance from the professionals at the Admiralty, Churchill continued to dream. He favored strikes against the German island of Borkum rather than Gallipoli.[4] He believed that the capture of this island would deny the Germans the use of the Kiel Canal, be a forward base for the invasion of northern Germany, and force the High Seas Fleet to fight a decisive battle with the more powerful Royal Navy. While Churchill held romantic views of the Middle East and wanted to destroy the Ottoman Empire, a campaign against the Dardanelles was simply not his priority—until outside events intervened.

During the final days of 1914, while Churchill schemed about the capture of this obscure German island, Russia was in dire peril. Russia had suffered massive defeats during the opening months of the war at the battles of Tannenberg and the Masurian Lakes but had avoided collapse and remained in the war.[5] However, Russia's position continued to be fragile, and it suffered further shock on October 29 when the Ottoman Empire launched a series of surprise attacks against its bases on the Black Sea. These surprise attacks were particularly disturbing for Churchill and the Admiralty because they were conducted by the former German warships *Goeben* and *Breslau*.[6] These two vessels had evaded British warships in the Mediterranean during the opening days of the war, fled to Constantinople, presented themselves as a gift to the Ottoman government, and been incorporated along with their crews into the Ottoman Navy. Although the German crews now wore fezzes to signify their new allegiance, this ruse fooled no one. The disturbing fact was that Churchill and the British admirals had been outmaneuvered and outwitted. These powerful warships had escaped, they had been used to induce the Ottomans into joining Germany and the Central Powers, and now they had attacked Russian bases in the Black Sea.[7]

The Russians had been begging the British for a diversionary strike against the Ottomans since October, but in late December, their pleas took on an increased urgency. On December 22, the Ottomans launched an ambitious winter campaign against Russian forces in the Caucasus. Initially, the

Russians were surprised, and it appeared that their position would collapse. As the reports of yet another disaster came in, the Russians redoubled their efforts to obtain additional support from their allies. The situation was believed to be so grave that Grand Duke Nicholas, the cousin of the czar and chief of Russia's armies, begged Britain's military attaché, Major General Sir John Hanbury-Williams, for an audience. When they met, the grand duke's loss of composure as he pleaded for assistance was so striking that it convinced Hanbury-Williams that prompt action was needed.[8] Hanbury-Williams reported the news of an impending Russian collapse in the Caucasus to Asquith's War Council, thus setting in motion British plans for an attack on the Ottoman Empire to relieve the Russians.[9]

These plans proceeded slowly at first. While it is unimaginable today, most of the British cabinet was away on a two-week Christmas vacation. Although each of the ministers received daily briefs and remained in contact through telegraph and courier, they did not meet as a group and could not be quickly recalled in the event of an emergency. Prime Minister Asquith, for example, was enjoying a working holiday at Walmer Castle in Kent.[10] Careful to reassure the grand duke, the head of the War Office, General Horatio Kitchener, sent a telegram promising that the British would "make a demonstration against the Turks" without offering much in the way of detail or committing the British to anything tangible.

While much of the Asquith government was enjoying their Christmas holiday, Churchill remained in London, ready for action. Sensing an opportunity to drive policymaking, win glory, and shorten the war, he began to develop a plan to aid the Russians and maneuver around the costly stalemate on the western front.[11] On December 29, 1914, he grappled with the problem, asking, "Are there no other alternatives than sending our armies to chew barbed wire in Flanders?"[12]

Churchill believed that the problem was finding a vulnerable area to strike where there was a reasonable prospect of achieving decisive results. Since the "race to the sea" had ended in a bloody stalemate in the war's opening months, little progress had been made as the two sides dug increasingly strong and sophisticated trenches from the English Channel to the Swiss border.[13] These defensive positions, combined with the awesome firepower of modern weaponry, made offensive operations and movements almost impossible up and down the entire length of the western front. As Churchill later described the situation at the end of 1914,

"When the old year closed a complete deadlock existed between the great combatants in the West by land and by sea. . . . The trench lines ran continuously from the Alps to the sea, and there was no possibility of manoeuvre. . . . Confronted with this deadlock, military art remained dumb; the Commanders and their General Staffs had no plan except frontal attacks which all their experience and training had led them to reject; they had no policy except the policy of exhaustion."[14]

In Churchill's mind, the Russian plea for help presented both a moral obligation and an opportunity to develop a new strategy.[15] Churchill, who had previously favored an attack on Germany via the North Sea, now believed that the Royal Navy must strike a decisive blow against the Ottoman Empire.[16] He soon began to propose a bold but risky course of action: attack and defeat the Ottoman Empire with a rapid naval strike through the Dardanelles.[17]

When the War Council finally convened on January 7, the British secretary of state for war, Lord Horatio Kitchener, was also pushing for an attack on the Dardanelles.[18] Kitchener summarized his views on the situation to the War Council, stating, "The Dardanelles appeared to be the most suitable objective, as an attack here could be made in co-operation with the Fleet. If successful, it would re-establish communication with Russia; settle the Near Eastern question; draw in Greece and, perhaps, Bulgaria and Roumania; and release wheat and shipping now locked up in the Black Sea."[19] Kitchener was by no means ignorant of the challenges of such an ambitious operation, but he believed that the "only place that a demonstration might have some effect in stopping reinforcements going east would be the Dardanelles."[20] Kitchener's leadership and the urgent desire to help the Russians thus set in motion planning for a campaign that would become a national tragedy for the British people.

What made the Dardanelles Campaign tragic was that it was initiated on false assumptions and misinformation from the very beginning: the need to avert a Russian collapse.[21] While it was not clear in the opening phases of the campaign, the Ottoman forces were ill equipped for the rigors of winter operations. The Ottoman Army soon suffered severe breakdowns in communications, logistics, and morale, and it faltered under the strains of battle and the elements. As the Ottoman advance quickly disintegrated into chaos, the Russians regrouped and fought well. Despite their initial panic, they were able to recover, coordinate a counterattack in the middle of winter, and win a decisive victory at the Battle of Sarıkamış.[22]

By early January 1915, the Russian Army had reversed the Ottoman advance and inflicted massive losses on their foe. This ended the immediate need for an attack on the Ottomans, yet planning for the Dardanelles operation continued.[23] In his memoirs, Churchill would minimize this reversal of fortune and imply that Russia was still in dire need of relief, but in reality, the Russians were stronger vis-à-vis their Ottoman foes than they had been only a few weeks before and were in no imminent danger of collapse.[24]

The plan to attack the Ottomans continued unchecked and began to take on a life of its own. Now Churchill, who had originally opposed the plan, began to imagine the possibilities of striking a blow against the Ottoman Empire. Churchill's energy, creativity, optimism, and romanticism appear to have gotten the best of him, as he now threw himself into planning this new operation. He passionately wanted to shorten the war, and, despite his previous reservations and the professional hedging of the Admiralty staff, he convinced himself that fate had now presented him the opportunity to do just that.[25] Churchill concluded that naval power alone could defeat the Ottoman Empire. If he could send his ships to boldly attack through the Dardanelles, plow straight through the Sea of Marmara, and anchor off the ancient city of Constantinople, the moribund Ottomans would see that continued resistance was fruitless and sign a separate peace. The war would be shortened, millions of lives would be saved, and he would get the fame and adulation for defeating an entire empire.

While such a grandiose plan was impractical in hindsight, Churchill quickly convinced himself that it would work. Moreover, his combination of authority, passion for debate, optimism, and energy appears to have silenced many of his critics in the Admiralty. Rather than debate the merits of the plan with such an energetic First Lord, many of the professional planners seem to have stated their reservations while doing their best to present a workable plan for execution. The subtle fact that professional military staff would do their best to work on a plan they opposed and that they might not directly state their objections was lost on Churchill. He minimized their concerns and interpreted his staff's ability to solve problems and answer his repeated questions in a timely manner as their implicit approval of the plan. In truth, the planners were anything but unified in their support of the Dardanelles Campaign; however, Churchill convinced himself that the opposite was true.

Exacerbating the tensions within the Admiralty was the belief that they must act quickly to save their Russian allies, achieve surprise, and move before the Ottomans could further fortify their positions in the Dardanelles. In addition, the Admiralty felt pressure to act on an intelligence report that the *Goeben* was temporarily disabled after striking a mine and would be unable to contribute to the defense of the Dardanelles.[26] This haste forced planners to make many unfounded assumptions about their foe and the challenges of the operation. The British also convinced themselves that the Ottomans were on the brink of collapse and that attacking the Dardanelles with naval vessels would force the government in Constantinople to beg for peace. This was fanciful at best, but the Admiralty did little to challenge this theory of victory in the coming weeks.[27] So confident were the British, French, and Russians that they even began diplomatic discussions as to what parts of the Ottoman Empire they would keep for themselves after the fighting was over.[28]

The operational details of the plan were similarly rushed and fundamentally flawed. In retrospect, it is clear that Admiralty planners had not properly accounted for the inaccuracy of long-range naval bombardment, the number of shells required to silence the Ottoman forts, the challenges of aircraft to perform artillery-spotting duties, the critical need for minesweeping, their ships' vulnerability to plunging artillery fire, or the threat from German submarines.[29] While it is never possible to account for every conceivable contingency, these basic issues were never properly addressed before Allied forces were committed to the campaign.[30]

These problems should have been obvious to Churchill, but he continued to drive forward, convinced that the plan would win a decisive victory at a minimal cost. Frustration with the futility of the war guided Churchill's decision-making, as did his belief that a navy-only operation would provide the option for a rapid and low-cost withdrawal. In the event of failure, all the Royal Navy would need to do would be to sail away and pretend the assault was nothing more than a hit-and-run strike, and the public and the Ottomans would be none the wiser. Churchill always insisted that the plan could be quickly abandoned in such a simple manner, yet it soon grew beyond his control.[31] Mission creep combined with unreasonable assumptions led to a plan that had little chance of success, and once ground troops were committed to the campaign, the navy was forced to support them.[32]

Had the British acted more quickly, it is possible that a naval assault through the Dardanelles would have been successful. Indeed, a December

1914 estimate by German intelligence predicted that the British could force the straits with warships alone and expect to lose only four or five vessels.[33] Similarly, the political situation was more panicked and uncertain in Constantinople during the early days of the conflict, but it stabilized when the anticipated British attack never materialized, and Ottoman officials reasserted their authority. While the Admiralty worked on their plan, the Ottomans and their German military advisers worked assiduously to strengthen the naval defenses in the Dardanelles Strait and on the Gallipoli Peninsula. By the time the Allies attacked, the moment for achieving a rapid victory with naval forces had already passed.

During the planning of the Dardanelles operations, Churchill also received inconsistent and unhelpful support from the First Sea Lord, Admiral John "Jackie" Fisher. The venerable admiral, who was known for his energy, vision, and decisiveness, failed when his strategic genius was most needed. While age and stress likely contributed to Fisher's poor performance, his failures were at least partially the fault of his friend, former disciple, and now civilian boss, Winston Churchill. Churchill had long admired Fisher, and the two were genuine friends. As a new First Lord, Churchill had consulted with him unofficially on a wide range of technical, personal, and bureaucratic matters despite the fact that Fisher was officially retired. After Prince Louis of Battenberg was forced to resign during the early months of the war because of his German birth, Churchill chose Fisher to replace him as First Sea Lord even though the aging admiral was believed to be past his prime and had made many powerful enemies during his career, most notably the king. The two frequently quarreled, they kept very different schedules, and both had colossal egos to manage, yet Churchill believed that their strange partnership worked well. He appreciated the debates, believed that their opposite schedules allowed the Admiralty to work around the clock, and, as egotists so often do, thought mostly about himself.[34]

Unfortunately, Fisher gave conflicting advice and seemed unwilling or unable to communicate his doubts to Churchill.[35] For example, in his letter to Churchill dated January 3, 1915, Fisher criticized the weakness of Asquith's War Council and argued for immediate action: "I CONSIDER THE ATTACK ON TURKEY HOLDS THE FIELD! But ONLY if it's IMMEDIATE."[36] However, the very next day, January 4, Fisher struck a timid note: "I think we had better hear what others have to say about the Turkish places before taking a decided line."[37] Fisher's January 18 letter argued for a landing in Holland as preferable to an attack on the Ottomans.[38] His March 31 correspondence again stated his preference for an invasion of Holland or a commitment to the North Sea but also stated that he was "prepared to risk the probable heavy losses in the ships and personnel now at the Dardanelles, in order to achieve success."[39] In his most dramatic reversal of course, Fisher exclaimed on April 5, "Damn the Dardanelles, they will be our grave."[40] A week later on April 12, Fisher complained that he had been pushed into the operation but said, "I think it's going to be a success."[41] Even in his later testimony to the Dardanelles Commission, Fisher claimed that he had gone in "totus porcus," or whole hog, despite his reservations.[42]

In regard to the Dardanelles operations, Fisher served Churchill poorly by giving unclear and contradictory advice.[43] For his part, Churchill heard what he wanted to hear and stubbornly refused to listen to the professional caveats of Fisher and the naval staff.[44] This was surprising given their close relationship, but in retrospect it is clear that Fisher became less forthright and consistent over time. These violent swings in opinion suggest that stress and age were finally taking their toll on the admiral, a fact that Churchill could not or would not face at the time.[45]

On the most basic level, Churchill fundamentally misread his relationship with Fisher. He focused on their mutual love and dedication to the success of the Royal Navy and minimized their differences. Churchill understood that Fisher had a volatile and histrionic temperament yet chose to ignore him when he acted dramatically and peevishly, or simply laughed these incidents off.[46] Ultimately, the stress of the Dardanelles Campaign and his work with Churchill would prove too much for Fisher, and signs of his mental and physical strain were already apparent during the planning phases. Fisher's moods and appraisal of the plan swung wildly. He varied from enthusiastic support and visions of glory to warnings of disaster and prophecies of doom.

While Churchill deserves much of the blame, he received poor and conflicting advice at every stage of the planning process. None of the Admiralty planners would say unequivocally that the project was a bad idea, and this led Churchill to equate their silence with support.[47] Initially, Churchill had his own doubts about the soundness of the plan, but he gradually became more confident in its prospects for success as he became more emotionally invested in the plan and received seeming assent from the Admiralty staff.[48]

Churchill would later claim that there were no major objections from the senior naval planners, stating: "No one at any time threw the slightest doubt upon its technical soundness. No one, for instance, of the four or five great naval authorities each with his technical staff who were privy said, 'This is absurd. Ships cannot fight forts,' or criticized its details. On the contrary, they all treated it as an extremely interesting and hopeful proposal; and there grew up in the secret circles of the Admiralty a perfectly clear opinion favorable to the operation."[49] This claim is clearly untrue, and it is one of the most self-serving passages in his memoir *The World Crisis*. The most charitable reading of the planning process is that Churchill deserves blame for hearing what he wanted to hear from his professional advisers, but this is still a very damning indictment of him as a First Lord.[50]

Particularly at this stage of his career, Churchill often failed to listen to others or heard what he wanted to hear unless he was strongly and directly contradicted. As Admiral David Beatty (who worked under Churchill in numerous capacities) noted in 1915, "The First Lord is obstinate when set on a thing, but really it only requires firm treatment to make him realize when he goes off the rails, but indeed it must be astonishingly firm."[51] The secret to working with Churchill was to possess the courage and strength of character to not be intimidated by the power of his personality. While he would ultimately learn to listen to professional advice from his subordinates, even his friends and supporters were sometimes exhausted by the task of continually advancing and defending their positions.[52]

Because Churchill inserted himself so deeply into the planning of the Dardanelles operation, he was an easy scapegoat for its eventual failure. These criticisms focus on the First Lord's enthusiastic amateurism as the basis for the failed campaign and suggest that a more mature and prudent strategist would have seen the dangers inherent in the plan. The Australian Official History, for example, endorses this assessment and bitterly asserts that the roots of failure were "Churchill's excess of imagination, a layman's ignorance of artillery, and the fatal power of young enthusiasm to convince older and slower brains, [in which] the tragedy of Gallipoli was born."[53]

While it is certainly true that Churchill had a strong personality and a willingness to force his opinions on others, this assessment is too harsh. Not only does this interpretation overstate the ability of one man to direct policy, but it also ignores the fact that dozens of civilian ministers and senior officers as well as hundreds of planners and bureaucrats all had a part in shaping the operation for better or worse. In addition, to blame Churchill for the entirety of the failed campaign also ignores the fact that he was removed from his position as First Lord at a relatively early stage of the operation and, much to his dismay, was largely ignored regarding matters of strategy and planning.

The more balanced view accepted by the Dardanelles Commission endorsed the notion that Churchill had not fully listened to the advice of those around him and had often taken overly optimistic views of the military situation but also that he had not received a clear and decisive rebuttal from his fellow ministers and professional advisers. According to a particularly revealing passage from the official report:

> Considering what Mr. Churchill knew of the opinions of Lord Fisher and Sir Arthur Wilson, and considering also the fact that the other experts at the Admiralty who had been consulted, although they assented to an attack on the outer forts of the Dardanelles and to progressive operations thereafter up the Straits as far as might be found practicable, had not done so with any great cordiality or enthusiasm, he ought not merely to have invited Lord Fisher and Sir Arthur Wilson to express their views freely to the Council, but further to have insisted on their doing so. . . . Without in any way wishing to impugn his good faith, it seems clear that he was carried away by his sanguine temperament, and his firm belief in the success of the undertaking which he advocated. Although none of the expert advisers absolutely expressed dissent, all the evidence laid before us leads us to the conclusion that Mr. Churchill had obtained their support to a lesser extent than he himself imagined.[54]

While much of the attention is focused on Churchill's relationship with the naval staff, he also deserves some blame for failing to fully include Lord Kitchener and the army in the planning process. This was a failure of leadership and oversight that exacerbated interservice friction between the army and the navy. Churchill failed to understand that he had not clearly communicated his vision to the army, however brilliant it may have been. Because both Kitchener and Fisher had strong opinions and personalities, Churchill was courting disaster by not receiving their explicit support for the operation, yet he did not believe it was necessary at the time. After the failures of the operation, Churchill was genuinely surprised that these two men turned on him, as he thought that they were trusted friends and colleagues.[55]

Churchill had unquestioning faith in the ultimate success of his plans. He was, at his core, an optimist. Despite his confidence, the audit of battle would tragically expose the flaws in his schemes and send thousands to their deaths.

A Narrative of a Failed Campaign

For the remainder of his long life, Churchill would remain bitter about his failure at the Dardanelles. Even after he had led Great Britain to victory during World War II, he felt that he needed to continue to make the case that victory was within grasp, only to be tragically lost by a combination of factors beyond his control. While this was self-serving, there is a measure of truth here as the operations in the Dardanelles present a series of missed opportunities and innumerable what-ifs. Initial victories were unexploited and insignificant, and they led to later failures that were devastating and profound.

The seeds of disaster in the Dardanelles were sown in the first days of November 1914. With war between the Ottoman Empire and Great Britain imminent, Churchill ordered the Royal Navy's Mediterranean Squadron to conduct an attack on the Dardanelles fortifications immediately after the outbreak of hostilities. Two British battle cruisers, *Indomitable* and *Indefatigable*, and two French predreadnought battleships, *Suffren* and *Vérité*, responded to Churchill's orders and began their bombardment on November 3, a few hours before war had formally been declared. The bombardment lasted approximately twenty minutes and was little more than a demonstration of force designed to probe the Ottoman defenses. Despite its limited objectives, this attack showed promising results. It caught the enemy unprepared, killed approximately 150 Ottoman and German troops, destroyed or dismounted approximately ten heavy guns, and ignited the magazine of a large fort at Sed del Bahr. The British and French escaped unscathed and were happy to claim a victory even if it occurred before war had officially commenced.[56]

The two foes learned very different lessons from this initial encounter. For the Royal Navy, it seemed that modern warships could use their long-range guns to engage and destroy the forts protecting the Dardanelles and achieve decisive results at a minimal cost.[57] Later engagements would disprove these assumptions, but the British felt hopeful.[58] The Ottomans recovered from their initial surprise and understood that their defenses were potentially vulnerable.[59] Within days, they began to reinforce the Dardanelles in preparation of a larger and more powerful Allied attack.[60] While increasing the numbers of troops, fortifications, and heavy artillery would take time, they were able to quickly sow additional rows of naval mines in the narrow waters of the Dardanelles. This development made the process of naval gunnery much more difficult as it forced ships to either engage the forts at greater range or risk destruction from unswept mines. The Royal Navy did not appreciate this development at the time, but it greatly complicated future Allied operations and limited the ability of their ships to accurately target the forts with their heavy guns.

The next Allied strike on the Dardanelles was anticlimactic. On February 19, a British force of two destroyers and the predreadnought battleships *Cornwallis* and *Vengeance* attempted to repeat the success from November and systematically destroy the Ottoman forts. With the destroyers providing a screen and drawing fire from the Ottoman guns, the old battleships began to fire on the enemy batteries beginning at 9:51 a.m. Despite the impressive sound and fury from the British twelve-inch guns, the results were disappointing. The British forces scored no direct hits on the Ottoman fortifications with their indirect fire, destroyed none of the enemy guns, and inflicted only a handful of casualties. While the British suffered no losses of their own, their initial estimates about the ability of long-range artillery fire to destroy the Dardanelles defenses were exposed as overly optimistic.[61]

When the British resumed their attack on February 25, the Ottomans had altered their strategy.[62] This time they withdrew their forces from the outer forts at the tip of the Gallipoli Peninsula and at Kum Kale on the Asian side of the entrance to the Dardanelles. The British exploited this by sending raiding parties of Royal Marines to attack these outer defenses. While the marines met little resistance, their quick hit-and-run raid was unable to do any serious damage on the Ottoman fortifications. A similar raid on March 4 was met with much stronger resistance from the Ottomans, resulting in the deaths of twenty-three Royal Marines for little military gain.[63]

On March 1, the British sent four battleships to attack the second row of fortifications but again made little progress. Because of the heavily mined waters, these ships were unable to get close enough to their targets to have meaningful results despite their impressive firepower.[64] While the battleships were accompanied by minesweeping trawlers, the civilian crews of these unarmed and unarmored vessels refused to clear the mines while under fire.[65] On the night of March 13, six minesweepers and the cruiser HMS *Amethyst* made additional attempt to clear the mines. The darkness did little to protect the British force as four of the minesweepers were hit by enemy fire. The *Amethyst* suffered the most severe damage as it attempted to draw fire away from the unarmored minesweepers and was struck by two shells, which hit its boiler and mess deck, resulting in the death or severe wounding of sixty of its crew.[66]

Frustrated by these ineffective strikes, Churchill demanded more aggressive action.[67] On March 15, the commander of the Dardanelles task force, Admiral Sackville Carden, presented a plan to attack the Ottomans during broad daylight using his entire fleet of eighteen capital ships. On the first day of the attack, these ships were to destroy all the fortresses guarding the first five rows of mines blocking the narrow waters of the Dardanelles. With these guns silenced, the minesweepers could work unmolested and clear the mines that evening. The Allied battleships would return the next day, eliminate any remaining forts, and allow the minesweeping trawlers to finish clearing the waters of the Dardanelles of the final five rows of mines that evening. After two days of silencing the guns and clearing the narrow waters of the ten rows of mines, they would open a path to Constantinople and victory.[68]

The boldness of the plan was impressive, but Admiral Carden's audacity belied his own crumbling constitution. While Carden had done his best to project confidence, he was physically and mentally faltering under the strain of command. In fact, on March 15, the very day he presented the plan, Carden suffered a nervous breakdown, was transferred to the sick list on the recommendation of his doctors, and was relieved.[69] Carden was replaced by his deputy, Rear Admiral John de Robeck, who was instructed to execute his predecessor's plan, "provided he thought that plans were wise and practicable."[70] De Robeck had doubts about the soundness of Carden's plan yet believed that he was honor bound to carry out the attack. Despite his reservations, de Robeck telegrammed the Admiralty that he would proceed immediately with the attack.[71]

As the Allied fleet prepared to fight a battle under a new commander who did not believe in the plan he was given to execute, the Ottomans were busy strengthening their defenses. Most critically, in the hours before the Allied assault on March 18, the Ottomans laid a new string of mines parallel to the shoreline. These mines were designed to hit the Allied ships as they turned away from their firing positions and exited toward the open waters of the Aegean Sea. Unfortunately for the Allies, their movements into and out of firing position had become predictable, and the Ottomans had positioned this new line of mines directly in the path the ships used to exit the narrow waters of the Dardanelles. Even though the mines had been laid in relatively clear and calm waters and could have easily been spotted from the air, the Allies' reconnaissance flights from March 13 to March 17 had searched a different area and been too early to discover this new threat.[72] In fact, on the basis of these sorties, the Allies were confident that they could safely navigate these waters, an assumption that would prove disastrous when their ships came into contact with the deadly obstacles.[73]

The Allied attack on March 18 began shortly after 11:30 a.m. when the British battleships opened fire on the Ottoman forts.[74] Twelve battleships were formed into three rows of four ships each, two British and one French, and were supported by six additional battleships in reserve. This formidable squadron sailed toward the narrowest portion of the Dardanelles, firing as they went. By noon, the ships were closing in on the heart of the Ottoman defenses. The plunging fire from the forts began to take its toll on the Allied ships. The *Gaulois*, *Suffren*, *Agamemnon*, and *Inflexible* all took critical hits, but it appeared as if their impressive firepower had suppressed the Ottoman defenses.[75] While it was unclear how many forts had been destroyed, their fire began to slacken around 1:25 p.m., and Admiral de Robeck decided to bring forward the second row of British ships as well as *Swiftsure* and *Majestic* from the reserve force to keep the pressure on the enemy batteries. At approximately 1:54 p.m., as the first two rows of ships turned to starboard to clear the path for the reserve ships, the French battleship *Bouvet* struck one of the mines that had recently been laid in the now-predictable path of departing Allied ships. The *Bouvet* sank within minutes, killing 639 of its crew.[76]

Despite this shocking loss, the Allied force continued to press its attack. At approximately 4:11 p.m., the British battle cruiser *Inflexible* was attempting to retire from the narrows when it also struck a mine in the same area where the *Bouvet* had sunk.[77] The battle cruiser was seriously damaged from this powerful explosion below the waterline. Thirty crewmen were killed, and the ship had to be temporarily beached to prevent it from sinking, but the remainder of the crew were safely evacuated. As the crew of the *Inflexible* was struggling to save the ship, the predreadnought battleship *Irresistible* struck a mine as it also attempted to retire from the Dardanelles narrows. Water flooded the ship's engine room, and the battleship floated helplessly back toward the Ottoman gunners, who found the defenseless British warship an irresistible target. As shells rained down, de Robeck ordered the predreadnought battleship *Ocean* to speed to the ship's aid and attempt to tow it out of harm's way. This heroic act only caused further disaster. The *Ocean* ran aground yet was able to free itself, but by the time it arrived at the side of the *Irresistible*, the ship was too badly damaged to be saved. The *Irresistible*'s survivors were transferred to the *Ocean* and the destroyer *Wear*.[78] As the *Ocean* attempted to flee, it was struck by a combination of Ottoman artillery fire and an underwater mine. The *Ocean* quickly listed to starboard as its coal bunkers and underwater compartments began to flood. The damage was fatal, and the survivors of the *Irresistible* and the *Ocean* were transferred to three British destroyers.[79] This action effectively ended the naval battle of March 18.[80] After the British forces withdrew, both the *Irresistible* and the *Ocean* sank at approximately 10:30 p.m., and a search for the ships and their survivors yielded nothing.[81]

The battle of March 18 had been costly for the Allies. In total, they had three battleships sunk, another three severely damaged, and over seven hundred men killed. While Churchill and others would later minimize the importance of these older ships, the fact that the plan to destroy the fortifications protecting the Dardanelles had been repulsed and three capital ships lost was psychologically damaging. Admiral de Robeck and Churchill both planned for renewed naval assaults in the coming days, but there appeared to be little enthusiasm for a naval attack when the War Council met to discuss the situation on March 19.[82]

While the loss of three obsolete ships that were destined for the scrapyard anyway did little to change the balance of power, it convinced Kitchener and others that naval power alone would be unable to achieve the desired results.[83] Although the British Army had been planning for possible amphibious operations on the Gallipoli Peninsula for several weeks, this contingency had little urgency until the repulse of the naval forces on March 18.[84] In a single day, Kitchener had made up his mind that victory in the Dardanelles would require ground troops to land on the Gallipoli Peninsula and to capture the Ottoman forts. He addressed the War Council on this point: "You know my views that the passage of the Dardanelles must be forced, and that if large military operations on the Gallipoli Peninsula are necessary to clear the way, they must be undertaken, and carried through."[85] Given Kitchener's almost unquestioned authority on military matters, these strong words effectively ended the debate. With only a cursory discussion, Britain was now committed to an amphibious assault.[86] After conferring with General Ian Hamilton, the cabinet allocated seventy-five thousand troops to the campaign.[87] The rapidity of the discussion surrounding ground troops would later allow Fisher to claim, with some degree of truth, that he was not properly consulted on the issue, and to disassociate himself from the subsequent failures.[88]

Despite his quiet and almost gentle manner, General Hamilton was the logical choice to command the ground forces. He was the overall commander of the Mediterranean theater, had a long and distinguished record of service going back to the Second Anglo-Afghan War, and enjoyed excellent political connections.[89] While he understood that his mission would be very difficult, he accepted his new command with his usual calm and reserved manner and began to gather his forces and plan for the coming campaign.

As the Allies assembled their forces, the Germans and Ottomans rapidly prepared to repel the anticipated assault. Under the direction of the German general Otto Liman von Sanders, the Ottomans and their German military advisers made the most of the month they had to improve their defenses. Von Sanders was not pleased with the condition of the Ottoman defenses but noted that the British delays gave him critical breathing room: "The British gave me four full weeks before their great landing. . . . The time was just sufficient to complete the most indispensable arrangements."[90] This was not false humility on the part of von Sanders. In fact, during this critical month he correctly anticipated where the majority of the Allied landing would occur and repositioned his troops accordingly. He also rebuilt many of the damaged fortifications and greatly improved the welfare and fighting spirit of his Ottoman troops.

Failure of the Allied Landings on April 25

At approximately 4:00 a.m. on April 25, 1915, the Allies began their amphibious assault on the Gallipoli Peninsula. They landed at the southern tip of the peninsula at Cape Helles and on the western shore at a place that would become known as ANZAC Cove. While the initial assaults achieved some degree of surprise and success, they were quickly checked by a combination of poor communications, exhausted men, uninspired leaders, vague orders, imposing terrain, inaccurate maps, and remarkable displays of bravery and sacrifice from the Ottoman defenders.[91] By the end of the first day, the Allies held on to a series of shallow toeholds along the peninsula but had achieved none of their main objectives.[92]

Over the next few days, both armies desperately tried to force a decision. The Allies brought ashore supplies, consolidated their positions, and conducted a series of assaults intended to capture key terrain features on the peninsula. The Ottomans reinforced their positions and conducted a series of desperate and costly assaults on the Allied lines. While the Allies were able to gain some ground and successfully repel the Ottoman attacks with a combination of small arms, artillery, and naval gunfire, they were unable to force the decisive battles they had planned. Within a few days, the Allies had exhausted their strength, and the Ottomans had brought up enough reinforcements to secure their positions. In May, both armies launched major offensives but were unable to break the deadlock, and a frustrating stalemate ensued.

Churchill was upset by the most recent failures. He had dreamed of a rapid victory that would avoid the attrition and devastation of the western front, and now his vision was in tatters as both armies dug in for a long and brutal struggle. Moreover, he was frustrated because he could do little to influence the outcome of the campaign. Once the troops landed, the conduct of the operations became primarily the responsibility of Kitchener and the ground commanders. While Churchill was upset by his inability to manage ground operations, the fact that these decisions were beyond his control should have absolved him of much of the responsibility of this phase of the campaign.

Despite this, Churchill would quickly become the scapegoat for the Dardanelles Campaign. He had been an early convert to action in the Dardanelles. He had pushed forward the plans for the initial naval operations. He had been a forceful and outspoken advocate for the operation's potential to shorten the war. He remained one of the few holdouts in the Asquith government who supported continuing the campaign even after it had become unwinnable. He would never admit that it was a mistake. Finally, Churchill lived four and a half decades longer than either Kitchener or Fisher and was the only key architect of the campaign remaining to receive blame.[93] For reasons both reasonable and petty, Churchill would become the man most closely associated with the failure at the Dardanelles. Holding him responsible for the entire disaster is truly unfair, but with the benefit of hindsight, it is appropriate to assign blame for the failure of the navy operations.[94] He was the civilian head of the Admiralty, and his view of the campaign was premised on unrealistic and romantic assumptions.

Even with this series of failures, Churchill could have likely survived as First Lord of the Admiralty had it not been for two political scandals that rocked the already-weak Asquith government: the Shell Crisis and the resignation of Admiral Fisher as First Sea Lord. These twin humiliations, combined with rising public frustration with the conduct of the war, failures in the Dardanelles, and the opposition's increasing willingness to bring pressure on the Asquith government, made Liberal control of the government increasing untenable. Asquith sensed that his position was extremely tenuous, and in the wake of these scandals, he felt it necessary to reinvigorate the war effort by shuffling key cabinet members and forming a coalition government that included prominent Conservatives and replaced Churchill as First Lord.

The Shell Crisis

The collapse of Asquith's Liberal government can best be understood as a gradual decline punctuated by two crises: the Shell Crisis and the bizarre resignation of First Sea Lord Jackie Fisher. These twin crises came after months of escalating frustration regarding the prosecution of the war and a shift in the political strategy of Asquith's opponents. While many expected a rapid victory, these hopes were soon dashed by events on the battlefield. Much of the British professional army was destroyed in the opening months of the war, and the horrific casualty lists revealed that the war would be significantly more costly and protracted than initially projected. In this moment of national emergency, Asquith's opponents understood that directly challenging the sitting government would be seen as unpatriotic and potentially dangerous. Therefore, for a mixture of patriotic and pragmatic reasons, the Tories chose to avoid direct criticism of government policies and present a unified front with their Liberal rivals.[95] This policy, known as "business as usual," was fragile at best.

As casualties mounted, public opinion soured. Yet despite this slow-moving crisis, Asquith appeared to take an apathetic approach to managing the war.[96] Indeed, he worked a relatively relaxed schedule, took ample time off, maintained a busy social calendar, and frequently wrote love letters to Venetia Stanley during cabinet meetings.[97] This seemingly half-hearted approach and the required general election to come no later than December 1915 made Asquith politically vulnerable.[98] Rivals such as Andrew Bonar Law seized on this weakness and began to look for a salient political issue to openly challenge the prime minister while appearing to serve the best interests of the nation. They found their issue in what became known as the Shell Crisis.

Since the beginning of the war, the British Army had been firing shells at a rate far greater than prewar planners had envisioned. In fact, the estimated expenditure of shells had been calculated in 1901 and was not reexamined until after the beginning of the Great War in 1914. This 1901 estimate was fundamentally flawed because it was based on the historical data from the Boer War and the assumption that the British Army would only field a force of seven divisions. The greater intensity of fighting and the increased size of the British Army exposed the flaws in these calculations, and British industry struggled to meet the increased demand for shells and a wide range of other war materials.[99]

The shortage of war supplies was by no means exclusive to the British, nor were these shortages anything new in 1915. Indeed, every nation that went to war in 1914 suffered from significant shortfalls in war supplies (artillery shells in particular), and these deficiencies had been apparent to the commanders in the field from the opening weeks of the conflict. In response to the defensive advantages of trenches, wire, and small arms, commanders on both sides turned to massed artillery barrages in the hope that they would smash their opponents and restore movement and decisiveness to the battlefield. Despite the awesome firepower of modern field guns, the grim reality was that they were remarkably ineffective at dislodging defenders holding modern trenches. These failures did not deter planners. Instead, they planned increasingly elaborate employments of artillery in the forlorn hope that the big guns might prove decisive. This led predictably to further increases in the use of shells, which placed increased strain on manufacturers, logisticians, and planners.[100] Indeed, although British munitions production increased nineteenfold over the first six months of the war, stockpiles of shells were critically strained.[101]

The British Army experienced these logistic failures firsthand in their spring 1915 offensives. At the Battle of Neuve Chapelle in March, British gunners experienced critical shortages of ammunition, expending over 30 percent of their shells in the initial thirty-five-minute barrage.[102] This shortfall, combined with poor communications, minimal progress, and a determined German counterattack, forced General John French to cancel follow-on assaults, which he had hoped would pierce the enemy lines and yield decisive results. In the aftermath, the British were left with few tangible gains and the loss of almost thirteen thousand men.[103] Similarly, at the Battle of Festubert in May, the British were unable to produce decisive results despite an impressive three-day barrage that expended over one hundred thousand rounds.[104] Again, the attack failed, and British had little to show for their efforts other than another gruesome butcher's bill of almost seventeen thousand casualties.[105]

These losses were shocking to the British public, and rumors of incompetence and mismanagement percolated behind the scenes. Sensing that this discontent was a critical liability for the Asquith government, the prominent Unionist politician James Gascoyne-Cecil, 4th Marquess of Salisbury, circulated an internal memo among party elites claiming that the chaos and mismanagement at the War Office were hindering the war effort.[106] For the time being, the Unionists chose not to act on this memo, but it indicates that Asquith's political enemies had already identified the conduct of the war in general and the shortage of shells in particular as political vulnerabilities.

Asquith was keenly aware that both elite and popular opinion were shifting against him and his government's conduct of the war. On April 14, he consulted with General Kitchener, who relayed assurances from General French that "with the present supply of ammunition he will have as much as his troops will be able to use on the next forward movement."[107] Armed with Kitchener's official reassurances, the prime minister traveled to Newcastle on April 20 and delivered a defiant speech in which he explicitly denied that there was a shortage of munitions and defended his government's conduct of the war.[108] This did little to convince Asquith's rivals, many of whom believed that, despite his hero status, Kitchener was largely to blame for the lack of efficiency at the War Office.[109] For the next month, Asquith's opponents bided their time, continued their whisper campaign regarding government negligence, and looked for opportunities to exploit their advantage.

This simmering issue would become elevated to the level of a national emergency when the Unionist-aligned "Northcliffe papers" ran a front-page article by Charles à Court Repington on May 14, 1915, that claimed that the recent defeat at the Battle of Festubert was due to a shortage of shells.[110] In bold font, the headlines proclaimed, "NEED FOR SHELLS. BRITISH ATTACKS CHECKED. LIMITED SUPPLY THE CAUSE."[111] The story quickly took on a life of its own, and in the ensuing weeks the Northcliffe press published dozens of stories on the shortage of shells and the broader malaise within the Asquith government concerning the conduct of the war. While Asquith was already involved in private discussions with the Unionist leaders about the possibility of forming a coalition government, the explosive nature of this headline, combined with the dramatic resignation of Jackie Fisher as First Sea Lord a day later, made it virtually impossible for the Liberal Party to retain its monopoly on power.[112]

Shockingly, two of the possible sources for the Northcliffe papers were none other than the First Lord of the Admiralty, Winston Churchill, and the commander of the British Expeditionary Force, General John French. While the exact details remain clouded in mystery and conjecture, Repington met with both men over the weekend of May 8–9 while Churchill was a guest at General French's headquarters. It is unclear what, if any, sensitive information was disclosed, but it has been suggested that Churchill and French were trying to force Asquith to provide more resources for the war, particularly men and shells. Churchill was passionate about the rigorous prosecution of the war in general and the issues of munitions and the draft in particular. In addition, Churchill, like his father before him, had cultivated close relationships with numerous reporters from across the political spectrum, and at various points in his career, he was not above leaking to the press. For his part, General French hardly denied his role in providing Repington with information regarding the lack of munitions and was apparently satisfied to see Asquith suffer politically in the coming weeks. Repington was well known as an opponent of the Liberal government, and in 1918 he would be convicted under the Defense of the Realm Act for his stories critical of David Lloyd George. In short, there is a large amount of circumstantial evidence, including timing, access to the reporter who broke the story, motive, a history of similar behavior, and a potential partner in General French. Thus, it is entirely possible, but not certain, that Churchill was responsible for inciting this scandal.[113]

If Churchill was the source for the story, he certainly miscalculated catastrophically, as the ensuing crisis would have disastrous personal consequences for him and for Asquith's Liberal government. Interestingly, the same Northcliffe papers that published the Shell Crisis story also failed to anticipate the consequences of breaking this scandalous news. While the headlines were shocking, the patriotic fervor the publishers hoped would sell newspapers and force Asquith out of power quickly backfired. Indeed, the public reaction was one of disgust as many elite clubs canceled their subscriptions to the *Daily Mail* and the *Times*. In protest, three thousand members of the London Stock Exchange built a public bonfire out of Northcliffe papers, and the circulation of the *Daily Mail* fell by almost two hundred thousand copies in the weeks that followed.[114]

Although he largely escaped blame for potentially inciting the crisis, Churchill remained extremely defensive about his role in it for the remainder of his life.[115] While he was willing to admit that the shortage of munitions for the army was real, he insisted that he and the Royal Navy were blameless. On the contrary, he claimed that thanks to his efforts, the navy was proactive in obtaining their own stock of ammunition and that by the time he left the Admiralty, the Royal Navy had four times as many shells as they had had prior to the outbreak of hostilities.[116]

In the context of the collapse of the Asquith government and later revelations that British naval forces were conserving their stocks of ammunition, it is clear why Churchill wanted to deny any responsibility for the Shell Crisis: he cared passionately about his place in history. To protect his legacy, Churchill wanted to distance himself from both the moribund Asquith government and the broader failures of British war policy. For a mix of genuine and self-serving reasons, Churchill insisted that he was entirely blameless for the Shell Crisis but highlighted it as the primary cause of Asquith's defeat. This provided a convenient means for explaining the collapse of the government and his removal from office while minimizing a less flattering episode from his own career: his melodramatic break with his friend Admiral Jackie Fisher.

Fisher's Resignation

The second of the scandals that would lead to the removal of Churchill as First Lord was the dramatic resignation and abandonment of his post by First Sea Lord Admiral Jackie Fisher. Although Winston and Jackie genuinely loved each other and had a similar passion for the Royal Navy, this scandal was perhaps inevitable as they were ill suited to work together. They frequently bickered, had powerful opinions on key policy issues, were suspicious of each other's motives, and believed that they could manipulate one another.

As the war progressed, a truly bizarre and dysfunctional pattern of behavior emerged. To try to force his opinions on the First Sea Lord, Churchill frequently tried to outdebate Fisher.[117] He would exhaust the older man with his repeated counterarguments, logic, persuasion, and energy.[118] In contrast, Fisher frequently threatened resignation (a total of nine times during his few months working with Churchill) and used his reputation for erratic and histrionic behavior to force Churchill to his preferred course of action.[119] Despite their near-constant feuding and the stresses of war, this unusual relationship held together for the first few months of the conflict.

Ultimately, it was the two men's diametrically opposed work schedules that forced a final showdown. Fisher woke very early in the morning, arrived to work between 4:00 a.m. and 5:00 a.m., and went to bed around 9:00 p.m. In contrast, Churchill preferred to sleep considerably later and take a midday nap but often worked until the early hours of the morning, just as Fisher was about to arrive at the Admiralty.[120] In theory, the fact that Fisher worked early in the morning and Churchill worked late into the night allowed for an around-the-clock schedule at the Admiralty and increased productivity—at least when there were no major disagreements between the First Lord and the First Sea Lord.

When there were disagreements over policy, these passionate leaders with very different schedules were almost destined to come into conflict. Both men were creatures of habit and could imagine no other way of going through their day even though they were out of sync with their counterpart. Compounding this dysfunction was that after Fisher left the Admiralty in the evening, Churchill often overrode his decisions without consulting him. Fisher would only discover this subterfuge after returning to work, often when it was too late to cancel the orders.[121] This led to a series of disputes between Churchill and Fisher, which disrupted Admiralty policy and coordination. In fact, Fisher threatened to resign if Churchill continued to countermand his decisions. A compromise was quickly arranged in which both Churchill and Fisher agreed to only make important decisions with the explicit approval of the other, and, for a few weeks, this commonsense truce held.

The Dardanelles debacle reignited these tensions. For months, the First Sea Lord had vacillated. At times he seemed to fully support the plan, while at others he spoke of the operation in apocalyptic terms. The most likely explanation for this wildly inconsistent advice was that Fisher was conflicted about the planned assault and was either unable to stand up to Churchill on important matters of policy or unwilling to resign despite his repeated threats. Fisher's contradictory advice and moods allowed Churchill to believe that he had in fact convinced the Admiralty about the soundness of his plans. In fact, they had serious objections to his policies, and Churchill was merely seeing what he wanted to see. In later years, Churchill would selectively use some of these statements in his testimony to the Dardanelles Commission and in his memoir *The World Crisis* to show that he had been fully supported by the professional naval experts, but they were far from unanimous in their opinion.[122]

While Fisher's frustration with the Dardanelles had been a serious issue, the proximate cause of his resignation was Churchill's broken promise to consult him on all major policy decisions. On May 14, 1915 (the same day that the Shell Crisis broke as front-page news), Churchill and Fisher had been conferring about sending more ships to the Dardanelles to support the foundering operation. After significant protest and debate, Fisher had agreed for limited reinforcements to be pulled from other stations and sent, but Churchill was still unsatisfied. Later that evening, Churchill called Fisher and feigned appreciation, stating that he was now pleased with the numbers of ships the First Sea Lord had agreed on. He told him, "We have settled everything, and you must go home and have a good night's rest." This apparently assured the admiral, who followed his friend and colleague's advice. However, Churchill used this opportunity to dictate an entirely new set of instructions, which ordered more ships into the Dardanelles than Fisher had agreed on.[123]

When Fisher returned to the Admiralty on the morning of May 15, he was shocked to discover Churchill's underhanded maneuver.[124] The notoriously volatile admiral flew into a rage of righteous indignation. He had been deliberately deceived by Churchill, who had broken his promise, pretended to care about his health, and then presented his altered plan as a fait accompli. While it is still uncertain to what extent Churchill had altered their agreed-upon reinforcement (sources differ, but most say that the only significant change was the transfer of two submarines to the Dardanelles), this was too much for Fisher to endure.[125]

In a fit of volcanic fury, Fisher wrote a terse letter of resignation explaining his motives in somewhat self-serving terms:

> First Lord:
> After further anxious reflection, I have come to the regretted conclusion that I am unable to remain any longer as your colleague. It is undesirable in the public interest to go in to details—Jowett said, "Never explain"—but I find it increasingly difficult to adjust myself to the increasingly daily requirements of the Dardanelles to meet your views. As

you truly said yesterday, I am in the position of continually vetoing your proposals.

It is not fair to you besides being extremely distasteful to me.

I am off to Scotland at once, so as to avoid all questioning.

Yours truly,

Fisher[126]

With a finely honed sense of the melodramatic, Fisher then stormed out of the Admiralty. He told no one where he was going and abandoned his post, much to the shock of the staff members.

Churchill was walking to his office when he heard the news. As he crossed Horse Guards Parade, he was met by his secretary, who was running toward him nearly out of breath. "Fisher has resigned and I think he means it this time," his secretary exclaimed as he handed Churchill the First Sea Lord's letter of resignation.[127] At first, Churchill dismissed this as yet another example of Fisher's melodramatic theater, as it was the ninth time he formally offered his resignation and it seemed to fit a pattern of resignations, threatened resignations, peevish behavior, and ultimate reversals.[128] However, this time was different—Fisher was determined to never work with Churchill again.

The immediate question was where Admiral Fisher was. While his letter indicated that he was leaving immediately for seclusion in Scotland, this was completely untrue. Rather, Fisher was very close to the unfolding melodrama. After departing the Admiralty, he briefly visited David Lloyd George at the Treasury to tell him that he was leaving and then walked up Whitehall, where he took a room at the Charing Cross Hotel, only a short distance from his office at the Admiralty. He shut himself inside his room and waited while the Admiralty staff and senior members of the Asquith government desperately tried to locate him. The increasingly frenzied staff made dozens of phone calls, checked departing trains, and even considered that Fisher might be taking a ship to France. For a few desperate hours, the whereabouts of the leader of the Royal Navy were completely unknown.[129]

Fisher probably wanted nothing more than to be found and pleaded with to return to his post.[130] Such an outcome would have satisfied his need for attention and allowed him a strong bargaining position to demand the removal of Churchill as a condition of his return.[131] Indeed, the fact that he did not depart for Scotland but decided to stay in close proximity to his office indicates that he expected to be found. This location would provide enough physical distance to accentuate his point that the two men's leadership styles were incompatible but not so much that he could not quickly resume his duties if his conditions were met. This, however, was a dangerous game to play and one that would ultimately lead to his ruin and disgrace.[132]

Fisher had abandoned his post during the middle of a war. This would have normally been cause for immediate removal from office, a court-martial, or criminal punishment, possibly including death.[133] Indeed, Asquith fumed that the First Sea Lord "ought to be shot for leaving his post."[134] However, Fisher's status as a legendary leader and reformer at the Admiralty ensured that he could not be dismissed in a simple bureaucratic matter. Moreover, in the context of the troubled Dardanelles Campaign, his feuds with Churchill, and the broader fragility of the Asquith government, this proved to be nothing less than a scandal of profound magnitude. Further exacerbating the crisis was a series of unsubstantiated rumors that the German fleet was preparing to put to sea and seek battle right as the Royal Navy's top military leader acted in such a petulant manner.[135]

Fisher's erratic and peevish behavior took on an element of absurdist humor despite the severity of the incident. Even Asquith did not take this latest resignation seriously, quipping that "Fisher is always resigning." His daughter Violet noted in her diary entry of May 15, "[He] told me the most astonishing piece of news in these words—'Fisher has levanted.' He had simply run away from the Admiralty—leaving his post, his work etc—pulling down all the blinds of his London house, & leaving a red herring trail in the direction of Scotland. Grave as the situation was Father cldn't [sic] help but laughing at its extraordinary comic aspects."[136]

The First Sea Lord had not levanted and was eventually tracked down and given a note from the prime minister, which demanded, "Lord Fisher in the name of the King I command you to return to your post!"[137] Anticipating that he would be fawned over by the prime minister, Fisher soon arrived at 10 Downing Street. Both men had apparently calmed down, and they spent approximately an hour in friendly conversation. The admiral was humorous enough to inspire tears of laughter from Asquith's assistant Maurice Hankey, but he refused to withdraw his resignation.[138]

On one thing Fisher was adamant: Churchill was "quite impossible to work with. He was always doing things without consulting him." Fisher attempted to discredit Churchill by blaming him for the entire Dardanelles operation and falsely claiming that he had opposed it from the outset.[139] Despite Fisher's mercurial mood, he would not return to work as long as Churchill remained First Lord. Asquith's frustration was clear when he shared his account of this meeting with his daughter Violet. She noted in her diary that her father was upset by both Fisher's and Churchill's antics. She described Fisher as acting in a "lower-more cowardly and more unworthy way" but admitted, "Winston may have been exasperating to work with."[140]

Sensing that Fisher might be serious about resigning, Churchill put aside his ego and wrote a heartfelt letter of apology asking him to return to work and promising better behavior. Mixing flattery with an appeal to friendship and duty, defensiveness, and desperation, he wrote:

> My dear Fisher,
> The only thing to think of now is what is best for the country and for the brave men who are fighting. Anything which does injury to those interests will be harshly judged by history, on whose stage we now are.
> I do not understand what is the specific cause which has led you to resign. If I did I might cure it. When we parted last night I thought we were in agreement. The proposals I made to you by minute were I thought in general accord with your views, and in any case were for discussion between us. Our personal friendship is and I trust will remain unimpaired.
> It is true the moment is anxious and our difficulties grave. But I am sure that with loyalty and courage we shall come through safely and successfully. You could not let it be said that you had thrown me over because things were for the time being going badly at the Dardanelles.
> In every way I have tried to work in the closest sympathy with you. The men you wanted in the places you wanted them, the ships you designed, every proposal you have formally made for naval action I have agreed to. My own responsibilities are great, and also I am the one who gets the

blame for anything that goes wrong. But I have scrupulously adhered to our original agreement that we should do nothing important without consulting each other. If you think this is not so, surely you should tell me in what respect.

In order to bring you back to the Admiralty, I took my political life in my hands with the King and the Prime Minister, as you know well. You then promised to stand by me and see me through. If you now go at this bad moment and thereby let loose upon me the spite and malice of those who are your enemies even more than they are mine, it will be a melancholy ending to our six months of successful war and administration. The discussions which will arise will strike a cruel blow at the fortress of the Army now struggling on the Gallipoli Peninsula, and cannot fail to invest with an air of disaster a mighty enterprise, which, with patience, can and will certainly be carried to a success.

Many of the anxieties of the winter are past—the harbours are protected, the great flow of new construction is arriving. We are far stronger at home than we have ever been, and the great reinforcement is now at hand.

I hope you will come to see me to-morrow afternoon. I have a proposition to make you, with the assent of the Prime Minister, which may resolve some of the anxieties and difficulties which you feel about the measures necessary to support the Army at the Dardanelles.

Though I shall stand to my post until relieved, it will be a very great grief to me to part from you; and our rupture will be profoundly injurious to every public interest.

Yours ever,
W.[141]

Despite the tone of Churchill's letter, it did not persuade Fisher. The First Sea Lord refused to work with Churchill and made this demand well known to Asquith and the Admiralty staff. He also emphasized this point in his reply to Churchill. Writing in a defensive and self-serving manner, Fisher dramatically claimed that he had always opposed the Dardanelles operation, citing a 1907 memo where he had argued against such an assault. His reply ended with a dramatic flourish:

> YOU ARE BENT ON FORCING THE DARDA-NELLES AND NOTHING WILL TURN YOU FROM IT—NOTHING. I know you so well. . . . I could give no better proof of my desire to stand by you to this last moment than my having remained by you in the Dardanelles business to the last moment against the strongest conviction of my life, as stated in the Dardanelles Defense Committee Memorandum.
>
> *You will remain* and I SHALL GO. It is better so. Your splendid stand on my behalf with the King and the Prime Minister I can NEVER forget, when you took your political life in your hands and I really have worked very hard for you in return—*my utmost*—but here is a question beyond all personal obligations. I assure you it is only painful having further conversations. I have told the Prime Minister that I will not remain. I have absolutely decided to stick to that decision. NOTHING WILL TURN ME FROM IT. You say with much feeling that "*it will be a very great grief to you to part from me.*" I am certain you know in your heart no one has ever been more faithful to you than I have since I joined you last October. *I have worked my very hardest!*
>
> Yours,
> Fisher[142]

Churchill received the letter but could still not comprehend that his friend was serious about quitting and that he had caused this decision.

Undeterred, Churchill again wrote to Fisher, this time in a softer and less defensive tone. Believing he could flatter his friend into a personal meeting and then win him over with charisma, Churchill listed the admiral's many accomplishments and appealed to his sense of duty before sheepishly ending his letter, "In any case, whatever, you decide, I claim, in the name of friendship and in the name of duty, a personal interview—if only for the purpose of settling what explanation is to be offered to Parliament."[143] Again, Fisher would not be moved by these appeals to friendship and duty. He responded by highlighting his unwillingness to meet with Churchill, lest he be tempted to return to office by Churchill's silver tongue: "As usual your letter is most persuasive, but I really have considered everything and I have definitely told the Prime Minister that I leave to-morrow (Monday). Please don't wish to see me. I could say nothing as I have determined not to. *I know I am doing right.*"[144]

As Churchill and Fisher exchanged letters reminiscent of jilted lovers, rumors began to circulate about the curious happenings at the Admiralty. Letters of support for Fisher poured in from members of the fleet, including Admirals John Jellicoe and David Beatty. Even Queen Alexandra wrote Fisher, advising him to "stick to your post like [Admiral Horatio] Nelson" and calling him "the nation's hope."[145] This swell of support appears to have strengthened Fisher's desire to continue to serve at the Admiralty, but not under Churchill.

On May 16, Churchill was in full damage-control mode. Fearful that he would be removed from office if he could not reassert his authority, he secured the agreement of Sir Arthur Wilson to replace Fisher as First Sea Lord and obtained personal assurances of loyalty from the Second and Third Sea Lords.[146] Churchill then spent much of the rest of the day preparing for an anticipated parliamentary inquiry into his conduct at the Admiralty. Yet, while Churchill was a whirlwind of energy, it was clear to his friends that he was deeply shaken. That same day, he met Violet Asquith. Violet immediately recognized that something was amiss. She saw that her typically cocksure friend's confidence was shattered and that he was vulnerable, so she asked him directly "if he knew he was on the edge of a volcano in his relations with Fisher—he said no—they had always got on perfectly well—differed on no principle—he had always supposed him perfectly loyal etc." This innocent and unassuming response saddened Violet, who lamented in her diary, "Poor Winston—there is a very naïve disarming truthfulness about him—he is quite insensitive to climactic conditions."[147] These comments were truer than even Violet could know. Her father had already begun discussions to form a new coalition government and would soon be forced to remove Churchill from his post at the Admiralty as the cost of Tory participation.

In an attempt to oust Churchill, Fisher penned a series of unhinged letters, which ultimately sealed his fate and fueled rumors that he was half-mad.[148] In his May 17 letter to Andrew Bonar Law, the leader of the opposition, Fisher made biblical allusions to rejecting "30 pieces of silver to betray my country," forecasted doom and a *"very great national disaster,"* wrote with even wilder punctuation and capitalization than usual, and insisted that Churchill was to blame for the failures in the Dardanelles. His repeated attacks on Churchill were hyperbolic: "W.C. (HE'S A REAL DANGER!) . . . W.C. MUST go at all costs! AT ONCE . . . *W.C. is leading them all straight to ruin* . . . W.C. is a bigger danger than the Germans by a long way."[149] Ultimately, Fisher's letters to Bonar Law were a severe miscalculation. Rather than helping expedite his return to the Admiralty, they gave Bonar Law the opportunity to exploit the internal fissures within the Asquith government, demand greater Tory participation in the cabinet, and force the removal of Churchill.[150]

Fisher's letter to Prime Minister Asquith was equally unreasonable, demanding his return to office:

> If the following . . . conditions are agreed to, I can guarantee the successful termination of the War. . . .
>
> That Mr. Winston Churchill is not in the Cabinet to be always circumventing me. . . .
>
> That there shall be an entire new Board of Admiralty, as regards the Sea Lord and the Financial Secretary (who is utterly useless). New measures demand new men.
>
> That I shall have complete professional charge of the war at sea, together with the absolute sole disposition of the Fleet and the appointment of all ranks whatsoever, and absolutely untrammelled sole command of all sea forces whatsoever.
>
> That the First Lord of the Admiralty should be absolutely restricted to policy and parliamentary procedure. . . .
>
> That I should have the sole absolute authority for all new construction and dockyard work of whatever sort whatsoever, and complete control of the whole of the Civil Establishments of the Navy.
>
> These conditions must be published verbatim so that the Fleet may know my position.[151]

These demands were clearly unacceptable.[152] They threatened to undermine civilian control of the military, bordered on insubordination, and indicated that Fisher might have gone mad as the rumors suggested.[153] Although Fisher had wildly overplayed his hand and incited a very real crisis within the

Asquith government, he was still not immediately terminated. Asquith was keenly aware of the admiral's strong support within the fleet, the press, and popular opinion.[154]

Churchill was less savvy in his approach. At first, he acted as if this was a relatively small matter and hoped for a reconciliation and a return to normalcy.[155] Despite his original faith that all would quickly be restored, Churchill eventually panicked and reversed course. Sensing that he needed to distance himself from Fisher, he actually contributed to the rumors about the admiral's mental condition. He whispered to friends that Fisher was mad and even put these thoughts into writing in letters to Kitchener and other key figures.[156] This underhanded behavior did little to alter the fate of either man, but it indicates that despite their friendship, Churchill could be remarkably two faced and self-serving, particularly when he feared for his political future.

Ultimately, Asquith accepted Fisher's resignation on May 22 with a terse one-sentence letter: "I am commanded by the King to accept your tendered resignation of the Office of First Sea Lord of the Admiralty."[157] Given the drama of the previous week, this was anticlimactic, but it signaled a profound change, nevertheless.

Churchill was in a state of shock. While he admitted that they had different schedules and styles, he could not accept that he and his old friend and mentor could not work together. As Violet Asquith noted, never had two men "disagreed more often and more passionately. . . . And yet he seems to have had no inkling that their relations had reached a breaking point."[158] Yet more shocking developments lay ahead for Churchill, ones that would further wound his confidence, deepen his despair, and jeopardize his political future.

The Collapse of Asquith's Liberal Government

The downfall of Asquith's Liberal government had been a long time in the making. Broad-based frustration over the conduct of the war, the inability to achieve victory, and Asquith's seemingly relaxed leadership style had been the source of simmering public frustration and speculation for months.[159] Yet, despite his flagging public support and the looming prospect of a general election, Asquith held on to power. However, military failures, the Shell Crisis, and the bizarre behavior of Jackie Fisher made this uneasy political peace untenable.[160] The Tories sensed this vulnerability and became increasingly vocal in their criticisms of Asquith, ending their previous pledge to observe the truce between the parties.[161]

Asquith now faced a revolt that would likely topple him from office. In early May, the prime minister approached the Conservative leader Andrew Bonar Law and began a series of secret discussions to broker a deal with his rivals that would allow him to retain his leadership position. Bonar Law understood that the Tories lacked the support to win control of the government outright and that his own party suffered from internal divisions.[162] He indicated that his party would accept a coalition government under Asquith on the explicit conditions that he could pick key Tories be included in the cabinet and that Richard Haldane and Winston Churchill would be removed from their posts at the War Office and Admiralty.[163]

From Asquith's standpoint, this was almost too good to be true. He would remain prime minister, avoid a likely electoral defeat, stack the cabinet in a way that would allow him to continue his policies relatively unchecked, and rid himself of two ministers who had become political liabilities. Haldane had been falsely accused of being a pro-German sympathizer, and Bonar Law and the Tory Party had a personal vendetta against Churchill.[164] In fact, many Tories were still hurt by Churchill's 1904 defection from the party over the seemingly minor issue of free trade. For many, this defection was not a sign of principles or even a policy disagreement but little more than a self-serving and opportunistic ploy to ride the ascendancy of the Liberal Party to higher office. Compounding this partisan resentment was the fact that Bonar Law was particularly wary of working with Churchill. Even though Bonar Law recognized Churchill's impressive array of talents, he believed that he was a dangerous liability.

The Dardanelles and the dramatic departure of Fisher from the Admiralty only confirmed what Bonar Law had long suspected. This personal distrust ran so deep, in fact, that over a year later, when Lloyd George wanted to include Churchill in his cabinet, Bonar Law objected, just as he had with Asquith. When Lloyd George asked him, "Is he more dangerous when he is FOR you than when he is AGAINST you?" Bonar Law replied, "I would rather have him against us every time."[165] While Churchill should have understood that Bonar Law and the Tories wanted him gone, he was desperate to retain his position as First Lord of the Admiralty. This led Churchill to approach Bonar Law for support, a request that was quickly refused.[166] While friends and foes alike had turned on Churchill, he seemed genuinely surprised that he was politically a persona non grata and that the opposition leader was refusing to help.[167]

For Asquith, giving in to the Tory demands would incur a high personal price. Haldane was one of Asquith's closest friends, and he had mentored Churchill for the past decade.[168] Asquith had grown increasingly frustrated with Churchill but detested that Bonar Law and the Tories were forcing him to betray his friends to remain in power.[169] While Asquith recognized that this was the price of remaining in public office, he privately felt betrayed and emasculated by the Tory demands.[170]

In addition to breaking with Haldane and Churchill, Asquith had also learned on May 12 that his paramour Venetia Stanley had accepted his protégé Edwin Montagu's proposal of marriage. While the exact nature of Asquith and Stanley's relationship remains a topic of debate, it is certain that they had formed an incredibly intimate intellectual bond. Starting in 1910, they exchanged hundreds of letters that disclosed personal and political secrets, and during times of stress, Asquith leaned heavily on Stanley for advice and emotional support. Since the beginning of the war, he had penned multiple letters per day, often during the middle of cabinet meetings. These letters revealed not only his private fears but also many of the political divisions within the government as well as highly classified information about British strategy.[171] Now he was losing Stanley, his personal confidant, to Montagu, a young Liberal MP whom Asquith had invited into his confidence and inner circle. Asquith felt abandoned and admitted, "This breaks my heart," adding, "No Hell can be so bad," but he had little choice but to compartmentalize his personal feelings and focus on making a rational decision about his political future.[172]

Asquith quickly chose political survival over personal loyalty and cast Haldane and Churchill aside to save his party and career.[173] While it carried a high personal price, Asquith's deal with Bonar Law was a political masterstroke. It allowed him to remain as prime minister, avoid a potentially disastrous December referendum, stack the cabinet with just enough Unionist Tories to ensure their support without having to yield on policy matters, and give the illusion that he would manage the war effort more actively.[174] On May 19, Asquith made a short public statement informing the nation that he would be forming a new coalition government with the approval of the king. With these few words, what would be the last Liberal government in British history came to an anticlimactic end.

The prime minister's speech was short on details, and despite the tumult of recent days and his troubled relationship with the opposition, Churchill still hoped that he could retain his position as First Lord of the Admiralty. On May 20 and 21, Clementine and Winston wrote separate letters begging Asquith to retain Churchill as First Lord. Apparently unaware that his dismissal was an explicit condition for Tory cooperation, Churchill pleaded, "Let me stand or fail by the Dardanelles—but do not take it from my hands."[175] Rather than bolster Churchill's case, these desperate appeals had the unintended effect of making it easier for Asquith to dismiss his troublesome First Lord.

Yet, despite all of the trouble he had caused, Asquith recognized Churchill's talents and wanted to soften the blow to his ego. To that end, he privately informed Churchill that he would be removed as First Lord of the Admiralty in the near future but that he should remain at his post until a successor was named. Implicit in these directions was that Churchill should make no major decisions and was merely a caretaker.

Churchill was stunned by the news. By chance, Violet Asquith encountered Churchill shortly after he had been relieved, and she noted in her diary that her friend was so depressed that he was uncharacteristically mute and resigned to his fate. Churchill kept repeating that he was finished and that his chance to make a meaningful contribution to the war effort had been taken from him.[176] Despite her loyalty to her father, seeing her typically boisterous and confident friend reduced to such a vulnerable condition shocked Violet. As she confided to her diary, "I felt heart-broken for him—for he has done his very damnedest."[177] In this moment of weakness, Winston admitted to Violet that he had chosen Fisher to serve under him because he believed that the admiral was old and weak and that it would allow him to direct policy as he saw fit. These confessions remained private for many decades, but they reveal both the level of trust the two friends shared and the fact that Churchill had miscalculated drastically regarding his power and influence at the Admiralty. Now he faced an uncertain political future and a loss of influence when he most desired it—in the middle of a worldwide war.[178]

Churchill officially resigned on May 21, and the press was quick to editorialize the controversial First Lord's downfall.[179] The *Morning Post*, which had been calling for his resignation since he temporarily abandoned his post in October 1914 to command the Naval Division's defense of Antwerp, was particularly brutal. The *Post* opined that it was a blessing: "The truth is that Winston Churchill is a danger to this country."[180] Even the German press noted Churchill's fall with a series of sarcastic comments lamenting the fact that they had lost one of their "most valuable allies" and claiming that "the coiner of the phrase 'Germany's deluxe fleet' seems himself to have become an expensive luxury for his country."[181]

While Churchill was at a very low point, he still believed that he could be of use to Asquith and the broader war effort. On May 21, 1915, the day of his resignation, he wrote a private letter to Asquith, saying, "Count on me absolutely—if I can be of any use [in the war cabinet]. If not, some employment in the field."[182] Churchill naively expected a prestigious post in the cabinet or a military assignment with high rank and significant responsibility. He quickly rejected Asquith's offer to serve as colonial secretary but then reversed course and begged him to reconsider him for the position. This combination of arrogance and desperation caused an upset prime minister to deny him the office and scoff, "The situation for Churchill has no other meaning than his own prospects."[183]

The uncomfortable fact was that Churchill was oblivious as to how far his reputation had fallen and how few friends he had in government.[184] As he often did, he schemed about how to return to power and come out on top again. Little did he know he would soon be offered a position that would keep him in the inner circle of the Asquith government yet ensure that he was virtually powerless—a cruel twist of fate indeed.

Kind Words from an Old Rival

Winston Churchill sat in his office at the Admiralty dejected and with little to do but wait. He had been told that he was going to be replaced as First Lord of the Admiralty but should remain at his post until a successor was appointed. He was to make no important decisions, only wait. For a man of almost boundless energy and enthusiasm, the quiet boredom was almost unbearable. A world was at war. Thousands of ships and millions of men were engaged in battle, the fate of empires hung in the balance, and Winston Churchill waited. As he idled away, Churchill pondered his political future and despaired. He had lost the trust of the prime minister, was being blamed for the unfolding disaster at the Dardanelles, and had now lost the job he had loved more than anything else. It appeared that his once-certain path to glory and fame was blocked and his once-promising political future ruined.

Churchill's depressive mood was temporarily interrupted by a knock at the door from an unexpected visitor, Lord Horatio Kitchener. As the senior member of the army, Kitchener was something of a mythic figure in British society. He had won great victories in the Sudan and South Africa, he directed the war effort with almost unquestioned authority, and his handsome visage was quite literally the face of the British war effort. What made this visit surprising was not Kitchener's fame but the fact that he and Churchill were rivals. Indeed, they had a long history of disagreements going back to war in Sudan, when Kitchener had repeatedly tried to block Churchill's transfer to serve in his command.[185] Eager to participate in the campaign, the young Churchill had used his political connections to circumvent Kitchener's refusal and was ultimately given a position as a member of the 21st Lancers. These lobbying efforts had the unintended effect of convincing the commanding general that Churchill was a selfish and entitled glory hunter who thought only about his own interests and not those of the British Army. As fate would have it, Churchill was the officer who had first seen the Dervish advance toward Omdurman and reported this information directly to Kitchener.[186] The general put his feelings aside, analyzed his young subaltern's verbal report, and used it to deploy his troops and ready them for the stunning victory that followed. Ultimately, this timely and accurate intelligence, the young officer's coolness under fire, and his willingness to personally lead his men in a daring cavalry charge softened Kitchener's opinion of Churchill.

These good feelings were not to last long, as Churchill was critical of Kitchener in his two-volume account of the campaign, *The River War*.[187] He was particularly unforgiving regarding Kitchener's treatment of the Dervish dead and wounded after the Battle of Omdurman and the purposeful destruction of the Mahdi's tomb at Khartoum a few days later.[188] While Churchill's private comments were even more critical, his written words were enough to permanently strain the relationship between these two strong-willed men. When World War I brought them together again as members of Asquith's War Cabinet, they did their best to act professionally, but they differed in personal style and frequently disagreed on matters of policy.

Given their history and the fact that Kitchener was busy with the ongoing war effort, his visit was truly unexpected. While Churchill might have anticipated gloating or peevishness from his rival, this was not Kitchener's style.[189] Instead, the most famous soldier in the British Army was remarkably humble and gracious. Churchill described his meeting with Kitchener:

> I was not at first aware of what it was all about . . . he asked me whether it was settled that I should leave the Admiralty. I said it was. He asked what I was going to do. I said I had no idea; nothing was settled. He spoke very kindly about our work together . . . he got up to go he turned and said, in the impressive and almost majestic manner which was natural to him, "Well there is one thing at any rate they cannot take from you. The Fleet was ready." After that he was gone . . . I was condemned often to differ from him, to oppose him and to criticize him. But I cannot forget the rugged kindness and warm-hearted courtesy which led him to pay me a visit.[190]

In the weeks that would follow, Kitchener's kind words were almost all Churchill had to cling to for reassurance and support.[191] In fact, much closer friends and political allies kept their distance from him, and, "with one exception, the only one of [Churchill's] colleagues who paid [him] a visit of ceremony was the over-burdened Titan whose disapprobation had been one of the disconcerting experiences of [his] youth."[192]

Despite Kitchener's kind gesture, Churchill remained in a state of shock. He had described his term as First Lord as "the four most memorable years [of his life]," and now the job that he had poured so much of his own energy into was gone, and for a time, so too was his own energy.[193] Friends noted that he now stooped when he walked, lacked energy, and looked haggard and aged by the ordeal. A war correspondent who saw Churchill at a dinner party wrote of this shocking transformation, "I am much surprised at the change in Winston Churchill. He looks years older, his face is pale, he seems very depressed, and to feel keenly his retirement at the Admiralty."[194] Churchill's family also noted his dark mood. His mother, Jennie, knew that her son craved action and attention, and noted, "I am afraid Winston is very sad at having nothing to do." She elaborated that because her son had been such a rapid riser and key figure in British politics, the blow must have been particularly cruel: "When you have your hand at the helm for four years it seems stagnation to take a back place and for why?"[195]

But the fleet had been ready.[196]

Chancellor of the Duchy of Lancaster

While Churchill had repeatedly lobbied Asquith for a high office in the new coalition government, there was little that the prime minister could or would do to meet these requests. The simple fact was that Asquith was politically wounded, the Tories had taken eight of twenty cabinet-level positions, and Churchill's political fortunes were at an all-time low. Despite his diminished political position, Asquith believed it was better to co-opt Churchill and keep him within the government rather than having him question government policy from the outside.[197] Much to Churchill's disappointment, Asquith offered him the job of chancellor of the Duchy of Lancaster.[198]

The position dated to the fourteenth century and sounded regal and impressive, but it was an unimportant role with little power. Officially, the chancellor was responsible for managing the king's properties held within the Duchy of Lancaster, collecting whatever rents these properties produced, and appointing magistrates and minor officials. However, as was the case with Churchill, this position was often used as a means of including prominent politicians in the cabinet without giving them any important duties. Recently, it had been used as a reward for loyal party members such as Charles Hobhouse and Edwin Montagu, a fact that was particularly frustrating for Churchill, who believed that he would be seen as a charity case or a has-been.[199]

Churchill could not accept that his appointment was an act of generosity on the part of Asquith. In fact, Churchill's initial refusal to serve as colonial secretary gave the prime minister an ample excuse to exclude his presumptuous and controversial young minister from the government entirely. This would have pleased Asquith's opponents, and it likely would have been easier to enact policy without the meddlesome Churchill fomenting dissent and debate from within. Yet Asquith chose to pay a political price and keep Churchill, while simultaneously attempting to limit his influence. Although this was ultimately a recipe for frustration on both sides, it was a genuine attempt at a pragmatic and mutually beneficial solution to an uncomfortable problem.

While this was the least prestigious cabinet-level position, it was still in the cabinet. On a practical level, Churchill desperately needed the salary of a cabinet official as his finances were perpetually strained during this period. Pecuniary considerations aside, neither the title nor the opportunity to appoint minor officials was his true motivation.[200] He passionately desired to wield power and influence over the conduct of the war, and this position allowed him to remain in government and serve on the newly formed Dardanelles Committee. The chance to continue to shape British strategy was Churchill's true reason for accepting the chancellery. To this end, he made much of the fact that he would retain his old seat at Lord Kitchener's side, even if it was in a greatly reduced capacity.[201]

In his postwar memoir, *The World Crisis*, Churchill admitted that inclusion in the war cabinet was his primary motivation and that the prime minister understood that his talents for war-making should not go to waste: "I should certainly not have felt able to accept it but for the fact that he coupled it with a promise that I should be a member of the War Council, or War Committee, of the Cabinet."[202] Churchill clearly realized that his prestige and influence had declined precipitously; as his cousin "Sunny," the Duke of Marlborough, wrote him, "You have been flung a bone on which there is little meat."[203]

Even though he believed the office was beneath his dignity, Churchill did his best to appear magnanimous in his reduced role. He promised to appoint qualified and honest magistrates and ensured continuity and efficiency by retaining Lord Shuttleworth as lord lieutenant of the county. Shuttleworth had worked with seven previous chancellors and was quite comfortable in running the relatively minimal day-to-day operations.[204] This delegation freed Churchill to focus on the conduct of the war and rebuild his own reputation—two tasks that held far greater interest than managing the king's estates.[205]

While Churchill still had an insider's view of the conduct of the war, this soon led to additional frustration. His fate hung by a slender thread, and he had little official power. While he should have been grateful for his inclusion on the Dardanelles Committee, Churchill believed that he was ignored, overruled, and surrounded by men he judged mediocre and uninspired. He was particularly bitter at his old friend turned rival, Arthur Balfour, for taking his position of First Lord of the Admiralty.[206]

Despite his feelings of jealousy, Churchill understood that he needed to appear gracious and wrote a very friendly letter to Balfour on May 26, 1915, wishing him success in the job.[207] Privately, Churchill seethed. He believed that he was better suited for the job and frequently mocked the reserved and quiet Balfour behind his back as a "tabby" cat.[208] This bitterness only grew with time, and Churchill would directly attack Balfour in a speech to the House of Commons in March 1916 and make many dismissive and petty comments in *The World Crisis*. He was quick to find fault, describing Balfour as weak, vain, stubborn, and ineffective as both prime minister and First Lord.[209] Churchill believed that he could do better, but the opportunities he so desperately sought were just out of his grasp.

Churchill's Political Obituary?

By the end of May 1915, Winston Churchill appeared to be finished. He had risen quickly and streaked through British politics like a meteor but had now come crashing back to earth. His friends lamented his fall, and his rivals rejoiced in the demise of a dangerous upstart. Even the typically cocksure Churchill doubted himself. He had a fear of dying young and had imposed the unreasonable goal of becoming prime minister before he turned forty-five, the same age his father, Randolph, had been when he died. Now, he privately questioned whether he was "Forty and Finished."[210] For a man known for his resilience and determination, this admission of self-doubt was unusual, yet Churchill had good reason to despair. His reputation was in tatters, his finances were strained, he suffered from bouts of depression, he had been cast aside by Prime Minister Asquith, and most importantly, he could no longer do what he loved most—lead the Royal Navy during a world war! In the twilight years of his life, after he had served as prime minister, led his nation through World War II, and won countless accolades, Churchill described his first term as First Lord of the Admiralty as his "golden age."[211] He loved that job. He loved the Royal Navy. He loved being a vital part of the Allied war effort. Now, the position that had so consumed Churchill's energies and given him a sense of purpose had been taken from him.

Churchill was now hardly more than an irrelevant scapegoat. He had little power, but as chancellor of the Duchy of Lancaster, he was provided a front-row seat to the conduct of the war and the inner workings of the government. He tried repeatedly to reinsert himself into the policymaking process, writing memos, proposing new strategies, and offering to serve as either a civilian observer or a combatant, yet action was often painfully slow, and he was often ignored. For a man with Churchill's energy and enthusiasm, being continually reminded of his irrelevance was crushing.

This was an inauspicious beginning to a year that would ultimately transform Winston Churchill into a great statesman. For the time being, all he could do was persevere and have faith in his ultimate destiny.[212] Over the next twelve months, he would struggle to find purpose and meaning and would ultimately win one of his greatest victories. Yet, in May 1915, the path forward seemed uncertain.

2

The Political Outcast

Churchill Turns to Painting

Winston Churchill was often frustrated but rarely bored. In fact, he was known for and defined by his seemingly limitless energy, ideas, and zeal for life. But at the end of May 1915, he was frustrated and bored. He had poured every bit of energy and passion into his role as First Lord of the Admiralty, and now he had little to show for his efforts but public scandal, a failed campaign, and a career that was once promising but now appeared to be at a dead end. When Churchill was bored, trouble often followed.

Despite the impressive-sounding title of Churchill's new office, the chancellery of the Duchy of Lancaster had little appeal for the ambitious former First Lord of the Admiralty. More than the reduced power and prestige, what bothered Churchill was the lack of excitement and relevance. Collecting taxes, appointing magistrates, and ensuring fair governance were noble and necessary pursuits, but they paled in comparison to the drama and urgency of leading the world's greatest navy in the world's greatest war. Churchill had little interest in his new position, but he understood that to have any political future he must put aside his ego and attempt to be a competent administrator. While Churchill largely deferred his duties to his deputy, who had served under seven previous chancellors and was happy to run the office, he did win a minor bureaucratic victory by obtaining more staff members and expanding office space.[1] He would later put a brave face on this period in his memoirs, yet he was clearly upset by his lack of power and influence.[2]

Initially, Churchill acted as if nothing had changed. He clung to the hope that his inclusion on the newly formed Dardanelles Committee would provide him significant influence over the conduct of the war but found that he had greatly limited authority and power in his reduced role. While he never gave up attempting to advance his ideas and shape the military and political issues of the day, he soon realized that he was largely irrelevant in his new position.

In addition to his fruitless attempts to direct the war, Churchill also channeled much of his boredom and frustration into a series of attempts to clear his name.[3] Even though the Dardanelles Campaign was just beginning and he had little to do with the failed ground operations, he was already being blamed for the stalemate and the sense of hopelessness that gripped the entire endeavor. Churchill's first attempt to clear his name came on May 19 when he was awaiting his replacement as First Lord. He requested that the Admiralty publish key documents from the planning phase of the operation, which he believed would show that the campaign had broad support from Admiralty planners and that it had been poorly executed by others, not poorly conceived by him. Given the need to maintain secrecy and the bureaucratic inertia of the Admiralty, Churchill was denied his request to publish the papers, and a protracted battle over the declassification and release of these documents ensued.[4]

While Churchill was unable to secure the documents, he was willing to talk in general terms to anyone who would listen to his side of the story. He was careful not to leak any classified information, yet he spoke freely and repeatedly asserted that he had been unfairly treated and his genius squandered, and that history would ultimately vindicate him once the full story was known.[5]

In an interview with newspaper owner Sir George Riddell a few days after he left the Admiralty, Churchill revealed his true feelings: "I am the victim of political intrigue. I am finished. . . . Yes. Finished in respect for all I care for—the waging of the war; the defeat of the Germans. I have had a high place offered to me, a position which has been occupied by distinguished men, and which carries with it a high salary. But all that goes for nothing. This is what I live for. I have prepared a statement of my case but cannot use it."[6]

It seemed that Churchill was left with only words. He could give his opinions on the conduct of the war but could not influence policy. He could tell his side of the story with access to classified documents but could not secure their release. He could complain to friends and the press, but these bitter words could not change his fortunes. Churchill was bored and depressed. In the words of his wife and best friend, Clementine, he almost "died of grief."[7]

Faced with political irrelevance and boredom, Churchill seriously considered fighting in a frontline capacity in May 1915. He had advanced his early career with military exploits and adventures, and now he wondered if he might do so again. These thoughts were encouraged by none other than his friend General John French, who was the commander of the British Expeditionary Forces in France. French and Churchill had long respected each other, and on May 20, the general wrote to encourage his friend to consider serving in a more active capacity: "I am always with you in deep affection and admiration. You know you are always welcome here."[8] This could have been dismissed as a simple courtesy had French not repeated the offer on May 29: "You have always spoken to me of the rest and happiness it gives you to be with the Army in the Field. . . . A view of the troops and the enemy will change your perspective. . . . Dark days come to all of us in turn and it is then we want to turn for help and sympathy to affectionate friends—and you have many here."[9] Although Churchill was flattered by these kind words, he was not ready to give up on politics just yet. Ever the optimist, he still believed that he could influence policymakers in London, clear his name, and stage a dramatic political comeback. To do this, he would need to avoid the siren song and escapism of military service.

Focusing on War Strategy

Whether fairly or not, Churchill's political future was intimately tied to the success of the Dardanelles Campaign. To this end, he could not admit defeat and instead argued repeatedly for reinforcements to be sent to the Gallipoli Peninsula. While the ability to focus his energies on an issue was one of Churchill's key strengths, this dogged single-mindedness quickly wore on the nerves of his fellow cabinet members. They were less wedded to the campaign and could see that it was a relatively minor part of the broader Allied war effort. Thus, many who had once supported the campaign were more willing to cut their losses and move on when it became apparent that a rapid victory was unobtainable. Not so for Churchill. Rather than aiding his cause or increasing his influence among the war cabinet, Churchill's obsession with the Dardanelles made it easier to ignore his proposals and supported the belief that he had been the sole author of the disastrous campaign.

The newly appointed chancellor of the Duchy of Lancaster refused to be limited to the administrative tasks of his office. On the contrary, Churchill spent much of the first week in office writing a memo on the current state of the Allied war efforts, which he presented on June 1. The memo was brilliant but almost completely irrelevant. After detailing the stalemates in other theaters, Churchill quickly pivoted and laid out his case for an immediate reinforcement of the Dardanelles. According to Churchill, the Russian front was stabilized and would improve with Italy's entry into the war; therefore, it would not have to be directly reinforced. He then considered action on the western front but concluded that direct attacks on German positions in France were wasteful and counterproductive, claiming, "I feel more than ever doubtful of our ability to break the German lines. . . . We should be ill-advised to squander our new armies in frantic and sterile efforts to pierce German lines. To do so is to play the German game."[10] He noted that the naval situation was favorable and that there was little chance of a German invasion of Great Britain.

Churchill then advanced his claim that the Dardanelles was the only theater where satisfactory results could be obtained:

> The position at the Dardanelles is at once hopeful and dangerous. The longer it lasts the more dangerous it will become. The sooner it is settled the sooner everything can again, if desired, be concentrated on the French and Flemish front. . . . If we delay longer in sending the necessary reinforcements, or send them piecemeal, we shall have in the end to send all, and more than all, that are now asked for. . . . It seems most urgent to try to obtain a decision here and wind up the enterprise in a satisfactory manner as soon as possible.[11]

This memo set a pattern of Churchill pouring significant time, effort, and thought into a problem only to be ignored by an increasingly frustrated cabinet.

The first meeting of the Dardanelles Committee was held on June 7, 1915.[12] The meeting was led by Kitchener, who presented three options: retreat, send major reinforcements, or send minor reinforcements.[13] Consistent with his June 1 memo, Churchill argued for major reinforcements, which he believed should have been sent "within 48 hours of Sir Ian Hamilton's telegram of May 17."[14] The committee was divided and adjourned without committing to any of the three options. For Churchill, who urged immediate action, this delay was exasperating.

With little else to do, Churchill traveled to his constituency of Dundee, Scotland, and gave a speech on June 5. His duties as First Lord had kept him away for over a year, but now he felt the need to reconnect with voters and defend his tattered reputation.[15] In his speech, he asserted that it was essential to remain optimistic and claimed that under his leadership "the seas have been swept clear; the submarine menace has been fixed . . . the personal ascendency of our men, the superior quality of our ships on the high seas have been established beyond doubt or question. . . . Everything is in perfect order." Churchill briefly praised his successor, Lord Balfour, before launching into a detailed defense of the Dardanelles operation. He told his audience to expect losses but claimed repeatedly that the prize was worth the risk. "There never was a great subsidiary operation of war in which a more complete harmony of strategic, political, and economic advantages have combined. . . . Through the narrows of the Dardanelles and across the ridges of the Gallipoli Peninsula lie some of the shortest paths to a triumphant peace."[16] Although these claims were factually dubious, the audience applauded Churchill's optimistic and defiant tone, his friends and constituents wrote numerous letters of support, and the press reports were generally favorable.[17] This support strengthened Churchill's resolve to act decisively on the Dardanelles, but his renewed confidence was soon met with frustration.

The Dardanelles Committee reconvened for additional meetings on June 9 and ultimately decided to reinforce General Hamilton. While Churchill had played a key role in the debate, he was distraught by the lack of decisiveness in these deliberations.[18] He noted later, "All the facts necessary to the decision were equally available; all the arguments were equally claimant. But from causes in which the enemy had no part, which arose solely from the confusion into which the governing instrument in this country had been thrown, from a fortnight to three weeks were lost forever. The consequences were momentous. Time was the dominating factor."[19] For Churchill, these meetings illustrated the broader malaise in the government and hammered home his own feelings of impotence.

A Friendship of a Lifetime

During this period of extreme frustration, Churchill solidified one of his greatest friendships in a life defined by friendships—that which he shared with Archibald Sinclair. The two had first met in London society circles in the months before the Great War, and Churchill was impressed by the young soldier, who was serving in the 2nd Life Guards. Despite the humble pay of a junior officer, Sinclair had independent means thanks to a hundred-thousand-acre inheritance. This wealth, combined with his rugged good looks, made him a striking figure and an eligible bachelor. The two mingled at parties held by Prime Minister Asquith and discovered that they enjoyed each other's company. Sensing the younger man's talents and charm, Churchill marked Sinclair as someone to get to know better.[20] Over the coming months, the pair formed a lasting friendship and respect for each other, based in no small part on their similar personal backgrounds. Indeed, both had American mothers, both of their fathers had died young from the probable effects of venereal disease, both were very close to their nannies, both had attended Sandhurst, and both enjoyed taking flying lessons in the early 1910s, when this was considered a very dangerous undertaking.[21] In addition, Sinclair had begun to show interest in politics, and Churchill was more than happy to serve as his political mentor, formally introducing him to various power brokers in the Liberal Party and planning out his future as a public figure.[22]

Although the outbreak of the war would interrupt Sinclair's political rise, it did not derail this friendship.[23] In fact, the relationship deepened. Churchill took a keen interest in Sinclair's career and even wrote to his commanding officer, the former Liberal war minister Jack Seely, to ensure that his friend received the coveted position as aide-de-camp. While Sinclair quickly found this role boring, he developed a reputation for efficiency, bravery, and coolness under fire.[24] Perhaps jealous of his friend's frontline experiences, Churchill wrote multiple times to implore Sinclair to be safe, often mentioning his own political trials. He even offered the opportunity to quit the army and promised, "I will fix up a constituency for you," but Sinclair spurned this offer and remained at the front.[25]

Churchill expressed his frustration and feelings of irrelevance to Sinclair in a letter dated June 9 and marked "Very Private." He mused about the future of the cabinet, Fisher's mental health, and the power of the Northcliffe press before confessing: "I am profoundly unsettled: and cannot use my gift. Of that last I have no doubts. I do not feel that my judgements have been falsified, or that the determined pursuance of my policy through all the necessary risks was wrong. I would do it all again, if the circumstances were repeated. But I am faced with the problem of living through days of 24 hours each:

and averting my mind from the intricate business I had in hand—which was my life. I do not think I can go on here."[26]

Throughout his public career, Churchill frequently complained about government policies in letters to his friends. Typically, he would grumble, get back to work, and either move on or figure out an alternative way to persuade others. The Dardanelles Campaign was different. While Churchill complained and dutifully got back to business, he soon found himself consumed by the topic. He was powerless and unable to move on or find an alternative means of influencing these critical war debates.

As was typical, Sinclair responded to his friend's ill temper with the youthful optimism that he would retain for the rest of his life. Instead of trying to rebut his friend's negative points, Sinclair focused on his own adventures and excitement on the front. Sinclair flattered Churchill, noting, "I am truly grateful to you for getting me this job. . . . It has been a great experience and enables one to see the war in a much truer perspective."[27] Sinclair's letter was meant to cheer up Churchill by reminding him of his own experiences at the front, which had been so formative in his early life and career. This appears to have had the intended effect, while also planting a seed in Churchill's mind that perhaps frontline service would again be the answer to his troubles. With a touch of envy, Churchill wrote back a letter of thanks, noting, "You at least in honourable definite real though circumscribed activities may feel confident. . . . You have done so well. If you survive you will always look back on these months as the true glorious period of your life."[28]

Strategic Frustrations

While Churchill would ultimately follow his own advice and seek glory and redemption on the front lines, for now he believed that his place was in London. As the details of the Allied plans were being debated and revised, he repeatedly argued for a significant reinforcement in the Dardanelles. His logic was straightforward—a few divisions more or less would make no difference on the western front, but they could make an impact in the Dardanelles. Therefore, a maximum effort should be made where it was most likely to meet with success, in the Dardanelles.[29]

Churchill was so sure of his strategy that "[he] therefore laboured by every means open to [him] to secure even larger reinforcements and above all their accelerated dispatch."[30] He composed another impressive memo dated June

11, which argued for an amphibious landing at the Bulair Isthmus to cut off the Ottoman Army's supply routes and provide a means of transporting fuel and food overland to British submarines stationed in the Sea of Marmara.[31] He followed this up with a June 15 letter to Kitchener, where he demonstrated a superb grasp of the geography of the Gallipoli Peninsula, anticipating the defensive measures of German general Otto Liman von Sanders and arguing for an additional reserve of "two or three fresh divisions" to be kept in Egypt in case the "three first divisions now under orders do a great deal, but not all and after three or four days' fighting are brought to a standstill with 10,000 or 15,000 casualties."[32]

Anticipating that these operational proposals needed additional strategic justification, Churchill completed a memo on June 18 titled "A Further Note upon the General Military Situation."[33] This memo was significantly longer than his June 1 memo but employed a similar style and structure to expand on his vision of Allied strategy. Again, Churchill began with assessments of other theaters and the pressures facing the Allied partners, and in each case the memo reached a convincing and sober conclusion that the theater was stalemated and provided little hope of victory. From there, the memo pivoted to a discussion of the Dardanelles as the only option that offered the hope of victory at an acceptable price.

Churchill's June 18 memo was considerably more hyperbolic than his previous memos and was filled with flowery language regarding the prospects of victory in the Ottoman theater. In particular, the conclusion of the memo read like a dramatic political speech:

> There can be no doubt that we now possess the means and the power to take Constantinople before the end of the summer if we act with decision and with a due sense of proportion . . . it will react on Russia. It will give the encouragement so sorely needed. It will give the reward so long desired. It will render a service to an Ally unparalleled in the history of nations. It will multiply the resources and open the channel for the re-equipment of the Russian armies. It will dominate the Balkan situation and cover Italy. It will resound through Asia. Here is the prize, and the only prize, which lies within reach this year. It can certainly be won without unreasonable expense, and within comparatively short time. But we must act now, and on a scale which makes speedy success certain.[34]

While this Churchillian rhetoric is impressive, it was almost certainly counterproductive. Indeed, these same turns of phrase that would later make Churchill so famous perturbed his fellow members of the cabinet. While we can see this use of rhetoric with the benefit of historical hindsight, at the time these prosaic lines had the unintended effect of convincing the members of the Asquith government that Churchill was a schemer and a political liability.

For his part, Churchill could not understand why his fellow cabinet members did not see his brilliance and refused to listen to his urgent appeals for action. He expressed his frustrations in a June 19 letter to his brother, Jack, who was serving at Gallipoli: "I have been having a hard battle all these weeks & have been fighting every inch of the road. My anxiety is that you will not have enough men to carry it [the planned offensive] through . . . the certainty [that the war would not be over in 1915] fills my mind with melancholy thoughts. The youth of Europe—almost a whole generation—will be shorn away."[35]

With little to do, Churchill attempted to micromanage the Dardanelles operations. He studied maps of the Gallipoli Peninsula, read intelligence reports, and made plans in minute detail about proposed lines of march and the employment of individual units. While these plans were not without their merits, this was incredibly presumptuous and unusual behavior. Understandably, the military professionals and cabinet members ignored Churchill's attempts to direct the campaign. With little influence, Churchill felt uneasy and nervous. The typically confident Churchill expressed his feelings in a particularly candid letter to his friend Archibald Sinclair dated July 30:

> I have now much time on my hands and can feel thoroughly everything, waiting passionately conscious of capacity for service, yet paralysed nearly always. It is like being in a cataleptic trance while all you value is being hazarded. But I have managed to bear it so far. It will comfort my soul to come out for a few months and serve with my regiment, & my mind turns over and over in its malaise to that. But till our victory is made at the Dardanelles my part is plainly here. . . . Would you believe it—I pass my days painting. It keeps my mind at peace . . . I have a small farmhouse beautifully placed in Surrey. Do come please—& let me know the earliest moment. Don't think of coming to England without warning me. . . . Do not let

my letters fall into the hands of the Germans when they storm your trenches. The swine will rejoice.[36]

Clearly, Churchill was bored and frustrated by his inability to influence events. Yet hidden within this revealing letter was the key to Churchill's salvation. He had rented a farmhouse and begun to paint. Of all the twists of fate and strokes of luck in Churchill's long life, this might have been the luckiest and most unexpected.

Painting as a Muse

Churchill's discovery of painting was the result of an extremely unlikely chain of events, the first of which involved financial prudence. Throughout his life, through good times and bad, Churchill spent lavishly. He was perpetually short on cash but would spend or borrow to obtain luxuries that he believed were necessary. While Churchill's position as chancellor of the Duchy of Lancaster provided him with a generous salary of £4,360 per year, he was deeply in debt during this period. Indeed, Churchill was so cash poor that he successfully petitioned for his salary as a cabinet minister to be disbursed monthly rather than quarterly as was customary.[37] Furthermore, he anticipated that Asquith's hold on power was tenuous and that he might not be able to rely on this salary for much longer. To this end, Churchill began one of his many attempts to economize. He resigned from four of his social clubs and moved his family from their rented home into a house that had been purchased by his brother, Jack. Although Jack was away fighting at Gallipoli, his family was present, and the home was rather crowded for Winston's taste. These cramped living arrangements, combined with the summer heat and frustrations with politics in London, led him to rent a property known as Hoe Farm with his brother's family.[38]

Although Churchill was reluctant to leave the city, the farm, which lay nestled in a wooded valley, was a blessing in disguise.[39] Churchill tried to make the most of his new retreat and, in a nod to the romanticism of previous generations, claimed that he enjoyed getting back to the country. In his June 19 letter to Jack, he noted that the family lived happily on the farm: "It really is a delightful valley and the garden gleams with summer jewelry, We live v[er]y simply—but with all the essentials of life well understood and well provided for—hot baths, cold champagne, new peas, & old brandy the essentials of life."[40]

This bucolic setting could not match the thrill of London, but it allowed Churchill to enjoy himself in ways that he had not anticipated.[41] For the first time in years, he had ample time to spend with his family. Freed from the demands of high office and society obligations, he was willing to relax and play silly games with his children, Diana, Randolph, and Sarah, and nephews, John and Peregrine. One of the children's favorites was "gorillas," where Churchill would hide and wait for the children to find him. When they were near his hiding place, he would spring up, hold out his arms, and make noises like a gorilla, much to the amusement of the youths.[42]

For both the children and Churchill, these games must have been unusually sweet. Churchill had grown up without the presence of his father and could remember only a few real conversations with Lord Randolph.[43] Now, he was a famous politician and was repeating the same pattern of neglect in pursuit of his career. For the moment, at least, this could be forgotten, and he could be the playful and doting parent his father had failed to be for him and his brother, Jack.

Churchill's increased interaction with his children and the slow pace of life at Hoe Farm had another unanticipated but profound impact: it introduced him to painting. One day (the exact date of which is unknown), while he was relaxing in the garden, he saw his sister-in-law, Gwendeline "Goonie" Churchill, sketching the idyllic scene spread before them. While Churchill had never cared much for high art, he asked Goonie about her picture. He quickly decided that he would like to try his own hand at painting, since he had little to do and was surrounded by the beauty of the English countryside in summer.[44] Amused by Churchill's sudden interest in art, Goonie suggested that he try his hand at her son's watercolor paints.[45] Taking the child's paint box, the famous statesman quickly began experimenting with colors, shapes, and techniques, applying pigment to paper. His efforts were tentative at first, but he quickly became transfixed by the new world that had opened to him.

While painting would quickly become an obsession for Churchill, he had given little indication of untapped potential or enthusiasm before summer 1915. He had enjoyed drawing as a schoolboy and had quit the school choir at Harrow and switched to drawing one hour per week beginning in January 1890.[46] He drew primarily landscapes and bridges, and with his minimal formal training, the results were predictably amateurish. Despite these uninspired efforts, the young boy appears to have persisted because of a mixture of professional and familial pressure. On the professional side, he knew that geometrical drawing and freehand drawing were part of the Sandhurst entrance exam and understood that because of his poor understanding of more academic subjects, he could not afford to miss points anywhere else.[47] In addition, a request from his demanding yet absent father that he focus on drawing rather than singing motivated the lonely schoolboy, as did a letter he received from his grandmother Duchess Frances "Fanny" Spencer-Churchill that specifically encouraged him to continue drawing.[48]

At Sandhurst, Churchill studied military drawing, but this had a practical focus on producing sketch maps and technical images of geographic features and buildings.[49] This may have contributed to his later skills as an artist, but at the time, he complained, "We have been doing a lot of sketching-maps etc. out of doors and it is very hot and uncomfortable work."[50] As a junior officer traveling on leave to Cuba, Churchill got a contract as a war correspondent to report on the fighting between the Spanish forces and the Cuban insurgents. As an unproven reporter, Churchill wanted to catch the eye of his editors, and he calculated that sketches of the action would help bring his words to life. Because he understood that his technique needed refinement, Churchill read a book titled *Making Sketches* before his 1895 departure to Cuba. Despite this attempt at self-improvement, his drawings were clearly hurried and amateurish, but they did reveal a sense of action and adventure.[51] The fact that these drawings were of poor quality and were not included in the newspapers did not deter the young Churchill, and he would continue to send drawings back from Cuba and other overseas postings in the days before pictures became a staple in newspapers.[52] Winston would also sketch pigs and other "gargoyle-like creatures" in his private letters to Clementine, but these were little more than loving doodles for his and her amusement.[53] Despite these faint hints of talent and interest, it is fair to say that Churchill had little exposure to or training in fine arts in general or painting in particular before 1915.

For a man who had done so much in his life, the possibility of trying something new and different for the first time held a true excitement. He had lived forty years but never attempted painting or even looked seriously at the works of others. Now, he could look upon the world in a completely different manner.[54] For Churchill, who was bored and frustrated, the newness of painting was a key element of its appeal; as he noted, "Change is the master key" for a hobby or mental diversion.[55] Despite its humble origins, the child's paint box had presented the worn-out politician an opportunity for revival and self-discovery; through "the illumination of another field of interest . . . the old undue grip relaxes and the process of recuperation and repair begins."[56]

As was his nature, Churchill wasted neither time nor expense in feeding his burgeoning hobby. He quickly instructed Clementine to purchase oil paints, brushes, an easel, and other accoutrements on her upcoming trip to the market in nearby Godalming. Clementine bought all the supplies she could find but neglected to purchase turpentine, an omission that would make it virtually impossible to paint with oils. This was remedied a few days later when Churchill was able to purchase more materials on a trip into London, where he indulged himself with a broad array of art supplies.[57] According to his private secretary, Eddie Marsh, Churchill "bought up the entire contents of Robertson's colour-shop in Piccadilly—easels, palettes, brushes, tubes and canvasses."[58] As he later explained, the cost of these painting supplies was low given their potential to provide "inexpensive independence," and the consequences of failure were minimal, as "the nursery [would] grab what the studio [had] rejected."[59]

Yet Churchill soon discovered that passion and tools are insufficient to create art. With a youthful enthusiasm, he set out to paint. He thought that a landscape of the pastoral countryside surrounding Hoe Farm would be a beautiful and simple subject for his first oil painting. He had grand ideas but soon discovered that he was having difficulties translating his visions to canvas. Indecision was not a common problem for Churchill, yet, as he would later admit, "the next step was *to begin*. But what a step to take! The palette gleamed with beads of colour; fair and white rose the canvas; the empty brush hung poised, heavy with destiny, irresolute in the air. My hand seemed arrested by a silent veto."[60] Struck by the complexity of the task, Churchill attempted to use logic to deconstruct the scene before him and translate the constituent parts onto the canvas in front of him.

Churchill made up his mind to paint the sky first, as it seemed the simplest in both shape and color, and hoped to move out from there to other sections of the canvas.[61] Armed with this new insight, he began to paint tentatively. But even this tiny step was so mentally exhausting and overwhelming that he nearly quit.[62]

As Churchill contemplated stopping, chance intervened as "a loud approaching sound of a motor-car was heard in the drive."[63] A few moments later, Mrs. Hazel Lavery, Churchill's neighbor, stepped from the car and approached.[64] For an artist struggling to find inspiration and guidance, this was an incredibly fortuitous meeting. Not only was Mrs. Lavery the wife of renowned portrait artist Sir John Lavery, but she was also an accomplished artist in her own right. In addition to her artistic talent, Hazel had legendary beauty and poise, which, combined with her charm and intelligence, propelled her to the top of British society. She was friends with influential artists, politicians, captains of industry, and writers, and was the subject of many of her husband's most famous portraits. She was also an outspoken advocate of Irish independence, a rumored informant for and mistress of notorious Irish Republican Army (IRA) leader Michael Collins, and, although she was American-born and lived in England, her image would grace Irish bank notes until the 1970s as the idyllic personification of Gaelic womanhood.[65]

This confident and accomplished lady approached a confused and overwhelmed Churchill and asked what he was doing. When he sheepishly replied that he was trying to paint a landscape, her strong and vivacious spirit sprang into action to encourage her friend. She asked for Churchill to give her one of his large brushes and began to pour her fierce spirit out onto the canvas, much to the amazement of her friend. "Splash into the turpentine, wallop into the blue and the white, frantic flourish on the palette—clean no longer—and then several large, fierce strokes and slashes of blue on the absolutely cowering canvas."[66]

The fact that Mrs. Lavery was able to apply her energy so fluidly to the canvas had a powerful effect on Churchill. It broke his mental stalemate. The blank canvas was not something to be intimidated by but rather a medium to express ideas and channel energies, a fact that he later explained with a pugilistic fury. "Anyone could see that it could not hit back. No evil fate avenged the jaunty violence. The canvas grinned in helplessness before me. The spell was broken. . . . I have never felt any awe of a canvas since."[67]

With this encouragement to be bold, Churchill would quickly develop a strong preference for oil paints. Oils were superior not only because of their more mature appearance and vivid colors but primarily because they allowed Churchill to apply them with greater energy.[68] With his newfound audacity, oils and pigments allowed him to paint from almost any angle he pleased and cover a greater area with a stroke, and they were more forgiving: if an error was made or a plan changed, "[he could] scrape it all away."[69] While Churchill's technique would undergo minor changes throughout his life, the constant themes were energy and expression. With Lady Lavery's encouragement, he found the courage to paint with bold colors and brushstrokes that gave expression to his inner passions.

Painting as a Substitute for War

So all-consuming was painting that it quickly became a substitute for politics and military action. In fact, Churchill would frequently describe it in military terms: "One begins to see, for instance, that painting a picture is like fighting a battle; and trying to paint a picture is, I suppose, like trying to fight a battle. It is, if anything, more exciting than fighting it successfully. But the principle is the same." Churchill extends this comparison by describing painting in a manner that is strikingly similar to the Clausewitzian concepts of unity of effort and coup d'oeil: "There must be that all-embracing view which presents the beginning and the end, the whole and each part, as one instantaneous impression retentively and untiringly held in the mind."[70] Moving on from a theoretical view of painting and warfare to a more tactical one, Churchill continues the comparison: "In all battles two things are usually required of the Commander-in-Chief: to make a good plan, thorough reconnaissance of the country where the battle is to be fought is needed."[71] Perhaps with a significant measure of self-flattery and projection, Churchill later argued that great painters were like great generals in their approach to their craft, with a study and reverence for the past.[72] Clearly, Churchill had a strong passion for both war and art and saw many similarities between these two seemingly disparate endeavors.[73]

In his 1930 book, *My Early Life*, Churchill explicitly made this connection between his creative outlets, writing, "I have noticed in my life deep resemblances between many different kinds of things. Writing a book is not unlike building a house or planning a battle or painting a picture. The technique is different, the materials are different, but the principle is the same. . . . The best generals are those who arrive at the results of planning without being tied to plans."[74]

Now that Churchill was politically marginalized, painting quickly became an obsession. According to his daughter Mary Soames, painting came "to him fortuitously and suddenly, at the moment of disaster in his political career after the Dardanelles catastrophe . . . painting opened up to him a complete new world of colour, of light and shade, of proportion and perspective.

But even more, this compelling occupation, I came to understand, nourished deep wells."75

A New World of Art

Art also opened new literal doors for Winston, as Clementine took him to the National Gallery for the first time soon after his initial experiments with painting. Amazingly, Churchill had never visited this world-class collection, which was only a few blocks from his office at the Admiralty, or any other art museum, for that matter.76 While it may seem unusual that someone as cultured and privileged as Churchill had never set foot in an art gallery, the fact is that at forty years of age, art again presented him with a new experience and outlet for his passions.77

During his first visit, Churchill was so overwhelmed that he could only view a few rooms before the gallery closed. Clementine described the experience: "When Winston took up painting in 1915 he had never up to that moment been in a picture gallery. He went with me to the National Gallery, and pausing before the first picture, a very ordinary affair, he appeared absorbed in it. For half an hour he studied its technique minutely. Next day he again visited the gallery, but I took him in this time by the left entrance instead of the right, so that I might at least be sure he would not return to the same picture."78

Churchill returned to the National Gallery many times over the coming weeks and throughout his life when he needed solace and mental refreshment. The National Gallery's collection instantly became precious to Churchill as he believed that they were an essential part of Great Britain's cultural heritage. He felt so strongly about this that in 1940, as prime minister, he refused to ship the collection's most precious items to Canada for safekeeping and instead had them transferred to a secret location in the English countryside. Consistent with his broader theme of defiance, he told the director of the National Gallery, Kenneth Clark, "No, bury them in caves and cellars. None must go. We are going to beat them [the Nazis]."79

Visiting art museums both at home and farther afield would become a lifelong passion. He would frequently interrupt official and private trips to visit art museums or to make the acquaintance of famous artists. Churchill described visiting the galleries of Paris with the painter Charles Montag, who introduced him to impressionists with mixed success:

Never having taken any interest in pictures until I tried to paint, I had no preconceived opinions. I just felt, for reasons I could not fathom, that I liked some more than others. . . . My friend said that this is not a bad thing to know nothing at all about pictures, but to have a matured mind trained in other things and a strong interest for painting. The elements are there from which a true taste in art can be formed with time and guidance, and there are no obstacles or imperfect conceptions in the way. I hope this is true. Certainly the last part is true.[80]

This habit of visiting galleries combined with his insistence on taking painting supplies with him when he traveled sometimes made scheduling very difficult. It particularly frustrated his bodyguards and personal assistants, who struggled to accommodate his impromptu artistic inclinations while keeping him safe and on schedule.[81]

Getting to Know the Masters

As an inexperienced painter, Churchill sought guidance and inspiration wherever he could find it, and he closely studied and copied the works of famous painters.[82] He appreciated many artists over the years, but the English painter J. M. W. Turner was always one of his favorites. He enjoyed the British landscapes and dramatic maritime scenes and flattered himself by thinking that his own artistic style was similarly bold and decisive.[83] While Churchill never came close to achieving Turner's mastery of painting, the fact that he could compare himself to such a renowned artist without a hint of irony is a clear indication that painting had the power to bolster his confidence and spirits.

In addition to studying great works of art and artists from ages past for inspiration, Churchill soon began to seek out great living artists. After the Laverys, the first prominent artist Churchill befriended was the Swiss landscape painter Charles Montag, whom he met on a trip to Paris during this period. Montag gave him private tours of multiple art galleries, encouraged him to present his work in shows under the pseudonym "Charles Morin," and tried to get Churchill to better appreciate the impressionist school of painting. The two would remain close friends until Montag's death in 1956 and would travel together and paint with each other many times over the coming decades.[84]

In addition to Lavery and Montag, Churchill became friends with and studied under the mentorship of noted painters Walter Sickert, Sir William Nicholson, and Paul Maze.[85] All of these artists saw true talent in the English politician and were happy to answer his torrent of questions and requests for technical expertise.[86] Of these, William Nicholson was one of the most influential in shaping Churchill as a painter.[87] In addition to providing Churchill with extensive art lessons in the 1920s and 1930s, he also painted a portrait of Winston and Clementine for their twenty-fifth anniversary and was "a great friend of the family" and "sort of a fairy godfather" to their daughter Sarah.[88]

It is also believed that Churchill befriended the noted seascape painter Julius Olsson. Olsson had worked as an artist for the British Admiralty during World War I, and he helped develop "dazzle-painting" camouflage schemes for warships and merchant vessels. This unusual form of camouflage involved painting bold and flamboyant geometric shapes on the hulls of ships. These garish paintings did not hide the ship but hampered an observer's ability to determine its speed, direction, and distance. These paint schemes were popular during World War I as they made it difficult for submarines to track and target ships through their periscopes and significantly reduced sinkings.[89]

While it seems likely that Churchill and Olsson knew of each other and remained in contact after they both departed the Admiralty, the letters they exchanged have gone missing. Family accounts confirm that they did correspond, but there is uncertainty as to the exact contents of the missing letters. Similarly, art connoisseurs note significant similarities in the two painters' seascapes but cannot definitively confirm that Churchill learned directly from Olsson. However intriguing this potential connection to the military history of World War I and Churchill's development as an artist may be, it cannot be conclusively established given the evidence currently available.[90]

What can be established is that, contrary to legend, Churchill did not order the Admiralty to adopt dazzle-painting schemes while serving as First Lord. While the naturalist John Graham Kerr had written directly to Churchill in September 1914 suggesting disruptive paint schemes similar to zebra and jaguar patterns, his ideas were never implemented during his tenure as First Lord. The Admiralty did send Kerr a letter, dated December 19, 1914, that thanked him for "valuable information" regarding his proposed camouflage schemes and transmitted the information to the fleet by way of a general order. However, the Admiralty chose not to institute these new paint schemes as an official policy and instead deferred the responsibility of painting ships to the individual officers in command. Ultimately, the Admiralty did adopt dazzle painting as an official camouflage pattern in early 1917, nearly two years after Churchill's departure.[91] If anything, Churchill's action delayed the implementation of dazzle-painting schemes, although it is amusing to speculate how he might have acted differently had he discovered painting earlier in his life. Perhaps as a tacit acknowledgment of his previous oversight, in August 1941, Churchill took time out of his frantic schedule to personally acknowledge Kerr's work on camouflage paint schemes during World War II.[92]

During his visits to London, Churchill was also a frequent guest at John Lavery's studio. Since they had been neighbors at Hoe Farm, the two became friends, and Churchill's newfound appreciation for art, which was assisted by Mrs. Lavery's timely intervention, made them even closer.[93] Sensing that Churchill had legitimate talent and that painting helped him cope with his political frustrations, Lavery was very accommodating of his new friend. He opened his studio to Churchill, provided private lessons and advice, and gave him a place to go when he needed to escape.[94]

While Churchill preferred the privacy of Lavery's studio, the two would also make trips to parks and gardens to paint landscapes. In his autobiography, Lavery described one time when they were painting in public and were spotted by one of Churchill's old rivals, Admiral Charles Beresford: "One such Sunday at Lady Paget's, at Kingston Hill, Winston Churchill and I were painting with no one taking much notice of us, when a hale-and-hearty voice behind called out, 'Hello, Winston, when did you begin this game?' Without turning round Winston replied, 'The day you kicked me out of the Admiralty, Lord Charles.' 'Well,' said Beresford, 'who knows? I may have saved a great Master.'"[95] While Admiral Beresford was not responsible for his removal from the Admiralty, this anecdote clearly shows that Churchill was still bitter about his treatment and still needed painting to distract him from his troubles.

Interestingly, Lavery was never comfortable with the notion that he was Churchill's mentor and would frequently claim that he learned copious amounts from Winston's flamboyant approach to art and life:

> Mr. Churchill has been called a pupil of mine, which is highly flattering, for I know few amateur wielders of the brush with a keener sense of light and color, or a surer grasp of essentials. I am able to prove this from experience. We have often stood up to the same motif, and in spite of my trained eye and knowledge of possible difficulties, he,

with his characteristic fearlessness and freedom from convention, has time and again shown me how I should do things. Had he chosen painting instead of statesmanship I believe he would have been a great master with the brush, and given a stimulus to the art world.[96]

These were more than hollow words. In fact, Lavery and Churchill painted portraits of each other during this period, and both were quite gratified with the results.[97] Lavery was so pleased by these two portraits and his friendship with Churchill that of the hundreds of paintings he could have added to his 1940 autobiography, *The Life of a Painter*, he chose to include both his 1915 portrait of Winston and Churchill's 1915 portrait of him. This was the only portrait of himself that Lavery included and, of the sixty-nine paintings, one of only two not by his hand.[98] Lavery also placed his professional reputation at stake and, in 1919, had this portrait exhibited by the Royal Society of Portrait Painters.[99]

Thanks to Lavery's encouragement, Churchill would continue to exhibit his work for the remainder of his life. In 1925, he won first prize at a London art exhibit. Fearing that his status as a prominent politician would influence the judges, Churchill left the work unsigned, and the judges believed it to be the hand of a professional painter.[100] In 1947, he entered two paintings into a contest sponsored by the Royal Academy of Art. He submitted the works under the pseudonym David Winter, and much to his delight, both were accepted for exhibition at the Royal Academy, a high honor for any artist, let alone an amateur who was largely self-taught.[101] In 1948, the Royal Academy further celebrated Churchill by making him an "Honorary Academician Extraordinary" and presenting him a diploma signed by the king. The inscription read, "In consideration of your eminent services to our Realm and People, and of your achievements in the Art of Painting." This membership allowed Churchill to present his works at future exhibitions of the Royal Academy, a privilege that he used every year until his death in 1965.[102]

Lavery would remain an intimate friend, tutor, and painting partner until his death in 1941. In this role, he was always encouraging Churchill to develop his own style and experiment with new techniques and subjects. Perhaps the most dramatic of these suggestions was that Churchill should explore the scenery of North Africa. In 1936, Churchill followed through with this suggestion and instantly fell in love with the natural and manufactured beauty of the region.[103] He would return many times over the remainder of his life to paint and write and developed a particular affinity for the scenery in Morocco. During World War II, he even used the natural beauty of Morocco's Atlas Mountains to induce President Roosevelt to extend his stay and make a side trip to Marrakech after the conclusion of the Casablanca Conference. This impromptu alteration to the president's schedule gave them time to discuss policy in a more private and informal setting. It was also in Marrakech where he painted his only picture during World War II, a peaceful rooftop view titled *Tower Koutoubia Mosque*, which he later gave to Roosevelt as a token of their friendship.[104] This painting has had an interesting history as it passed through the hands of several private collectors before being purchased by the American actress Angelina Jolie in 2011. In 2021, Jolie sold it at auction for $11.6 million, a record price for a Churchill painting.[105]

A Visit from a Poet

In August, the poet Wilfrid Blunt visited the Churchills at Hoe Farm. Despite an age difference of more than three decades and very different political views on the question of Ireland, Blunt greatly admired Churchill. As early as 1903, Blunt had helped him organize letters, provided editorial advice for his biography of his father, Lord Randolph, and generally encouraged his literary ambitions.[106] Blunt quickly became enamored with the young politician, and the two would remain friends for the remainder of his life. While Blunt was frequently frustrated in his own forays into politics, he predicted that Churchill would eventually become prime minister, and he would reiterate this assertion even after Churchill's disgrace.[107]

Despite his fascination with the young politician, Blunt's writer's eye quickly noted Churchill's sense of ennui. When he arrived, Blunt was amused to discover that Churchill was in the middle of painting a portrait of Clementine's younger sister, Nellie Hozier, but quickly understood the importance of painting to his friend. He did his best to praise Churchill's work, noting its similarities to the futurist school of portraiture, a fact that apparently satisfied his host. In a moment of unusual reflection and candor, Churchill told the poet, "There is more blood than paint upon these hands. All those thousands of men killed. We thought it would be a little job, and so it might have been if it had begun in the right way."[108] This statement of uncertainty and grief from the typically cocksure Churchill clearly made a strong impression on Blunt, who would remark that Clementine and painting saved his friend during this uncertain period. An astute observation indeed.[109]

While Churchill was still profoundly unhappy and restless during this period, painting, family, and the bucolic setting of Hoe Farm sustained him in ways that he had not anticipated. As he noted, "Painting came to my rescue in a most trying time. . . . Happy are the painters, for they shall not be lonely. Light and colour, peace and hope, will keep them company to the end, or almost to the end, of the day."[110]

Painting as Soulcraft

So why did Churchill suddenly, at the age of forty, develop such a powerful love of painting? Part of the answer is that he was a romantic idealist. For his entire life, he was trying new things and searching for beauty and meaning.[111] Another reason is that it simply gave him something to fill his day when his role in Asquith's cabinet was decidedly marginal. Also, as described above, there was a sense of planning, strategy, and attacking a canvas that vaguely resembled the military operations he was now powerless to control. However, the most important reason is that it allowed him to escape from the overwhelming pressures of being Winston Churchill. Indeed, he frequently suffered from his own unreasonably high expectations for himself as well as bouts of melancholy or depression, which he termed his "Black Dog."[112]

Although the popular image of Churchill is one of unflinching confidence, on a personal level he was often anything but. In fact, during World War II, Churchill even confessed to his personal physician, Dr. Charles Wilson, later Lord Moran, that for several years as a younger man, he had to stand far back from the tracks in a station as trains approached. He was afraid that in a moment of weakness, he might be tempted by the notion that "a second's action would end everything."[113]

Churchill's daughter Mary witnessed her father's depressive tendencies firsthand and would come to understand how important painting was to revive his spirit. She claimed, "Winston Churchill in his earlier years was no stranger to depression—he labeled his depressive times 'Black Dog.' But in my opinion two events or circumstances in Winston's life increasingly and effectively kennelled 'Black Dog.' The first was his marriage and the relationship with Clementine. The other was when, in his 41st year, painting literally 'grabbed' him, thereafter playing an increasingly and abiding role in his life, renewing the source of his great inner strength and enabling him to face storms, ride out depressions and rise above the tough passages in his political life."[114]

While Churchill rarely admitted weakness, his family knew that he was plagued by self-doubt and that painting was one of the best means of reviving his spirits. In moments of extreme stress, fatigue, and depression, painting provided a fantasyland of total escape from the imperfections of the outside world. Churchill would describe the all-encompassing power: "Painting is complete as a distraction. I know of nothing which, without exhausting the body, more entirely absorbs the mind. Whatever the worries of the hour or the threats of the future, once the picture has begun to flow along, there is no room for them in the mental screen. They pass out into shadow and darkness. All one's mental light, such as it is, becomes concentrated on the task."[115]

Violet Asquith described the effect similarly: "As he painted, his tensions relaxed, his frustration evaporated." But then with a flash of her quick and biting wit, she noted, "This was the only occupation that I had ever seen him practice in silence . . . rapt in intense appraisal, observation, assessment of the scene he meant to capture and transfer to his canvas."[116]

The fact that painting could be such a wonderful distraction for Churchill during uncertain times would serve him well throughout the remainder of his life.[117] Indeed, he would have other periods of seclusion when he was again a political outcast. The longest of these, the so-called Wilderness Years from 1929 to 1939, were in fact the most productive period for Churchill as an artist.[118] During this time, he painted over half of his more than five hundred known works and was also unusually prolific as a writer and amateur bricklayer.[119] Similarly, in the aftermath of being voted out of office in 1945, he retreated to Lake Como and the French Riviera and restored his spirits by painting, resting, and planning his literary and political future.[120] As late as 1949, when he had led the nation through World War II and achieved everything he could have possibly hoped for, he still admitted that he needed painting, noting to Sir John Rothenstein, the director of the Tate Gallery, "If it weren't for painting, I couldn't live; I couldn't bear the strain of things."[121]

Even in his twilight years, painting was a constant theme. As his health declined and he struggled to recover from a stroke that severely strained his body and threatened to limit his physical, mental, and rhetorical powers, he and his family were relieved that "[he'd] still be able to paint; his right hand [was] alright."[122] According to both his family and his doctor, Lord Moran, painting helped relieve his tension and focus his recovery from this and other maladies. In fact, painting was such a part of his zest for life that even on his deathbed, "his hand would begin to move in painting gestures, and we would know that he was happy. Needless to say, we wondered what particular scene was crossing his mind."[123]

For the moment, however, Churchill told very few outside of his immediate family and inner circle about his newfound means of escapism. This was very unusual behavior for Churchill, who typically liked nothing more than to talk about himself and his exploits. Yet, at first, Churchill wrote and spoke very little about painting; he seems to have been somewhat embarrassed or afraid to broach the subject. Perhaps he thought that his hobby would be seen as effete or unusual, or perhaps he was not yet confident enough in his own talents to expose his works to a broader audience. Whatever the reason, Churchill kept a close hold on his new love of art during this critical period.

Churchill's atypical silence has made the biographer's task much more difficult. Indeed, during the critical summer of 1915, the only contemporary evidence of Churchill's paintings comprised brief and sometimes cryptic references to painting in letters to close confidants like his brother, Jack, and Archibald Sinclair. While we now know that painting played a key role in developing Churchill's character, few appreciated this critical fact at the time. However, this lack of contemporary documentation should not diminish the importance of Churchill's unexpected discovery. On the contrary, Churchill would rely on art to help aid him through one of the most trying months of his entire life. While he ultimately survived this tumultuous period, it was a very near thing at the time as the future that once seemed bright now seemed anything but.

Only after surviving this difficult period was Churchill confident enough to publicly admit that painting was a critical source of amusement and distraction. Starting in the late 1910s and continuing for the remainder of his life, he became open about painting. He often made grand displays (painting at the pyramids and on the beaches of southern France), he wrote articles about it, advocated for arts education, and frequently recommended painting as a source of renewal and rest to his friends. Much like his trademark cigars, exuberant drinking, and love of hats, painting became something of a prop for Churchill. He understood the power of images and desperately wanted to display an intriguing picture of urbane sophistication and embody a romantic approach to life. To that end, painting eventually helped Churchill project the cocksure image he wanted the world to see. However, in the uncertain days of 1915, he was nearly broken, and painting provided an unexpected means of personal succor.

Churchill's Continued Marginalization

Despite the arrival of the reinforcements, the Dardanelles Campaign remained deadlocked, and Churchill remained marginalized.[124] After the Shell Crisis, he asked about the production of munitions but got no answer. In an attempt to break the stalemate on the Gallipoli Peninsula, he asked Balfour about the possibility of using naval aircraft to bomb Ottoman munition dumps but again received no answer. Churchill was so desperate for power and influence that he even tried to create a new cabinet-level position for himself as air minister.

For partially self-serving reasons, he believed that this new role would provide power and influence over the conduct of the war, but he also believed with good reason that he was uniquely qualified for the position.[125] While serving as First Lord of the Admiralty, he had been a pioneer for naval aviation and had taken a particular interest in the technical and operational details of early airplanes. He had even created the name *seaplane* for aircraft that could take off and land on water, authorized the first aircraft carrier, and passionately promoted independent naval air service.[126] Now he argued that joining the army and navy air forces under a single Air Ministry would provide maximum efficiency and unity of effort.[127]

In early June, he wrote a memo detailing his views and making the case that he should be made minister of air. When Maurice Bonham Carter passed this memo along to Maurice Hankey on June 10, he did so with the comment, "It looks to me like a scheme for providing Winston with something to do, and though I would gladly see his engines suitably employed at first sight I cannot say that I like it."[128] Despite the fact that Churchill was far better qualified, the responsibility was delegated to David Lloyd George instead. This upset Churchill, but he kept his feelings private as Lloyd George was a rising figure in the Liberal Party and he understood that he could not afford to jeopardize his already-tenuous standing within the party.

Throughout this period, Churchill argued repeatedly against renewed offensives on the western front. However, for political reasons, the cabinet felt pressure to conduct further offensives to show solidarity with France in the west and to relieve pressure on Russia in the east. Churchill argued that these offensives were bound to fail, would cause "useless slaughter on a gigantic scale," and would do little to relieve pressure on Russia or open the Dardanelles.[129] Interestingly, his old rival Lord Kitchener largely agreed but highlighted the need to bow to political pressure. Kitchener admitted, "There is a great deal of truth in what Mr. Churchill has said, but unfortunately we have to make war as we must and not as we should like to."[130]

Despite his marginalization within the cabinet, Churchill did have direct access to General John French, the commander of the British Expeditionary Force in France. The two had known each other since the Boer War but became confidants because of their membership in several prominent London clubs during Churchill's tenure as home secretary. Since the Agadir Crisis of 1911, French had believed that war with Germany was increasingly likely and that conscription was a necessary precaution to deter Germany. French trusted Churchill with secret information about the German Army and the broader strategic situation facing Great Britain. Churchill appreciated this special access, and both men maintained this relationship out of a combination of genuine bonhomie and self-interested calculation. Their mutual trust and respect deepened after the outbreak of the war as they shared similar views on Allied strategy. In addition, they soon found that they also shared a common impediment to their execution of that strategy in the person of Lord Kitchener, who did his best to rein in the desires of both French and Churchill.[131] For as long as Churchill remained in the cabinet, he would share critical information with French and coordinate with him on matters of strategy. While they sometimes differed, they had an excellent working relationship and mutual respect.[132] Now, in 1915, both men believed that Britain faced the prospect of a protracted stalemate and a looming political crisis.

Under pressure to renew offensive operations, French traveled to London to confer with senior British leaders. In his statements to the cabinet, French was not optimistic about the prospect of a successful offensive on the western front. The general stated that he lacked the necessary supplies and manpower to succeed in the near future and counseled patience. However, despite these reservations, the cabinet wanted to show solidarity to their French allies and to help support their planned offensive. General French put aside his personal objections, played the role of the dutiful soldier, and promised that he would do his best to attack with his full energy if so ordered.

After briefing the cabinet, French met Churchill at Lancaster Gate and privately discussed the decision to launch a new offensive. Already doing his duty to vigorously implement the orders from the cabinet, General French underscored the political need to support the impending French offensive. He stressed the massive scale of this effort, which was planned to include forty divisions, and did his best to project confidence. Despite these assurances, Churchill had his doubts.[133] The decision to emphasize action on the western front infuriated Churchill, who saw it as wasteful and unlikely to succeed. In fact, for the remainder of his life, he would conveniently blame the failure of the Dardanelles Campaign on the prioritization of the western front.[134]

A Canceled Trip to Gallipoli

In July, Asquith proposed that Churchill travel to Gallipoli on a fact-finding mission for the cabinet.[135] The British were planning a new offensive farther north of their current beachheads, at a place called Suvla Bay. Churchill had long advocated for such an assault and was the ideal person to send to inspect the troops.[136] Kitchener, perhaps happy to temporarily rid himself of the meddlesome Churchill, quickly approved. This mission appealed to Churchill because it would give him an official duty that he believed was critical to the war effort but would also provide an opportunity for adventure and a visit to his brother, Jack, who was serving in the campaign.[137] However, like so many of his other efforts during that year, this proposed trip would only lead to further frustration and heartbreak.

With the blessing of Asquith and Kitchener, Churchill threw himself into planning the trip. He prepared to depart for Gallipoli on July 19 and be gone for three to four weeks. Once in theater, he intended to confer with army and navy leaders, visit the front lines, meet with the troops, and summarize his findings in a written report for Asquith and the cabinet.[138] The news that Churchill was preparing to travel to Gallipoli worried Clementine. She knew that he could not help taking risks and perhaps thought that his political marginalization would exacerbate this tendency. To assuage her fears, Clementine made him assure her that he would be as careful as possible while fulfilling his duties.

While Churchill did not have a death wish, he understood that this would be a dangerous trip. To this end, he purchased an additional life insurance policy to provide financial security for his family. He paid the Phoenix

Assurance Society £147 for a £10,000 policy to cover him from "risk of fire of the enemy, so long as you do not serve as a soldier or take an active part in the hostilities."[139] The wording here indicates that the insurance company was afraid that Churchill might take a more active role in the fighting than his position as a civilian minister allowed. This stipulation reveals significant sophistication and insight on behalf of the underwriters. Indeed, while serving as a civilian newspaper correspondent during the Boer War, Churchill had fought to repel an ambush on his armored train and taken great personal risks to evacuate the wounded before being captured and imprisoned. Despite his protests, his captors refused to treat him as a civilian and even considered executing him as a spy because he was not in uniform. His well-publicized escape had made him a celebrity and launched his political career, a fact that was likely remembered by the insurance firm, which anticipated that he might be tempted to again cross the line between combatant and noncombatant.[140]

Churchill also wrote two "last letters" for his family, to be opened in the event of his death. The first outlined his finances and was left in the care of the chair of his bank, Cox and Co. Churchill was afraid that the news of this letter and purchase of insurance would be a potential breach of operational security, so he had the managers of Cox and Co. take an oath promising that they would not spread this compromising information and that they would only forward it to Clementine "in the event of [Churchill's] death." This letter specifically mentioned that "insurance policies are all kept up and every contingency is covered. You will receive £10,000 and £300 a year in addition until you succeed my Mother."[141]

In addition to these pecuniary details, this letter also instructed Clementine to secure his papers at the Admiralty. Thinking of his posthumous political reputation, he instructed her, "[James] Masterson Smith will help you secure all that is necessary for a complete record. There is no hurry: but some day I should like the truth to be known. Randolph will carry on the lamp."[142] While Churchill would live for another five decades, these instructions provide insight into how he planned to shape his historical legacy, and they would prove quite prescient. In the coming years, he would fight numerous battles for the release and rights to publish the official documents, and ultimately his son Randolph would try with mixed success to follow in his father's footsteps as a politician and his official biographer.

His other "last letter" to Clementine was more personal. As a loving husband and father, he understood that there would be dangers involved with his trip and felt it was necessary to explain his love and sense of duty:

> Do not grieve for me too much. I am a spirit confident of my rights. Death is only an incident, & not the most important wh [sic] to us in this state of being. On the whole, especially since I met you my darling one I have been happy, & you have taught me how noble a woman's heart can be. If there is anywhere else I shall be on the look out for you. Meanwhile look forward, feel free, rejoice in life, cherish the children, guard my memory.
> God bless you.
> Good bye.
> W.[143]

Even though Churchill was happy to go on this mission and some in the cabinet were glad to get rid of him, this was not to be. Last-minute objections from key Tory cabinet members, Lord George Curzon and Bonar Law, made Asquith withdraw his support for the mission.[144] Curzon and Bonar Law personally detested Churchill for his defection from the Tory Party years before, as well as for his personal quirks and desire to have a say in every facet of cabinet policy. They were surprised that Churchill was chosen for such a sensitive mission and argued that he was a biased observer. Worse yet, he might take personal control of the troops as he had during the defense of Antwerp or use his trip to help return him to an influential position in the government.[145] According to Violet Asquith, Curzon was so upset that he personally intervened to force her father to cancel Churchill's trip.[146] Asquith, fearful of a Tory challenge to his fragile hold on power, gave in to the demand that Churchill be removed and instead replaced him with Maurice Hankey.[147]

Churchill was deeply hurt by this latest development.[148] Not only did he feel betrayed by Asquith and the Tory members of the cabinet, but he also believed that his opportunity for adventure and vindication had been taken away from him. Violet described the cancellation of the trip as "one of the bitterest disappointments of Winston's life" and claimed that he was still angry about this issue as late as 1956.[149] According to Violet, Churchill was particularly anxious about the impending amphibious assault at Suvla Bay, and he believed that his presence would ensure success, break the stalemate, and by extension restore his political fortunes.[150] Churchill's feelings of bitterness and betrayal were also magnified by the fact that a similar but less ambitious trip to Calais to discuss military strategy had already been blocked in early July.[151] This second last-minute cancellation suggested a pattern of being purposely thwarted by his political enemies.[152] These twin cancellations in July, combined with the failure of the landings at Suvla Bay in August, seemed to underscore how powerless to influence events Churchill actually was.[153]

During this period of extreme frustration, Churchill leaned heavily on the friendship of Archibald Sinclair. As he confessed in a July 15 letter to Sinclair: "I do not want office but only war direction. . . . I am profoundly unsettled: & cannot use my gift. . . . I am faced with the problem of living through days of twenty-four hours each day; & averting my mind from the intricate business which I had in my head—which is my life."[154]

Churchill's July 30 letter to Sinclair had a similar tone: "It is a horrible experience remaining here in the midst of things knowing everything, caring passionately, conscious of capacity for service, yet paralysed nearly always."[155]

While Sinclair clearly understood his friend's frustrations, he urged him to remain at his post and keep up his spirits. In his reply dated August 8, Sinclair employed his well-developed skills for positivity and flattery to dissuade his friend from abandoning his post and going to the front:

> Above all things, don't come out here. . . . You would be wasted, your position would be hopelessly anomalous and difficult, you would see so much of what you strongly disapprove and which you are powerless to alter, your seniors in rank would not trouble to exercise much politeness or unlimited decorum in dealing with you here and on the contrary there would be a tendency to show you that out here a Privy Councillor and an ex-Minister is no better than a Major. . . . The Army is a jealous Army. . . . [In Parliament] your influence may decide a Cabinet Council or some vital question of policy. . . . Your value to the country out here is incomparably smaller.[156]

Sinclair's advice had the intended effect of calming Churchill, if only temporarily.

In his September 28 letter to Sinclair, Churchill again questioned his role in the cabinet and wrote about his desire to serve in a more active capacity:

"My heart is all with the Army now fighting well against such difficulties, and also with our poor friends in the Dardanelles. . . . We shall see clearly and then I shall know exactly what to do and where my duty leads me. I shall try my hardest to do what is right."[157]

While Churchill was debating what to do with his own political future, he found distraction in planning a future for Sinclair. Without consulting the presumptive candidate about the matter, he directly approached Asquith about finding a constituency for Sinclair. With Asquith's blessing, he decided on Stirling Burghs because its longtime Liberal MP, Arthur Ponsonby, had defected to the Labour Party, while the constituents remained solidly Liberal. Churchill told his friend in the same September 28 letter that this "would suit [him] admirably," saying, "During the war you would get in without difficulty."[158] Sinclair was unwilling to run for this seat, but the incident shows that Churchill was in desperate need of something to occupy his time and that his political instincts were still sound, as the district would flip back to the Liberals in 1918.

When additional troops and the August offensive at Suvla Bay failed to produce results, many resumed their attacks on Churchill. This was understandable as Churchill had been the public face of the campaign since its inception, but it was unfair as he had left the Admiralty in May, Kitchener was responsible for the overall war effort, and General Hamilton was in command of the ground troops.[159] The failures at Suvla in particular were clearly not Churchill's fault as he was denied his trip to the theater and had argued for a more aggressive attack that involved landing troops farther north.[160] While it is unclear if his plan would have fared any better, Churchill correctly predicted that the Allied assault would not produce the desired results and was distraught when his warnings proved prescient.

Desperate to contribute in a more active capacity, Churchill asked Asquith on September 10 if he could resign and take command of an army corps. Asquith deferred the matter to Kitchener, who promptly declined, thus giving the prime minister the official cover to refuse this presumptuous and politically untenable request.[161] While command of a corps was an impractical pipe dream, this unusual request speaks to Churchill's frustration with his political irrelevance, his inflated sense of his own importance, and his genuine desire to serve his country.

This refusal of a major military command revitalized Churchill's efforts to influence policy. He presented two more strategy memos on September

21 and September 24. In these documents, Churchill expressed frustration about the high losses at the Battle of Loos and used this most recent defeat on the western front as the basis for arguing against withdrawing from Gallipoli.[162] In his mind, the Dardanelles Campaign had been perpetually starved of resources yet still had the potential to achieve decisive results.[163] On September 30, he explained succinctly, "With one quarter of the military effort which has been needed to take the village of Loos, we should have been able to get through to the Narrows."[164] Churchill returned to this line of argument the next day in an October 1 letter to Lloyd George: "The same effort and expenditure which had given us the village of Loos would have given us Constantinople and command of the Eastern world."[165] On October 6, he sent a letter to First Lord of the Admiralty Lord Balfour asking for renewed naval action in the Dardanelles. He circulated yet another memo on October 15 arguing for more aggressive action in the Dardanelles and concluding that Allied failures had been a result of uninspired leadership and that an Ottoman victory would "stand as an example of the triumph of superior willpower over superior resources."[166] While there were significant merits to each of these requests, their unintended effect was to annoy those with power and make it easier to dismiss Churchill as a perpetual nuisance.[167]

The Relief of Hamilton

On October 16, Sir Ian Hamilton was relieved as the commanding general of the Dardanelles Campaign.[168] Although this was an understandable decision, Churchill was unhappy. Hamilton had been his friend for two decades and had provided access to firsthand information and an ability to directly influence the campaign. Hamilton was ordered to return home and await further instructions, but he was now a scapegoat and would never receive another command.[169]

Perhaps inevitably, Churchill was displeased with Hamilton's replacement, General Charles Monro.[170] In addition to replacing his friend, Monro had transferred from France, and therefore Churchill believed he would be unfairly biased in favor of action on the western front: "He belonged to that school whose supreme conception of Great War strategy was 'killing Germans.' Anything that killed Germans was right. Anything that did not kill Germans was useless."[171] Churchill believed that this closed-minded approach was dangerous as the exact same way of thinking had already resulted in a stalemate on the western front. Although key cabinet leaders such as Lloyd George and Bonar Law began to openly discuss evacuation, Churchill refused to consider retreat.[172] This fixation on the Dardanelles caused Lloyd George to exclaim, "The Dardanelles have become an obsession with him. He is anxious to achieve victory at all costs because he feels that failure will probably ruin his career."[173]

Increasingly frustrated and desperate to save the floundering campaign, Churchill wrote yet another memo, dated October 20. He hoped to reverse the situation on the ground before Monro could travel to the theater and recommend evacuation.[174] Here, he proposed the use of poison gas on the Gallipoli Peninsula.[175] This recommendation demonstrated how committed he was to achieving rapid results:

> Some time ago our troops on the Peninsula were provided with the earlier patterns of respirators . . . [but] it seems very probably that the respirators have deteriorated and that the men have not been practiced in their use as are our troops in France . . . we ought without delay to send out a complete new outfit of the latest helmets and to make sure that during the period of inactivity while we are making up our minds the troops are duly practiced in their use . . . I trust that the unreasonable prejudice against the use by us of gas upon the Turks will now cease. The massacres by the Turks of Armenians and the fact that practically no British prisoners have been taken on the Peninsula, though there are many thousands missing, should surely remove all false sentiment on this point, indulged in as it is only at the expense of our own men. Large installations of British gas should be sent out without delay. The winter season is frequently marked by south-westerly gales, which would afford a perfect opportunity for the employment of gas by us.[176]

Churchill's willingness to deploy poison gas is a clear indication of his desperation to win a decisive victory; his recommendation, however, must be viewed in the proper context.[177]

While the initial British response to the German introduction of chlorine gas at the Second Battle of Ypres on April 22, 1915, had been one of outrage and disgust, generals and politicians immediately saw the battlefield potential of these weapons.[178] The very next day, April 23, General French officially asked Lord Kitchener for permission to retaliate in kind. Kitchener supported this response but believed that it was imperative to defer the final decision to Asquith and the cabinet. The cabinet, which included Churchill, acted quickly and enthusiastically endorsed the creation of chemical forces as a new branch of the army, created a panel of experts from leading British universities, and commissioned a series of studies on how to employ these new weapons to the greatest effect. Although British politicians and generals would still claim the moral high ground, they actively supported the creation of their own chemical forces.[179]

For the remainder of the war, the use of chemical weapons steadily increased in the British Army and became an increasingly important part of their offensive doctrine. The belief that gas could enable offensive operations by suppressing defensive firepower was enticing as it would provide the opportunity to achieve decisive victory. The reality never fully matched the hopes of the military planners, but adaptation and experimentation continued for the remainder of the war as new chemical agents and delivery methods were introduced. Even though military and civilian leaders recognized the brutal and indiscriminate nature of these weapons, once they became a part of the fighting, they put their humanitarian considerations aside and focused on winning the war, not on banning their use.[180]

The fact that chemical weapons were never introduced to the Dardanelles theater appears to have been a matter of availability, not humanitarianism. In fact, the supply of chemical weapons rarely met the demand of commanders on the western front, and the British saw themselves as playing catch-up with the Germans in this new arms race. Consistent with Churchill's complaints, poison gases were kept for use on the western front, and the troops fighting there were given priority for supplies of defensive equipment like gas masks.

In this context, Churchill's comments take on a different light. While his willingness to use chemical weapons strikes modern audiences as barbaric, it was entirely consistent with British thinking at the time on the value of gas to restore the offensive and break the bloody stalemate that faced their forces on multiple fronts. Churchill was desperate to achieve victory, but his desire for gas was not seen at the time as unreasonable.[181] Rather, this was a small part of his obsession with the operations in that theater and his beliefs that the western front was receiving an undue share of British resources.[182]

Monro's fact-finding mission to Gallipoli seemed to confirm Churchill's suspicion that the general had already decided to end the campaign and that his visit was mere formality: "General Monro was an officer of swift decision. He came, he saw, he capitulated."[183] The fact that Monro then left the theater and delegated command to his deputy further angered Churchill, who believed that it was a clear indication of his bias and weak character.[184] This effectively ended the Allied attempt to force decisive action in the Dardanelles. Although Monro was expected to recommend evacuation, his formal report still shocked the cabinet.[185] While Churchill still hoped that Kitchener would continue to support the campaign, the powerful effect of Monro's report was undeniable.[186]

The Conscription Issue

During this period of extreme frustration, Churchill wandered into a political minefield over the issue of conscription.[187] This was an extremely divisive issue politically. It cut across class, party, and regional lines, it struck many as a desperate and defeatist measure, and it pitted Churchill against his own prime minister and most of the cabinet. Neither Kitchener nor Asquith supported conscription, fearing that it would anger the population, implicitly admit failure, induce panic, and lead to the collapse of the coalition government.[188] Rather than address the issue, both men denied that there was a problem. They highlighted the fact that Great Britain had enjoyed an extraordinarily high rate of volunteering, approximately 43 percent of eligible men, a figure that far surpassed all the other major powers. In total, approximately 2.5 million troops volunteered for service in the British Army, an impressive statistic that allowed the issue to go largely unaddressed for the first year of the conflict.[189]

In contrast, Churchill had publicly supported conscription from the outset of the war.[190] His early predictions that the conflict would be long and costly and require a massive levy of human capital were correct. However, in the early months of the war, volunteers flooded recruiting stations, and the issue was not yet obvious. In July 1915, Churchill submitted to the cabinet a report on conscription that was critical of government policy and proposed adopting a national draft. This report was prescient but controversial, and it was quickly seized upon by Tories such as Neville Chamberlain, George Curzon, and William Waldegrave Palmer, 2nd Earl of Selborne, who believed that Churchill's dissent could be a wedge issue to undermine Liberal support for Asquith.[191]

In August, as pressure mounted on Liberal members of the government to address the conscription issue, two significant events occurred. An official commission was established under the leadership of Lord Robert Crewe-Milnes to study the issues of manpower, and David Lloyd George joined Churchill in support of conscription. These two events were significant, as it was the first time the government even hinted that there might be a manpower issue and Lloyd George's defection threatened to break up Asquith's coalition. Lloyd George addressed the newly formed Crewe Commission on August 18 and argued forcefully that the longer conscription was delayed, the closer Great Britain would come to disaster.[192] This was essentially an endorsement of the position Churchill had held since the beginning of the war. Churchill was frustrated that Lloyd George had stolen much of his attention and credit, but he saw this support as a means to reassert himself within the Asquith government.

The single biggest impediment for Churchill and Lloyd George was the venerable minister of war, Lord Kitchener. The famously stubborn general had opposed conscription from the beginning of the war for a mix of personal and professional reasons and remained unwilling to change his position despite increasing evidence that new drafts of manpower were necessary.[193] Kitchener himself was called to testify before the Crewe Commission on August 24, 1915. Arguing from his position of authority, he made repeated assurances that future manpower needs could always be met with calls for voluntary enlistment and appeals to patriotism.

Churchill was unconvinced. As a member of the Crewe Commission, he asked Kitchener under oath if it would not be better to begin the process of conscription before public opinion turned against the war and limited the willingness of citizens to volunteer. Much to Churchill's disgust, Kitchener dismissed the question as the concern of a politician and refused to make a prediction about the potential impact of public opinion on the conduct of the war.[194] While Kitchener was able to rely on his stature as the most famous living British soldier to avoid answering this important question, this shocking breakdown in civil-military affairs underscored the dysfunction in the Asquith government.[195] In this divisive atmosphere, the Crewe Commission failed to reach a consensus regarding conscription policy.[196] In fact, four of the six members of the committee, including Churchill, wrote their own reports about the conscription issue, further highlighting the divisive nature of the issue as well as the ineffectiveness of the government.[197] Fearful of the political consequences of taking a firm stand on either side of the issue, Asquith did nothing.

Frustrated by his inability to force meaningful change on conscription, Churchill had dinner with Lloyd George and Lord Curzon on September 14 to plot their next moves. Despite their personal and political differences, each of these three cabinet members agreed that Asquith must act on the matter of conscription. Curzon was ready to force the issue and indicated that his fellow Tories were on the verge of openly breaking with the government. In addition, the Tories were prepared to demand the removal of Kitchener, whom they believed was impeding the progress of the war in general and conscription in particular. This was a bold proposal. It meant not only breaking with the policy of working with the Liberals in the name of national unity but also directly targeting a larger-than-life hero, Lord Kitchener. Sensing an opportunity, Lloyd George and Churchill agreed to join Curzon and the Tories as a means of breaking the deadlock on this critical war policy. Both men recognized that they might be shunned by their fellow Liberals for their disloyalty, but they concluded that action was needed and that the prize was worth the risk.[198]

For a brief moment, Churchill saw the looming Tory rebellion over the conscription issue as a means of toppling Asquith and again holding a powerful office. However, Asquith was a keen politician in his own right and would not be forced out of office without a fight. As early as September 18, just four days after the dinner where the rebellion was planned, Asquith had learned about the plot and begun to privately tell other ministers that Churchill and Lloyd George were disloyal and not to be trusted. In addition, Asquith began to alter his stance on conscription, suggesting that he had always supported it but that he had wanted to wait until the time was right to implement this controversial policy.[199] Asquith's shrewd maneuvering made Churchill and Lloyd George suspicious, and they privately accused each other of treachery. In October, Asquith again outmaneuvered his political rivals by backing a new voluntary recruiting scheme proposed by Edward Stanley, the 17th Lord of Derby. This allowed the prime minister to have it both ways on the issue rather than be forced into supporting or rejecting conscription. This plan ultimately failed, but it undermined Churchill's wedge issue and made him feel increasingly irrelevant in terms of influencing policy.[200]

Even after he had left for the front, Churchill carefully followed the conscription debate. He quickly saw the need for additional manpower and harbored secret hopes that the issue would break the government and help return him to power. Ultimately, the government did pass conscription legislation and avoided collapse over this issue. Although Churchill's political schemes were dashed, he was relieved that the issue of manpower was finally being addressed, and he celebrated the news at the front and noted his approval in letters to family and friends.[201]

Resignation

As British failures continued to mount, Asquith was under increasing pressure to dissolve the Dardanelles Committee and remove Lord Kitchener from his position as minister of war.[202] The prime minister was keenly aware that some change would be needed to save his tenuous political position, yet he refused to sack Kitchener.[203] In Asquith's estimation, Kitchener's fame made him untouchable, and any attempt to remove him would create a public outcry that Lloyd George and Churchill would happily exploit. To demonstrate that he was willing to shake up a stalled war effort, Asquith instead decided to dissolve the Dardanelles Committee.[204] This decision was both wise politically and in the best interest of the nation. The Dardanelles Committee had failed to produce results, and if eliminating this inefficient bureaucratic entity would improve policymaking while outflanking his political opponents, then so much the better.

From his own selfish perspective, Churchill was unhappy to learn of the demise of the Dardanelles Committee. While it often frustrated him, it had given him a place to at least pretend that his views were being heard and to produce a paper trail of documents that he could later use to promote his own cause. In fact, he had only accepted Asquith's offer to serve as the chancellor of the Duchy of Lancaster, a job that he believed was beneath him, because it would allow him to serve on this committee.[205]

What Churchill was too stubborn and self-absorbed to recognize was that he had been a major source of the division and inefficiencies of this committee. His strong opinions and dissenting views, while often correct, clashed with those of others, particularly the minister of war, Lord Kitchener. This division made it incredibly difficult to make decisions, as neither man would yield. In the words of Balfour, Kitchener and Churchill had "very strong personalities with very incompatible temperaments. They would not work with each other, and neither of them would have tolerated for a moment the independent examination by any member of the committee of experts belonging to their own department. . . . I am convinced that we never should possess it [responsibility] in a committee of six or eight of which Kitchener and Winston were members."[206] While Churchill would blame the size of the committee for its failures, this was an all too convenient half-truth.[207] The fact was that he and Kitchener were the two greatest impediments to effective policymaking.

The Dardanelles Committee met for the last time on November 6. Appropriately enough, it could reach no consensus about the future of the Dardanelles Campaign or the broader strategy for the war.[208] It was dissolved and replaced with the triumvirate of Asquith, Kitchener, and Balfour.[209] Churchill remained in Asquith's cabinet as the chancellor of the Duchy of Lancaster but was now excluded from discussions regarding the conduct of the war.

With little left to do that he considered interesting or important, Churchill despaired. He wanted to contribute to the war effort, but the path forward appeared to be blocked. The safest course of action would have been to do nothing, to continue to accept the significant ministerial pay, and to wait for another opportunity to present itself, but this was not Churchill's way. He could not stand idly by when his country was in the middle of a worldwide conflict. Churchill had been dreaming of frontline service for months, but his inclusion on the Dardanelles Committee had given him hope and reason to remain in politics. Now, he was free of this great responsibility. He quickly concluded that he could do more for the war and his political future by resigning from the government and serving on the front lines.[210] He would later describe his decision: "I knew too much and felt too keenly to be able to accept Cabinet responsibility for what I believed to be a wholly erroneous conception of war."[211]

On October 30, Churchill privately offered Prime Minister Asquith his resignation.[212] Asquith refused and asked Churchill to remain. He agreed to continue for the time being, but Asquith understood that there was little he could do to change the stubborn Churchill's desire to leave. Much to his credit, Churchill continued to serve loyally and did his best to aid the British war effort. On November 2, Churchill prepared a dossier defending his and the government's conduct in the Dardanelles and presented it to Asquith. He hoped that the prime minister would use it in a speech to Parliament on his conduct of the war but was disappointed when Asquith neither used these materials nor defended Churchill in his speech.[213]

On November 3, Asquith asked Lord Kitchener to personally travel to the Dardanelles and inspect the situation.[214] Kitchener had long opposed withdrawal, yet he dutifully departed on November 5, hoping that seeing the terrain and the troops' dispositions would help him finally break the deadlock. While Asquith had lacked the courage to sack the popular Kitchener, the old field marshal understood that he could be removed at any point and chose to take the seals of office with him on his trip, a move that would theoretically allow him to remain in power until they were transferred to his appointed successor. Asquith had a more devious scheme in mind—to exclude Kitchener from the policymaking process for a month without having to pay the political price for removing him from office.[215] As Asquith described this political maneuver to Lloyd George, "We avoid by this method of procedure the immediate suppression of Kitchener as War Minister, while attaining the same result."[216]

With Kitchener gone, Churchill also sensed an opportunity to advance his own interests. On November 6, he asked Asquith to make him governor-general and commanding general of British East Africa.[217] He had long taken an interest in African affairs, and this role appealed to his sense of adventure and desire to contribute to the war effort.[218] It would have also come with the rank of major general, a fact that was not lost on the ambitious young man, who had already asked for a generalship twice before.[219] If provided this opportunity, Churchill claimed, he had a bold plan for employing armored cars to conduct surprise attacks on German forces in East Africa.[220] Despite many logistic and operational challenges, Churchill believed that a rapid victory could quiet his critics and propel him to fame and prominence and that an armored strike would provide the desired results.[221] While armored vehicles would eventually prove their worth in desert warfare, this plan was short on details and did not have the support of the British government. Had it been enacted without serious revisions, this half-baked plan would likely have led to disaster and further tarnished Churchill's reputation.[222]

Churchill found an unlikely ally in his attempt to become the governor-general of British East Africa—Andrew Bonar Law. Despite his personal dislike of Churchill and doubts about his qualifications, Bonar Law was anxious to get him as far away as possible and supported this unusual request. Asquith, however, refused on the grounds that it would be seen as favoritism. He feared any scandal that might threaten his tenuous grip on power and was sure that such an appointment would be met by spirited debate in the House of Commons.[223] Ultimately, the prospect of a position in East Africa was exciting for Churchill and kept him distracted for a few days, but nothing came of it, and he quickly returned to his feelings of hopelessness. In an unusual twist of history, the man who was chosen for this position was none other than Jan Smuts, who in 1899 had fought for the Boers and had interrogated Churchill as his prisoner.[224] Despite his history of opposing British rule in Africa, Smuts was an inspired choice. He was an effective military commander and civilian administrator in both world wars, was an impassioned advocate for South African home rule, and ultimately became a close friend and political ally of Winston Churchill.

On November 11, Asquith exploited Kitchener's absence to reshuffle his cabinet. Asquith appointed a five-member War Committee, which included himself, Balfour, Lloyd George, Bonar Law, and Reginald McKenna, all of whom were skeptical about the prospects of the Dardanelles Campaign. The three strongest advocates of the campaign, Churchill, Kitchener, and Curzon, were purposely excluded, a clear indication that Asquith wanted to end the discussion of the campaign and terminate it as quickly as possible.[225]

Surprisingly, the trip to the Dardanelles had a powerful effect on Kitchener.[226] Witnessing the rugged terrain that the Ottomans occupied as well as the misery and hopelessness of the Allied troops caused the old general to reverse his position and conclude that further efforts would be fruitless. This, combined with the reordering of Asquith's military advisers, ultimately ensured that the discussion shifted to how best to evacuate the men from the peninsula. While Kitchener was frequently obstructionist, his willingness to adapt his views to the situation on the ground and put aside his ego speaks well to his character and suggests that he had the best interests of the country in mind.

That the Dardanelles would be abandoned was now a foregone conclusion, and Churchill had no duties that involved the war effort. While he was still the chancellor of the Duchy of Lancaster and there was no reason to believe that Asquith was about to remove him from this office, he again submitted his resignation on November 11, shortly after hearing of the composition of the new War Committee.[227] Having no use for Churchill, Asquith accepted this resignation, and for the first time since April 1908, Churchill was without a cabinet office.[228] Life as a backbencher was something the young politician dreaded. It interrupted his rapid and seemingly unbroken path to the very top of British politics and left him with little to do but paint and despair.

Asquith personally broke the news of Churchill's resignation to Violet. Like many of Churchill's close friends, she was shocked and could not accept that he was being forced out of government at such a time. She asked her father what he thought Churchill would do. Asquith replied, "He will go to the front. . . . It is a terrible waste. I think he has more understanding of war than any of my colleagues."[229]

Asquith was correct; Churchill had decided to join the army. He had no actual plan as to how he could serve, but he desperately wanted to contribute to the war effort. While Violet and her father understood Churchill's decision, it struck many as a ridiculous and desperate act. Rather than focus on his future in the army, for the time being, Churchill poured his energies into a final bit of political theater and posturing before his departure for the western front.

A Magnificent Final Speech

Churchill's resignation did allow him one additional perk—the traditional opportunity of a departing cabinet member to address Parliament on the cause of their exit and their conduct while in office.[230] He understood the importance of rhetoric and theater and made sure to use this opportunity to maximum effect.[231] Churchill's resignation speech was scheduled for November 15. Because no one knew what he might do or say, the speech had the potential for drama and was eagerly anticipated by the members of Parliament and press alike.[232]

Churchill began by graciously thanking the Asquith administration before then going into a wide-ranging defense of his tenure as First Lord. He strongly asserted that he still believed in the Dardanelles operations: "I have offered the same counsel to the Government—undertake no operation in the West which is more costly to us in life than to the enemy; in the East, take Constantinople; take it by ships if you can; take it by soldiers if you must; take it by whatever plan, military or naval, commends itself to your military experts, but take it, and take it soon, and take it while time remains."[233] As he had repeatedly argued to Asquith's cabinet, the Dardanelles operations had the greatest potential for winning the war at the lowest cost. True, they were a risk, but a risk justified by the significant rewards for aiding Russia and knocking the Ottoman Empire out of the war.

In his speech, Churchill described his calculation as a "legitimate gamble," a phrase that, while innocent enough on the surface, would later be taken out of context and used as evidence that he had wagered recklessly with the lives of Allied troops.[234] Unaware of this unfortunate choice of words, Churchill continued and, as he would so often do, met defeat with defiance or at least the appearance of defiance, stating, "Time will vindicate my administration of the Admiralty, and assign my due share in the vast series of preparations and operations which have secured us the command of the seas."[235]

Churchill concluded his speech with a flourish of rhetoric and strategic insight that resembled his defiant speeches during World War II:

> We are passing through a bad time now and it will probably be worse before it is better, but that it will be better—if only we endure and persevere—I have no doubt whatever. Sir, the old wars were decided by their episodes rather than by their tendencies. In this war the tendencies are far more important than the episodes. Without winning any sensational victories, we may win this war. We may win it even during a continuance of extremely disappointing and vexatious events. It is not necessary for us to win the war to push the German lines back over all the territory they have absorbed, or to pierce them. While the German lines extend far beyond their frontiers, while their flag flies over conquered capitals and subjugated provinces, while all the appearances of military successes attend their arms, Germany may be defeated more fatally in the second or third year of the War than if the Allied Armies had entered Berlin in the First.[236]

Churchill returned to his seat to a strong ovation from the House of Commons.

The speech was a bittersweet triumph. While he had made numerous enemies among the Tory and the Liberal Parties, his patriotic rhetoric still had the ability to stir the hearts of all but the most jaded members.

Next, Prime Minister Asquith rose to say a few words of tribute: "I desire to say to him and of him, that having been associated with him now for ten years in close and daily intimacy, in positions of great responsibility and in situations varied and of extreme difficulty and delicacy, I have always found him a wise counsellor, a brilliant colleague, and a faithful friend."[237]

While Asquith appears to have been genuine in his respect for Churchill, it must be remembered that these were the carefully chosen words of a politician. Nevertheless, these accolades captured the overall mood of respect for Churchill as a talented political foe and of a broad willingness to show gentleness to a defeated political rival. In the debate that followed, his rival, Bonar Law, echoed these kind words to the House of Commons, noting, "He has the defects of his qualities, and as his qualities are large, the shadow which they throw is fairly large also; but I say deliberately, in my judgement, in mental power and vital force he is one of the foremost men in our country."[238]

While the response was largely positive, some MPs took issue with Churchill's speech. A few believed he had been too harsh in his assessment of the First Sea Lord. True, Churchill had pointed out where he and Fisher had differed, but, overall, he had done his best to minimize their disagreements. Other critics focused on his claim that the Dardanelles was a "legitimate gamble." While in Churchill's mind this simply meant that the risks of the operation were outweighed by the potential rewards, to some it was further "proof" that he was and had always been a dangerous gambler who could not be trusted. In fact, this phrase was held against him for years to come and would become a source of considerable frustration and contention for Churchill.[239]

Overall, the speech was a much-needed success amid Churchill's broader failures. It allowed him to make the best case he could to clear his name and reminded onlookers of his extraordinary powers of rhetoric. It was generally well received in the press, and even his political rivals were surprisingly gracious, perhaps because they truly believed that Churchill was finished as a major player in British politics.[240]

Violet Asquith had a brief meeting with Churchill as she exited the House of Commons after watching these events from the gallery. While she knew that her friend was deeply hurt, she saw that the "afterglow of his speech shone in his eyes." She asked him how he thought the speech had gone, and he replied that he believed it had gone well but that "there was more to say [he] didn't." He then went on to describe his critics as "foolish—sheepish—oafish—blank," a clear indication that despite their attempts at kindness, he had not forgotten that they had wronged him personally. Not knowing how to say goodbye, Violet blurted out, "In a fortnight you may be under fire in France—can it be true?" Churchill replied, "Yes—and in a fortnight you will be married [a reference to her pending nuptials with Maurice Bonham Carter]—that's just as strange and just as true." After this witty quip, he then devolved into a tirade of profanity about the cruelness of fate, which was so crude that Violet chose not to preserve it for posterity.[241]

In response to this outburst, Violet attempted to philosophize about the heavens and her belief that Churchill had a destiny. She concluded, "Don't forget you've got a star." Churchill replied, "I shan't forget it—I may see rather more of it than I shall like during the coming months." As the two friends parted ways, Violet tried to imagine Churchill huddled in the mud and cold of the trenches. She had a difficult time with this thought as she could not imagine him deprived of either the many luxuries he enjoyed or the thrill of being at the center of British politics. While she believed in Churchill's star, Violet, like many of the political elite who knew him, wondered, "Could he endure it?"[242]

While Churchill did not know exactly what the best path forward would be, he did believe that fate was not done with him. To this end, he desperately wanted to clear his name regarding his role in the Dardanelles. He believed that censorship and the need for discretion in discussing ongoing Allied operations had muzzled him and allowed his critics to make baseless attacks on his record, which he could not properly address and counter. If only Churchill could have the official documents published, he believed the truth regarding his role in the operation could be known. In his November 15 farewell speech, he explicitly requested that the documents concerning his role in the Dardanelles be published as soon as possible.[243] This began a battle for the release of critical documents that would last for over a decade. It would see him disgusted at the government for refusing to publish documents and threatened with a parliamentary inquiry over the use of official documents in his memoirs, and it would ultimately provide significant vindication, just as he had hoped.[244]

On November 15, Churchill also got a much-needed letter of encouragement from his friend Archibald Sinclair. Despite Sinclair's earlier warnings to remain in politics and avoid frontline service, he welcomed his friend:

> I'm so glad that you have taken the plunge and that you are coming to join us out here [at the front]. . . . Do write me of your plans. If there is a difficulty about a higher formation surely the command of a Kitchener battalion would be a better position than that of 2nd in command of a yeomanry regiment. . . . Why not get a battalion— no-one could object to that on any grounds? A Scotch one as you are

a Scotch member for the Scotch divisions of the King's armies (9th and 15th) have fairly eclipsed the others. I know nothing whatever about infantry drill and organisation but I know a bit about conditions out here and if I could be of any service and if my General would spare me you know how proud and eager I would be to serve under you in any capacity.[245]

While Churchill had yet to finalize the details, he was already thinking along similar lines as his friend. As he confessed to Clementine in December, "Taking a battalion means living with strangers of a common class, but I hope that if it is settled thus Archie will come as Adjutant or something—as I must have a pal."[246]

Although he did not know exactly how he would contribute, Churchill felt a powerful desire to depart London as quickly as possible and fight as an officer in the army. He would serve with the fighting men in the trenches, and the details would of course fall into place once he arrived at the front. As Churchill's daughter Mary would later explain, "An honourable door was open to him," and he now chose to rejoin the army on active duty.[247] Churchill later described this decision to leave his old life behind: "I thought it necessary to quit their councils and betook myself to the Armies."[248]

While Churchill had been privately considering a return to the army for months, his decision shocked many. He had told few about it before his resignation, and now he planned to depart for the front in only a few days' time. Rumors abounded. Could he be serious? Why give up the comforts of home and risk life and limb in the squalor of the trenches? What did Churchill have to prove? Did he have a death wish? Was this a political stunt? To Churchill's critics, his patriotic decision to serve in the army was particularly curious. It was broadly maligned and put forward as further evidence of Churchill's impetuousness and unreliability. Many of Churchill's friends and colleagues tried to talk him out of going, yet he refused to consider anything else. He had made his decision and would not be cajoled into changing his mind. Churchill was, after all, a very stubborn character.

However, this return to the front was more than escapism, a death wish, or a willingness to fight. Churchill had always believed that he was lucky and that he had been chosen for some great thing. Now, when even he could not see the path out, he clung to this vision that he was special. Either he would continue to be lucky and survive or he would die a hero's death.[249] Whatever the outcome, he would be satisfied living for a bigger purpose and trusting that fate had chosen him for something greater.

Farewells

Churchill's decision to serve on the front lines was met with a mixture of disbelief and dismay among the political elite. While some believed it to be another stunt, most felt a genuine sense of sadness and loss. Edward Grey believed it to be a horrible thing that deepened his already intense hatred of war. Lloyd George thought that it was a waste to lose a man of Churchill's talents, even though he considered him a rival for the premiership. Asquith was privately sad to see Churchill leave, but he remained quiet on the matter. This did not stop his daughter Violet from asking if she could provide any piece of additional equipment, such as a luminous watch or a muffler, that would make her friend's time in the trenches more comfortable.[250] Letters and telegrams of support and encouragement flooded in from a wide range of military leaders, politicians, and common people. For a fleeting moment, Churchill was again the talk of London.

While Churchill was typically unconcerned about fiscal matters, he now acted decisively to get his finances in order. In the week before his departure, he purchased a full war-risk insurance policy from the Phoenix Assurance Society for the cost of £472 and secured a loan of £1,000 from Cox and Co. These were significant expenditures as Churchill was already highly leveraged, owing more than £9,000 in loans, and was struggling to pay his previous debts. In fact, he had already taken out another loan from Cox and Co. five weeks before and was only able to obtain this second loan because it had been guaranteed by his cousin, Freddie Guest. While Churchill's debt was primarily the result of profligate spending, this loan was made necessary because of his loss of cabinet salary and the grim fact that the £420 per year he would earn as an army major would be insufficient to service his accrued debts.[251]

In fact, Churchill was so worried that he visited Sir Ernest Cassel, his financial manager, on November 18, the very day he departed for France. Cassel was semiretired but still tended to Churchill's finances. Cassel promised an immediate advance of an additional £1,000 to cover Churchill's family's expenses and promised to care for their needs even if he exhausted the entirety of his remaining funds and credit—a generous offer that spoke to his admiration for Churchill.[252] These preparations are an indication not only that Winston cared for his family but also that he was serious about seeing active service on the front line.

On November 16, Churchill hosted a farewell lunch for his friends at his home at 41 Cromwell Road.[253] The house was a chaotic whirlwind of activity and emotion. As the honored guests entered, they had to maneuver around the massive heap of uniforms, food, military equipment, and luggage that had been piled in the hallway in preparation for Churchill's departure for France.[254] Once inside, the scene was a surreal combination of sadness, patriotism, and revelry as guests attempted to say goodbye to their friend and provide love and support. Some guests cried openly, most notably Edward Marsh, Churchill's private secretary. Even though Churchill faced an uncertain future, he did his best to project calm and reassurance. He seemed to thrive in moments of crisis, and this time was no different as he was apparently confident that he would either die a hero's death or emerge from the fighting with pride and redemption.[255]

Ever the political operator, Churchill had invited the Asquith family to the party, and both Margot (Asquith's second wife) and Violet (his daughter by his first wife) attended. Apart from his wife, Clementine, Violet was Churchill's closest female friend, and it would have been awkward to not invite her. Moreover, Churchill enjoyed both ladies' sharp wit and strong personalities. Despite the celebratory nature of the occasion, politics intervened, and a tense moment ensued. Margot felt the need to defend her husband by asserting that he had not been forced to accept a coalition government but that he had always wanted such a political arrangement. Churchill felt as if he could not let this comment go unanswered. He countered that had Asquith wanted to form a coalition, he could have easily done so when conditions were favorable, but the fact that he waited until after the Shell Crisis was a sign of weakness. Margot then responded that if the Liberal Party had been stronger, then they could have avoided being forced into a coalition government, and then she proceeded to detail her views about the shortcomings and failures of various Tory politicians.[256]

This awkward moment hung in the air and remained unresolved, but Churchill did his best to ensure that the remainder of the party was as pleasant and lighthearted as possible. Violet would later describe the scene by highlighting the mixed emotions on display, noting Clementine's stoic presence and the fact the Eddie Marsh was choking back tears. Churchill alone "was at his gayest and best."[257] Despite these accolades for her friend's cheerfulness, she agreed with her stepmother, Margot, that the party was something of a pathetic anticlimax.

The tense atmosphere of the lunch and tearful goodbyes did not slow down Churchill. After his guests departed, he attached his sword to his belt and marched around the house giving orders to Clementine and his assistant Eddie Marsh. They worked late into the night packing and preparing for his upcoming trip to France. As it would turn out, Churchill packed far too much equipment and too many personal effects for his trip to France, but he had a long history of extravagance when it came to his kit at the front. For the moment, however, he contented himself with knowing that he was prepared for any eventuality and would bring the comforts of home to the trenches of the western front.

In addition to these comforts, Churchill packed a .45-caliber Colt model 1911 pistol he had recently purchased. This weapon, engraved with "WINSTON SPENCER CHURCHILL," would accompany him throughout his time at the front during World War I.[258] This sidearm was not only a symbol of his role as an officer but a clear sign that he planned on seeing active service.[259] While this was a relatively new type of pistol at the time and not standard-issue, he had a well-established love of firearms as well as a desire to carry the deadliest and most modern types currently available.[260] The Colt .45 would remain a treasured item that reminded him of his service in the trenches and provided peace of mind when he carried it again after receiving death threats from the IRA in the 1920s and while serving as prime minister during World War II.[261]

As Churchill directed the packing of the pistol and his other accoutrements in the entryway of his home, his mother, Jennie, was waiting upstairs in seclusion. She was tearful and distraught. She feared for her son, and with good reason. As a socialite, Jennie had worked to raise funds for military hospitals during the Boer War and the Great War, and through her visits, she knew firsthand about the horrors of modern combat. She also understood that her beloved son was a risk-taker and was hungry to again prove his bravery and burnish his reputation as a military leader. In addition to death or dismemberment, she feared that her son's physical constitution had been too diminished by the previous decade of desk jobs to survive the rigors of the trenches and tearfully advised him to be cautious and take no unnecessary risks.[262]

Churchill, for his part, was worried about his family's conditions much more than his own. Despite his significantly constrained finances, his parting instructions for the care of the household were far from Spartan: "I really don't think you or Goonie should deny yourself any reasonable comfort or convenience. Keep a good table: keep sufficient servants & y[ou]r maid: entertain with discrimination, have a little amusement from time to time. I don't see any reason for undue skimping."[263]

While Churchill faced great uncertainty, he seemed to be looking forward to leaving London and returning to the comradeship of military life. To this end, he sent a letter dated November 17 to his friend and fellow Liberal MP J. E. B. Seely. Like Churchill, Seely had also served in the Asquith government, as the secretary of state for war, but had been forced to resign in the wake of the Curragh mutiny in Ireland in early 1914.[264] Since the opening weeks of the war, Seely had served with the army in France, and now he was a brigadier general in command of a Canadian cavalry brigade. The two had been good friends, attended the Harrow school together, and helped establish the Royal Flying Corps and Royal Naval Air Service, and now both were disgraced politicians trying to win glory through military service.[265] In addition, Seely's aide-de-camp was Churchill's close friend Archibald Sinclair. Anticipating the need for influential allies in the army and the opportunity to renew their friendship, Churchill wrote:

> I cross to-morrow to join my regiment near St. Omer. I have no plans to remain with them. It will give me real pleasure if you and Archie [Sinclair] could come to see me there, and 'though it is hardly for a general to visit a major, I dare say you may be able to contrive an occasion.
>
> I am extremely pleased with the way my own affairs have gone; but miserable about the situation in the near East [the Dardanelles]. However, it is a relief to let all that slide off one's mind, and I shall be so glad to be back again with the army.
>
> Write me and let me know.[266]

As Churchill anticipated, he and Seely would have frequent contact during their time serving at the front together, and Seely would write in glowing terms of his friend's prowess as a military leader.[267]

Given that Churchill was a master of political theater, his departure for France was anticlimactic. On November 18, he made a final visit to his financial adviser, said goodbye to his family, and boarded a ferry to France.[268] He could only guess at what awaited him. He had vague plans to return to his old reserve unit, but nothing firm. He had friends and well-wishers in the ranks, but would they help him in his time of need? He wanted action and the possibility of redemption, but he was guaranteed neither. He did have faith in himself and tenacity to carry him through the months to come. In the relative anonymity of the trenches, he would fight and win some of his least appreciated but most personally rewarding battles.

3

The Hellish Landscape
Churchill Rejoins the Army

Winston Churchill did not know what lay ahead as he boarded a steamer and crossed the English Channel on November 18, 1915. He knew he was leaving London and entering active military service. His plan was to rejoin his old unit, the Oxfordshire Hussars, and ask to be given a combat role. He knew that Britain needed officers, and as a member of the upper class, he was likely to be granted his request. He wanted to escape and contribute in some meaningful way, yet he had no certainty, only a belief in his own destiny. That was enough for now.[1]

As he crossed the channel, Churchill was surrounded by British veterans who were returning from leave, and his fresh uniform and enthusiasm certainly made him stand out from the crowd. He arrived in Boulogne with no expectation of a welcoming party, but "as the crowd of officers and men returning from leave was streaming off the steamer in the French port, [he] heard [his] name called out by the Military Landing Officer and was told that the Commander-in-Chief, Sir John French, had sent a car to take [him] at once to his headquarters."[2]

This was a fast start, and Churchill welcomed the opportunity to meet his old friend and lobby for a position of some importance. Although Churchill and French had differed over policy during the Boer War and its immediate aftermath, they had since become both warm friends and trusted political allies. In the early days of the Great War, the First Lord and the commanding general had worked closely with each other to transport the British Expeditionary Force safely and efficiently to France, and as Churchill said, "I had been thrown constantly into the most intimate relations with him."³ Now, Churchill's relationship with French was opening doors. Although this struck some (including the popular humor magazine *Punch*) as a clear sign of favoritism, Churchill was happy to accept French's kindness and see what he had to offer.

After a brief wait, a staff car arrived and drove Churchill to French's headquarters at the Chateau of Blendecques, near Saint-Omer. The two exchanged pleasantries, and Churchill happily accepted the general's offer to have dinner with him and several other officers.⁴ They dined together in a small but convivial group, and Churchill felt at home surrounded by fellow officers who shared a common sense of purpose. As was typical of French, the meal was informal, served quickly and without pomp, and discussion of the war was strictly prohibited.⁵ This casual approach soothed Churchill's ego as the two old friends talked as equals and avoided unpleasant topics of conversation.⁶

French was a gracious host but kept Churchill guessing as to the purpose of their meeting. In fact, French did not ask him directly about his plans until the next morning, when he inquired simply, "What would you like to do?"⁷ Sensing an opportunity for advancement if he did not overplay his hand, Churchill answered humbly, "I said that I would do whatever I was told."⁸ The general responded, "My power is no longer what it was. I am, as it were, riding at single anchor. But it still counts for something. Will you take a Brigade?"⁹ Careful not to appear too eager, Churchill accepted, noting that he was "proud to do so," on the condition "that before [he] could undertake any such responsibility, [he] must learn first-hand the special conditions of trench warfare."¹⁰

For a man as ambitious as Churchill (who in the previous few months had repeatedly asked Asquith to make him a general), this was an incredibly humble and self-aware request.¹¹ Not only would this insulate him from charges of favoritism, but it would also give him significant time to acclimatize himself to the faster and deadlier pace of modern war. As he later recalled, "However presumptuous it may have been, I did not feel incapable of discharging the duties in question, provided I had a month or two in the line to measure the novel conditions of the Great War for myself."¹² French agreed to this reasonable request. "[French said] that he would attach me for instruction to any Division I liked. I said that the Guards was the best school of all. He thereupon invited Lord Cavan [General Rudolph Lambart, 10th Earl of Cavan], who commanded the Guards Division, to come and see him a few days later; and after a pleasant conversation I found myself duly posted to this famous unit."[13]

Serving with the Grenadier Guards

The choice of the Grenadier Guards was interesting. In a world that still valued social connections, this was a unit of unusually high status. It was nominally commanded by the king, provided pallbearers for royal family funerals, and claimed among its ranks many wealthy and well-educated members of the British elite. The unit also had a rich history dating to its formation in 1656 and had distinguished itself in various conflicts ever since.[14] In addition, the Grenadier Guards also had an attractive family connection for Churchill. Winston's ancestor, John Churchill, 1st Duke of Marlborough, had served as the regimental colonel during the early 1700s and had won some of his early battles in command of this unit during the War of Spanish Succession.[15]

During the Great War, the Grenadier Guards had continued this proud tradition, fighting in some of the bloodiest and most famous battles on the western front, including Mons, Marne, First Battle of Ypres, Neuve Chapelle, Festubert, and Loos. While these battles killed or wounded many of the older and more socially prestigious members of the division, it remained a famous unit with a reputation for gallantry and fighting spirit.[16] The Grenadier Guards were currently holding a quiet sector of the front, and because of the prevailing cold weather, no major offensives were anticipated. While there would be frequent shelling and trench raids, this would also be a relatively safe place for Churchill to acclimatize himself to the conditions of the front while being embedded with a high-quality unit.[17]

Before officially reporting to the Grenadier Guards, Churchill had lunch with the unit's commanding officer, Lord Cavan, who was happy to assign him "to one of the best Colonels [he had] . . . his battalion goes into the line tomorrow."[18] The next day, Churchill arrived at the Guards' divisional headquarters near Merville, where he was again welcomed by the divisional commander. He thought he had packed a minimal amount of baggage, a notion that would prove comically wrong in the coming hours.[19] Before officially joining his unit, Churchill and Lord Cavan rode to the front lines in the general's car.[20] By the time Churchill arrived, most of the troops had already begun to move toward the front, and the battalion staff were packing the final items and preparing to follow.[21] After some perfunctory exchanges with the battalion officers, Lord Cavan drove away, leaving Churchill "very like a new boy at school."[22] The battalion staff was not entirely welcoming of their newest member, but they provided Churchill with a pony, and the group set off to catch up with the main body, which was now about a mile ahead. They caught up quickly and rode among the men. A freezing rain began to fall, and for the next half hour, not a word was spoken.[23]

The silence was broken when the colonel in command of the battalion, George Jeffreys, gave voice to his frustrations about having a high-profile politician attached to the unit, noting, "I think I ought to tell you that we were not at all consulted in the matter of your coming." Churchill tried to be understanding and replied that he had no idea what battalion he was being assigned to. He added, "We must make the best of it." Despite this genuine attempt at bonhomie, his words were met with further awkward silence.[24]

Churchill's next interaction was friendlier but similarly jarring. Because of the Spartan conditions in the trenches, the battalion adjutant informed him, "We have had to cut down your kit rather, Major."[25] Churchill, who was accustomed to living in comfort even while on campaigns in India, South Africa, and Sudan, did his best to appear unconcerned and insisted that he understood and would make himself comfortable.[26] For the remainder of his time on the western front, he would write to his wife, Clementine, asking for luxury items and additional pieces of equipment and clothing, but he was sensitive to the fact that he was new to the unit and something of a burden, so he chose not to complain and instead put on the affectation of a stoic warrior.

As the battalion approached the front in silence, Churchill got his first view of the battlefield that would be his home for the coming weeks. He was struck by the numerous shell holes that marked the shattered landscape and saddened by the remnants of homes and leafless trees.[27] As troops dispersed to their positions along the lines, Churchill dismounted and went to the battalion headquarters, which was set up at a ruined place known as Ebenezer Farm. The crumbing brick building had been reinforced with sandbags and had three or four rooms to serve as unit headquarters. A charcoal fire provided some heat and comfort, but the general appearance was decidedly shabby.[28]

After the troops were in their positions and the reports had been received from the Coldstream Guards unit, which they had replaced in the line, Churchill and the other officers at headquarters shared a meal supplemented by tea and condensed milk. The mood was generally businesslike, and some of the officers seemed reluctant to talk too much in front of their commanding officer. Around eight o'clock, the body of a dead enlisted man was brought into the headquarters and kept there to await burial the next day, a grim reminder that even in this relatively quiet sector of the front, death and danger were constant companions.[29]

Churchill was given his choice of places to sleep, either the signal office in the battalion headquarters or a dugout approximately two hundred yards away. Shunning the cramped and chaotic conditions of a room shared by four telegraph officers and their machines, he decided on the colder but quieter dugout. Churchill and the battalion second-in-command walked through the sleet and wet grass to find it but were unable to use a flashlight for fear of exposing their position to the enemy. They wandered for a quarter of an hour before stumbling on the four-foot-deep pit, which contained at least a foot of frigid and muddy water on the floor. Churchill thanked the deputy commander for showing him his prospective home, but he quickly changed his mind and decided that the chaos and heat of the headquarters signal office were preferable to the wetness of the dugout. The two briefly discussed the dangers of trench foot, which was a near-constant danger in these wet and unsanitary conditions, and the "sockatorium," where socks were continually being laundered, dried, and returned to their owners. The two walked back to headquarters through the cold night as a steady stream of bullets and shells whistled over their heads.[30]

Despite the danger, hardships, and initially frosty reception, Churchill threw himself into life at the front with his typical energy and enthusiasm. He would later claim that he immediately made himself at home and within forty-eight hours had overcome most of the prejudices and suspicions of the men.[31] While this is likely something of a self-serving exaggeration, Churchill made a conscious effort to maintain his military bearing and positive attitude and to project his genuine desire to learn about modern warfare. This approach eventually paid dividends as his gruff commanding officer, Colonel Jeffreys, began to incorporate Churchill into the command structure of the unit and trust him with greater responsibilities. On Churchill's own suggestion, Jeffreys allowed Churchill to accompany him on his daily rounds, and he said, "Always ask me anything you want to know. It is my duty to give you all information." Churchill graciously accepted this offer, and the two spent two to three hours each day discussing countless military subjects.[32] In just a few short weeks, Churchill had proved himself to his once skeptical battalion commander and made a true friendship.[33] Jeffreys would rise to the rank of major general and become a Conservative MP before Churchill made him a baron in 1951 during his second term as prime minister.[34]

When the battalion's deputy commander went on leave, Churchill was invited to temporarily assume his duties. This opportunity was a genuine sign of trust and confidence in his leadership abilities, and he considered it one of the greatest honors he had ever received. After serving as the deputy commander, Churchill made the unusual request of being allowed to sleep in the trenches for the ostensible purpose of improving his understanding of life on the front lines; he would later confess that he was primarily motivated by his desire to drink alcohol.[35] Battalion headquarters was strictly dry, but at the company level, the men were allowed greater latitude to flaunt the regulations.[36]

In addition to the warmth of spirits, Churchill also had an old friend in the unit, Edward Grigg, who was serving on the front lines.[37] Grigg was born in India into a respected civil service family; attended Oxford, where he won prizes in classics; and worked as a journalist before the war. At a time when journalistic standards were very different from today's, Grigg covered Churchill's rise to power and quickly grew to admire this talented upstart who was only a few years older than himself. The two became friends, both passing along information and political gossip. Grigg was even an occasional guest aboard the HMS *Enchantress*, the magnificent yacht used by the First Lord of the Admiralty for official state business.[38] At the start of the war, Grigg voluntarily enlisted in the Grenadier Guards and, because of his Oxford education and social status, was quickly commissioned as a lieutenant. By the time Churchill joined the unit, Grigg was serving as a brevet captain despite his relatively advanced age of thirty-six. He would serve honorably for the remainder of the war, rising to the rank of lieutenant colonel and winning numerous decorations for his service. After the war, he would enter politics, serving as a Liberal MP and governor of Kenya before, like Churchill, switching over to the Conservatives. Like Churchill, he was also wary of a resurgent Nazi Germany, and during the 1930s, he penned two books arguing for increased armaments and defense spending.[39] Grigg would serve in a number of positions under Churchill during World War II, including undersecretary of state for war, minister in residence for the Middle East, and privy counsellor.[40] While Churchill could not have known this at the time, he anticipated "the most cordial welcome" from his friend and kindred spirit.[41]

Despite the harsher conditions and increased danger, Churchill genuinely loved his time on the front lines. As Grigg noted, "Winston accepted the situation with great cheerfulness and we had quite a good time . . . he is strictly amenable to discipline, and salutes the Commanding Officer as smartly as any of us when he comes around."[42] Not only did he bond with Grigg and the troops, but he was able to distract himself from politics for the first time in years by focusing on the daily trials of military life. Rather than dwelling on the political questions of the day, Churchill could simply worry about staying alive and being an effective soldier.[43]

Churchill loved the simple duties of military life, particularly the act of digging trenches. He understood that improving these defenses helped provide distraction while also increasing the odds that his men would survive German attacks. His long-standing interest in fortifications went back to his days at Sandhurst, and he had an urgent need to learn as much as he could about fieldcraft before taking command of his own unit.[44] Churchill was also eager to demonstrate that he was an active and inspirational leader who shared the same risks as his men. They typically worked at night, and Churchill frequently bragged about his long nights spent out in the cold with his men digging trenches.[45]

In an almost routine manner, the next morning the German artillery would get to work attempting to undo the efforts of the previous evening. This led to repeated complaints from the men, but Churchill was satisfied that the trenches were quite effective at limiting casualties and keeping his unit in fighting shape. The predictable nature of German artillery fire was matched by the routine the unit quickly fell into during this relatively calm period. The unit would spend forty-eight hours on the front lines, followed by another forty-eight in support of the frontline troops. It would maintain this schedule for twelve days and then rotate to six days in divisional reserve, where it could rest and refit before another twelve days at the front.[46] Despite this grim and sometimes deadly routine, Churchill and his fellow officers did a remarkable job of maintaining discipline and morale.

Although Churchill had displayed courage under fire and an unbreakable spirit countless times before on the battlefields of India, Sudan, and South Africa, the trenches were different. In this more modern form of warfare, battles lasted months, the enemy was largely unseen, and death was often impersonal and random. There were no cavalry charges where in a moment a soldier could gain glory or the grave; rather, there was a slow, inglorious grind punctuated by moments of extreme danger and little recourse. This postheroic warfare forced Churchill to channel his courage and leadership into a new direction, one that would serve him well not only in the months that would follow but during his greatest test during World War II.

Light in the Darkness

In this and other dark moments of his life, Churchill was able to maintain his spirits and encourage those around him because of an abounding faith. While he was not a particularly religious man, he believed that he was part of a divine plan. This gave him the ability to carry on and show strength and confidence while others doubted and wavered.[47] He reasoned that there was little one could do to avoid a well-aimed bullet or a randomly shot artillery projectile launched from miles away. Rather, he had to trust that fate had saved him for something special or that he was destined to die serving heroically—either way, Churchill believed that he could do little more than trust in fate and act as bravely as possible.[48] While such a fatalistic view of life may strike readers as unusual, such attitudes were quite common among soldiers of World War I. Moreover, Churchill had always lived by the belief that he was lucky and destined for greatness, so he had little reason to fear death.

One prominent example of Churchill's good luck was the story he would frequently retell about when he was summoned to meet with the corps commander, Lieutenant General Richard Haking, on November 24.[49] Churchill had been in his frontline position for about a week and was using a break in the shelling to write letters home. After writing for about a quarter of an hour, he was interrupted by a courier who delivered a telegram. He was to report to the Rouge Croix crossroads no later than 3:15 that afternoon, where a car would be waiting to drive him to a meeting with his corps commander.[50] While this was an unusual request, it could not be ignored, and Churchill promptly put away his letters and prepared to go and meet the general.

Churchill was somewhat piqued at this interruption and the prospect of having to walk across cold and muddy fields to reach the meeting point, but Haking had been an acquaintance before the war, and the general outranked him, so there was little choice in the matter.[51] He had his servant accompany him to carry his coat and to serve as a guide because he knew the way back in the dark better than Churchill. As the two men walked across the field, four or five shells screamed down and hit the very trenches where they had been moments before. The Germans then proceeded to barrage the British lines for about an hour, but Churchill gave it little thought. He was now a safe distance from the crashing shells, and his mind was busy anticipating the meeting with the corps commander.[52]

When Churchill arrived at the appointed location, he was surprised to see that there was no car waiting for him. He waited impatiently for about an hour before a staff officer walked up and asked, "Are you Major Churchill?" After he confirmed his identity, he was informed, "There was a mistake about sending the car for you. It went to the wrong place, and now it is too late for you to see the General at Merville. He has already gone back to his Headquarters at Hinges. You can rejoin your unit."[53]

While disappointed, Churchill tried to engage in polite small talk and asked the staff officer what exactly the general had wanted to discuss at the planned meeting. The response piqued Churchill, as apparently the general only wished to make a social call and had no military purpose for his visit.[54] Churchill had a lifelong habit of missing or being very late for trains, meetings, dinners, and other scheduled events, but he was unhappy about being pulled out of the line during his limited leisure time and vented his frustrations on the messenger. He made little effort to conceal his anger, and a brisk argument ensued.[55]

Churchill walked away cold and upset as darkness approached. He soon lost his way and, despite the cold rain, spent two hours sweating from his exertions under his full uniform. He was cold and tired and dispirited when he stumbled into the company mess for a drink and a short rest.[56] The officers present quickly recognized him and said, "You're in luck to-day." Churchill could not see why and responded gruffly, "I haven't seen much of it. . . . I've been made a fool of." The officers assured Churchill, "Well, you're in luck all the same . . . as you will see when you get back to your Company."[57] Churchill still did not fully grasp what he had been told. He quickly downed some much-needed whiskey and water before going back out into the cold and mud to rejoin his company in the line.[58]

Churchill was met by a sergeant who saluted and informed him, "We have shifted your kit to Mr. ____'s dug-out, Sir." Not knowing the meaning of this, he asked, "Why?" "Yours has been blown up, Sir," was the reply. Concerned, he responded, "Any harm done?" The sergeant replied, "Your kit's all right, Sir, but ____ was killed. Better not go in there, Sir, it's in an awful mess."[59] Only then did Churchill begin to understand the meaning of his fellow officers' words a few minutes before. Shocked, he asked, "When did this happen?" "About five minutes after you left, Sir. A whizzbang came in through the roof and blew his head off."[60]

Astonished at his narrow escape, Churchill "felt [his] irritation against General ____ pass completely from [his] mind. A sense of grievance departed in a flash."[61] As Churchill walked to his new dugout, he "reflected how thoughtful it had been of him to wish to see [Churchill] again, and to show courtesy to a subordinate, when he had so much responsibility on his shoulders."[62] Consistent with Churchill's belief in his own destiny and his own willingness to perpetuate the myth that he was destined for greatness, he would tell and retell this tale countless times over the coming decades as proof that "a hand had been stretched out to move [him] in the nick of time from that fatal spot." However, in typical Churchill style, he hedged on the existence of God, concluding, "Whether it was General ____'s hand or not, I cannot tell."[63] For the remainder of his life, he bragged about the many near misses he experienced during his time at the front. Close calls such as this one seemed to confirm his sense of destiny and emphasize his willingness to serve in an active capacity and expose himself to danger.[64]

Interestingly, while he was happy to boast about his bravery to almost anyone who would listen, he minimized these dangers to his wife, Clementine.[65] He knew she was worried about his safety, and he had promised her not to take unnecessary risks. To this end, he purposely understated the risks in his letters from the front. While this would seem two faced, it fits a larger pattern of Churchill attempting to put on a brave face for Clementine and shield her from the horrors of the front while also trying to get maximum public adulation for his bravery in confronting the dangers of active service.

Such an approach also fits with Churchill's lifelong fixation on more romantic and civilized notions of war from days gone by as well as his desire to remain positive and energetic amid horror and uncertainty.[66] For example, his letter to Clementine of November 27 makes the idealistic claim that returning from the front lines was "like getting to a jolly good tavern after long days hunting, wet & cold and hungry, but not without having good sport."[67] While the front was relatively calm during this period, Churchill must have known that it was more dangerous and less sporting than a fox hunt. This language, therefore, seems to have been an attempt to make the best of a bad situation by finding a happier analogy and exuding confidence, an ability that would serve him well in dark days for the remainder of his life.

A perfect example of Churchill's ability to project confidence and optimism was on display during his forty-first birthday on November 30, 1915. During his visit to the front lines, he was under very heavy shelling for three hours before he returned to the rear areas for what he described as a "most cheery dinner."[68] He largely glossed over the brush with death and his own aging and instead used the opportunity to brag about his strength and vitality to Clementine: "It has not caused me any sense of anxiety or apprehension, nor does the approach of a shell quicken my pulse, or try my nerves or make me about to bob as do so many. It is satisfactory to find that so many years of luxury have in no way impaired the tone of my system. At this game I hope I shall be as good as any."[69]

Despite Churchill's desire to put on a brave face, this birthday must have been personally disappointing. He had long dreaded aging and feared that he would die young like his father, Randolph, before him. Because of this belief that his time on earth would be short, he had set the overly ambitious goal of becoming prime minister by the age of forty-five.[70] Now, like his father, it seemed that he was finished. Finished for breaking with his party. Finished for being seen as a brilliant but reckless show-off. Finished for resigning his cabinet position out of principle. Finished when the future had seemed so bright.[71] While Churchill always believed in himself, here, in the cold and danger of the trenches, the grandiose visions of the young statesman must have seemed very distant indeed.

It may have been difficult for Churchill to see, but his time in the trenches and away from the politics of London was already paying dividends. He was learning valuable insights about the character of modern warfare, making lifelong friends, and generally enjoying the comradeship and adventures of military life. While the day-to-day hardships were taxing, the cumulative effect was that Churchill was on the path to personal growth and renewal.

Growing as a Leader

Churchill's efforts to learn as much as he could in preparation for brigade command appeared to be bearing fruit. His humble approach, generosity, and inquisitive nature converted many skeptics in the Grenadier Guards and elsewhere while giving his patron, General French, ample evidence to support his promotion to brigadier. According to his friend General J. E. B. Seely, Churchill had exceeded all expectations: "At the start Jeffreys did not approve of the arrangement and said so. But in a very few weeks he reported that Churchill had gained an exceptional knowledge of trench warfare in all its forms, and was fully competent to command a battalion . . . the officers and men loved Churchill, and would have followed him anywhere."[72] Churchill was quick to praise the officers and men and credit them with teaching him about modern warfare firsthand: "It was a comfort to be with these fine troops at such a time, to study their methods, unsurpassed in the Army, of discipline and trench warfare, and to share from day to day their life under the hard conditions of the winter and the fire of the enemy."[73]

The simple fact was that Churchill enjoyed the comradeship of living with the officers and men and not having to worry about the politics and political intrigue of London. In the trenches, he was too busy to think about politics and instead took pleasure in practicing martial virtues and living in the moment. He made this very point when describing his first time in command of a small raiding party:

> As in the shades of a November evening, I for the first time led a platoon of Grenadiers across the sopping fields which gave access to our trenches, while here and there the bright flashes of the guns or the occasional whistle of a random bullet accompanied our path, the conviction came into my mind with absolute assurance that the simple soldiers and their regimental officers, armed with their cause, would be their virtues in the end retrieve the mistakes and ignorances of Staffs and Cabinets, of Admirals, Generals and politicians—including, no doubt, many of my own.[74]

Indeed, there was an authenticity to these men who shared the same fate, and all contributed to the same small part of the war. The typically self-centered Churchill recognized this and insisted, "The kindness with which I was received during my period of instruction with the Guards Divisions will ever be gratefully remembered by me."[75]

Although Churchill reveled in the Spartan simplicity of the military life, he did not wish to do without the amenities of home. To this end, he almost immediately began to write Clementine to ask for additional food and luxury items. He had drawn the scorn of his fellow soldiers by bringing far too much luggage and equipment with him when he first arrived, and he quickly cut his kit down to a relative minimum. Now, almost as quickly, he began to build his supplies back up to a more comfortable level. To this end, Clementine was obliging as she often sent multiple care packages per week as well as newspaper clippings that mentioned him or other key events.[76] She truly missed her husband and worried about his safety, so despite the significant expense, she obliged his repeated requests.[77] This near-constant flow of luxury goods helped win Churchill friends as he freely shared his food, tobacco, and wine with his fellow officers, and this largesse turned many skeptics into friends.[78]

Churchill repeatedly thanked Clementine for these packages and often attached additional requests to his grateful replies. She still feared for her husband but felt that her frequent letters and care packages would see him through this trying period. In fact, they communicated so frequently and extensively (writing over one hundred letters) that Churchill's time at the front is by far the best-documented period of their long and successful marriage.[79] On December 8, Winston was able to call Clementine on the telephone. Although they only spoke a few minutes, international phone calls were a rare privilege in those days, and she felt comforted to hear her husband's voice, if only briefly.[80] While Churchill is remembered as a stoic and pugnacious warrior, beneath this masculine veneer was a romantic and emotionally vulnerable heart. Churchill needed almost constant love and affirmation, and he was fortunate that Clementine understood and nurtured him.

The Promise of Brigade Command

In only a few weeks with the Grenadier Guards, Churchill had proved that he was serious about serving in an active capacity and had won over many of his skeptics.[81] General French was quite pleased with Churchill's progress, and the two met on December 3 and 10 to discuss his progress and next assignment. In the first of these meetings, Churchill asked for a battalion in the immediate future, to more slowly acclimatize him to command and to protect him against claims of favoritism. Perhaps sensing that his own position as commander of the British Expeditionary Force was increasingly tenuous, French instead insisted on him taking command of a brigade as soon as one became available.

Churchill understood that this would open both men up to criticism but also knew that after he had taken command of a brigade, it would be difficult to remove him. Once in command, he would succeed or fail on his own merits. Since French would approve the transfer, he also reasoned that he would appear to only be following orders as a dutiful subordinate and could claim that he had not asked for the assignment. Although he clearly wanted to command larger formations, Churchill would maintain this pretense of feigned humility in his letters and memoirs for the remainder of his life.

In the second meeting on December 10, French informed Churchill that he would be given command of the 56th Brigade of the 19th Division, currently holding a sector of the front adjacent to the Grenadier Guards.[82] Churchill was pleased with this news and began to prepare for his promotion and transfer, which he anticipated would occur in the upcoming weeks. Shortly after getting word from General French, Churchill relayed the good news to his friend General Seely, who noted, "Winston told me this with great glee, naming the brigade. He was heart and soul in the business, spending all the spare time he could find in thinking out new methods of attack and defense for this novel kind of warfare, and writing memoranda on the subject."[83]

Despite Clementine's constant urging for Churchill to remain grounded and humble, his excitement was similarly evident in his letter to her dated December 10: "Of course there will be criticism & carping. But it is no good paying any attention to that. If I had a battalion for a few weeks, it must equally be said 'he has used it merely as a stepping stone etc.' I am satisfied this is the right thing to do in the circumstances, & for the rest my attention will concentrate upon the Germans."[84] Ever a lover of military uniforms and pomp, he also requested that she obtain for him a complete set of brigadier general uniforms and badges of rank.[85]

With the promise of brigade command, Churchill's work with the Grenadier Guards took on an increased intensity. Seemingly every day provided the opportunity to learn something new, which he hoped would serve him well in the coming weeks. Even though he was actively engaged in learning about tactics and fieldcraft on the western front, he never stopped thinking about the larger strategic picture or the fact that he had once been one of the most important drivers of war policy. For example, on December 7, 1915, he was musing with his friend Captain Edward Spears about how to use the Royal Navy to take offensive action against the German fleet in the North Sea. This issue had troubled him greatly during his tenure as First Lord, as the Germans had employed a multilayered defense that included mines, torpedo boats, submarines, and aircraft to protect their capital ships from the more powerful and numerous British fleet. Much to the frustration of Churchill, who had wanted to force out the German High Seas Fleet "like rats from their hole," the more conservative British admirals had preferred to stand off the German coast and wait. This prudent strategy would slowly strangle the German economy rather than force the Royal Navy into the confined and heavily defended waters off the German coast, yet it held little appeal for Churchill.[86]

Now, in the mud of the western front, Churchill had an idea. He could use Royal Navy aircraft armed with torpedoes to strike at the German fleet while at anchor.[87] For Churchill, this brilliant idea was a logical extension of his work as a pioneer in naval aviation. Indeed, he had been an early supporter of the Royal Navy Air Service, had fought for their budget and autonomy, had invented the term *seaplane*, had funded newer aircraft models, and had defended their officers when they likely violated Swiss neutrality during a bombing raid on German zeppelin hangars.[88] While nothing came of this daring plan, it was an amazing bit of strategic insight into the vulnerability of capital ships to torpedo attacks from the air, twenty-six years to the day before the Japanese attack on Pearl Harbor.[89]

These mental exercises were more than simple fantasy or musings to his friends during idle time. Rather, they indicated just how active and creative his mind was and how much he still wished to be included in key discussions even though he was only a major serving in a quiet section of the front.[90] To this end, Churchill spent significant time in late November and early December recording his thoughts about how to break the stalemate on the western front in a memo he titled "Variants of the Offensive."[91] This impressive document synthesized many of Churchill's previous writings about the character of modern war and the importance of new technologies such as the tank for restoring mobility and decision to the battlefield.[92] In it, he argued for a mass armored assault on German lines, which would overcome the defensive advantages provided by machine guns and barbed wire. If the Allies could husband their resources until they had sufficient numbers of tanks and then employ them en masse, then there would be hope of achieving real results.[93] Barring this, the Allies must choose to not waste their strength in piecemeal assaults. Churchill understood that the Allies were locked in a bloody war of attrition, and he argued for the importance of conserving lives rather than wasting them on taking relatively worthless pieces of terrain. Given the massive scale of the western front, Churchill reasoned that no single piece of real estate was important since either side could simply conduct a fighting retreat and inflict horrific losses on the attacking force. In Churchill's words, "After all, it is the enemy's *army* we are fighting and not the enemy's *position*."[94] This understanding that the true German "center of gravity" was its army and not its fortified positions was an insightful application of the classic Clausewitzian principle, which speaks to the lucidity of Churchill's mind even when faced with the deprivations of the trenches and the uncertainty of political exile.[95]

Perhaps the most remarkable feature of this memo was that it had a wide readership despite Churchill's status as a political outcast and midlevel officer. Consistent with his long history of providing unsolicited advice to higher-echelon commanders, Churchill circulated drafts of this document around French's headquarters and sent copies to influential friends in London.[96] While this presumptuous and insubordinate approach may have endangered the careers of other officers, he had support from above in French. Moreover, the merits of his ideas were significant as they provided a potential path out of a seemingly hopeless military situation.

After French's removal, the incoming commander, General Douglas Haig, also read the memo with significant interest. Despite his need to distance himself politically from the disgraced former First Lord, Haig was interested in the potential for tanks to transform the nature of war. In April 1916, Haig met with Colonel Ernest Swinton, who had worked at the Admiralty under Churchill on armored vehicles and overseen the British tank force.[97] This sequence of events would later allow Churchill to claim partial credit for the creation and introduction of armored vehicles into modern war, but his contributions have been overstated.[98] Brilliant insights aside, Churchill's work ultimately had little impact on the course of the war or the future of armored warfare. In Churchill's mind, fate seemed to conspire against him to yet again thwart a war-winning idea. While Churchill's memo was ultimately ignored, a few weeks later it did provide for a moment of panic and a lifetime of self-deprecating humor when he thought it had fallen into enemy hands.

Although his strategy memo did not have its intended impact, Churchill remained pleased about his prospects. He had learned much about modern warfare. He had made friends and converted his skeptics. He was in good spirits. All seemed to be turning in Churchill's favor. However, Churchill seemed to have forgotten General French's warnings that his position was tenuous, and he was "riding at single anchor."[99] His patron had suffered from poor health for months and, in the aftermath of the Battle of Loos, had lost the confidence of both the king and the prime minister.

A Battalion, Not a Brigade

Despite Churchill's exile to the western front, he could not fully escape the political intrigue of London. The Asquith government was facing renewed public frustration regarding its conduct of the war and was desperate to provide bold and decisive action. Churchill's friend and patron General French was an obvious target given that he had commanded the British forces since the beginning of the war and had been blamed for the repeated failures to achieve victory. For both the king and Asquith, French's defeat at the Battle of Loos was the final blow. While many of the criticisms of French were unfair, particularly the claim that he would have achieved victory at Loos if he had acted more aggressively, the damage was done.[100]

After repeated requests from the king and increased public pressure, Asquith decided to act. He polled key members of his cabinet, including Lloyd George, Bonar Law, Grey, and General Sir William Robertson. All agreed that French was a brave and dedicated soldier, but he had outlived his usefulness. On November 23, Asquith decided to relieve French and to dispatch Reginald Brett, the 2nd Viscount of Esher, to personally deliver the news to the general's headquarters. Esher and French met on November 25 and discussed the matter privately. Acting on Asquith's instructions, Esher told French that if he resigned gracefully, he could continue to serve as the commanding officer of British forces stationed at home and could expect a peerage and a grant from Parliament after he retired. French's initial reaction was surprise, but his mood hardened after he had dinner and thought further on the matter. He decided that he would not accept this generous offer of a graceful exit and instead would fight to keep his job.[101]

French traveled to London on November 29 and met with Asquith. While the talk was pleasant, it was clear that French would be relieved. French insisted on several conditions for his departure, such as naming his successor, but Asquith was determined not to give in to these demands since he had already chosen Haig. French left the meeting and again tried to convince Asquith to agree to his demands by writing a letter outlining his terms for resigning. This was met with a letter from his friend Walter Long written on Asquith's behalf to suggest that French should resign his command at once. Faced with the blunt but heartfelt advice from his friend, the general decided to resign. French's resignation was formally accepted on December 6. The War Office did not formally announce French's resignation until

December 15, and the official transfer of command would not take place until December 18.[102]

This development had profound consequences for Churchill. In addition to replacing his patron, Asquith also chose to formally deny Churchill the brigade command that he had been promised.[103] To soften the blow, French telephoned Churchill on December 15 to warn him of his own imminent relief and the fact that his promotion had been at least temporarily blocked. French apologized for this turn of events and informed his friend that both decisions had been made by Asquith. French later shared private correspondence from Asquith that read, "With regard to our conversation about our friend [Churchill]—the appointment might cause some criticism—& should not therefore be made. Perhaps you might give him a battalion."[104] Churchill appreciated that French had done everything he could but had been blocked by the prime minister. On December 18, General John French was officially relieved of command and replaced with General Douglas Haig.[105] While French had warned Churchill about his tenuous position and pushed for his promotion to brigade command on the belief that he might not remain in command much longer, this news was still a shock.

Haig was aware that Churchill had been promised a brigade and discussed this delicate situation with French when he was turning over his command. According to Haig's account of the meeting:

> He [French] did not look very well and seemed short of breath at times. He expressed a wish to help me and the Army in France to the best of his power at home. Then he said that "There was a delicate personal matter" which he wished to speak about. This was that he wanted to give Winston Churchill an Infantry Brigade. This had been vetoed but he was anxious that Winston should have a battalion. I replied that I had no objection because Winston had done some good work in the trenches and we were short of Battalion COs.[106]

While the assignment of a major was typically well below the normal concerns of an incoming commanding general, Haig understood that he needed to be careful. He and Churchill had crossed paths many times and had respected each other. Yet Churchill's star was in eclipse, and Haig needed to remain in good standing with his political supporters.[107] This pressure combined with the fact that Churchill's present rank of major (he would be promoted to lieutenant colonel in January) was only appropriate for the command of a battalion made Haig unwilling to back Churchill at this juncture.[108] In addition, denying Churchill command of a brigade would test his true motives. If he actually desired to command a frontline unit, then he would put aside his ego and accept this reduced role. If, however, he only wanted high rank and prestige, this would force him to refuse command of a battalion and expose him as the dilettante that his rivals had long alleged him to be.

Eager to conclude this unpleasantry, Haig called Churchill in for a one-on-one meeting to deliver the bad news. According to Haig, "Winston Churchill then appeared and I told him what I had said to French."[109] Haig got to the point quickly, telling Churchill that he would not be getting the brigade that French had promised.[110] Haig was apologetic and praised his subordinate's "excellent work" in the field with the Grenadier Guards, but despite Churchill's protests, he held firm, insisting that he could only offer a battalion. This direct and personal approach appears to have somewhat softened the blow to Churchill's ego, as he appreciated both his old friend's candor and his delicate position.

Churchill wrote Clementine later that day to break the bad news and to help make sense of the incident in his own mind:

> Haig came to see French who told him the whole position. I was called in and had an interview with Haig. He treated me with the utmost kindness of manner & consideration, assured me that nothing w[oul]d give him greater pleasure than to give me a Brigade, that his only wish was that able men sh[oul]d come to the front & that I might count on his sympathy in every way. He had heard from Cavan of the "excellent work" that I had done in the trenches . . . I was greatly assured by his manner wh[ich] was affectionate almost. He took me by the arm and made the greatest fuss. I used to know him pretty well in the old days when he was a major & I a young MP, but I am bound to say the warmth of his greeting surprised me. . . . So I am back on my perch, again with my feathers stroked down.[111]

Despite his attempt to be stoic, this latest reversal of fortune was devastating to Churchill. He had been preparing to command a large body of troops and hoped to win glory and redemption. Now, when he was so close to beginning this new chapter in his life, he was denied for a political reason, not a military one. His bitterness was increased by his belief that Prime Minister Asquith had betrayed him yet again. Asquith had forced him to resign as First Lord, then marginalized and ignored him on the Dardanelles Committee, failed to include him in his reconstituted war cabinet, and now felt it necessary to again cast him aside to bolster his own political position.

For Churchill, this latest betrayal was too much of an insult to pardon.[112] In fact, he never fully forgave his old friend. On December 18, Winston wrote Clementine, "I am inclined to think that [Asquith's] conduct reached the limits of meanness and ungenerousness. . . . Personally I feel that every link is severed . . . all relationship should cease."[113] In the coming months, Churchill increasingly backed Asquith's rival, David Lloyd George, in political matters and plotted his revenge. Ever one to use analogies from the animal kingdom, Churchill made frequent references to Asquith "throwing him to the wolves" to save himself, a revealing if not particularly gracious reflection of his thoughts on the matter.[114] Churchill's belief that he was wronged even strained his relationship with Violet. Churchill never said anything to her about this, but she understood that it had hurt him deeply and would later recognize that it had changed their relationship.[115] Although in the long run distancing himself from Asquith was advantageous, this nevertheless was a painful betrayal and a dramatic break with a man who had been instrumental in Churchill's rise to prominence.[116]

As a gesture of solidarity and support, Churchill accompanied French to his change of command ceremony and noted that his old friend was obviously under a great strain: "His pain giving up his great command was acute. He would much rather have given up his life."[117] While this statement likely contained a significant amount of hyperbole and projection, Churchill was genuinely sad to see his friend and patron depart under such inglorious circumstances.

Shortly after Churchill received the bad news from Haig, his friend J. E. B. Seely saw him and recorded his impressions in his memoirs:

> In forty years of close friendship I have never seen him so deeply disappointed and hurt. Indeed, he had every reason. He had served through every rank in the army from a second lieutenant to a lieutenant-colonel commanding a battalion in the field. He had been through Sandhurst, and either as an observer or a combatant

officer, had served in five campaigns with distinction, mentions in dispatches, medals and clasps. He had come up to the exacting standard of the Guards brigade. It was an extraordinary instance of the rigid exclusiveness of the old-fashioned military mind. The fact that he could write well should have taught them that he could think well. The fact that he could rise in parliament [*sic*] from a private member to be first Secretary of State and the First Lord of the Admiralty should have taught them that here was a man with a strong constitution and a powerful, alert and clear brain. I said at the time that if Napoleon had had the opportunity he would, without doubt have promoted him to command an army straight off on the chance that the qualities that had made for his meteoric rise in peace might be of equal value in war. Of course Napoleon would have ruthlessly shorn him had he failed. But it is certain he would have given him the opportunity.[118]

Although Seely's memoirs are technically mistaken in their assertion that Churchill was already a lieutenant colonel in command of a battalion in the field, there can be no doubt as to the fact that they accurately capture his friend's sense of rejection and injustice at this cruel twist of fate.

With the opportunity to command a large unit taken from him, Churchill again felt as if he was floundering. The path forward, which had looked so promising with the prospect of brigade command, was again unclear. He knew that for the foreseeable future, he must continue to play the role of a dutiful soldier and do his best to be the military hero he believed he had always been.[119] While this is a tribute to his personal loyalty and desire to fight, it is also a reflection of the fact that he had committed himself to the strategy of redemption through military service and had little choice but to continue.[120] To do otherwise would have only proved his critics right in saying that he was an impetuous glory hunter, not a serious soldier.

As he would so many times, Churchill responded to crisis and misfortune with bravado. He chose to accept the command of a battalion without further complaint and threw himself into the task of learning any additional details he could about battalion-level tactics and assembling a staff for his future command. Seely noted that despite his "sore heart," Churchill was "making the best of it."[121] While his public persona projected confidence, he was clearly still emotionally fragile, and he described himself candidly as "The Escaped Scapegoat."[122]

If Churchill was going to command a battalion, he would do his damnedest to leave his mark on it and do his best. This began with selecting a staff. While Haig had denied Churchill higher rank and brigade command, he helpfully allowed Churchill to select his own deputy battalion commander. In their December 18 meeting, Churchill "asked for an officer—Archie or [Edward] Spiers [Spiers would legally change his name to the English Spears in 1918]—and he went off and arranged at once that I was to have what I wanted." Haig understood that "the need for a few competent professionals is very important, every step [Churchill] take[s] is watched by curious eyes. [He] must be well supported."[123] Both Spears and Sinclair were excited about the opportunity to reunite with their friend. Both had been serving in a series of posts that kept them busy with staff work and did not allow them to see frontline combat. Service with Churchill promised adventure and action in addition to comradeship and conviviality.

A Frustrating Wait

On December 20, Churchill left the trench line with the Grenadier Guards for the last time and returned to the divisional staging area to await orders. He still did not know what battalion he would command, but he knew that he would have time to wait and ponder his future. He did not enjoy this period of inactivity as it allowed him to dwell on his own situation rather than focus on the details of military life. In his typical mixture of candor and bluster, Churchill expressed these feelings in his letter to Clementine:

> I am simply waiting d'un pied a l'autre for orders. It is odd to pass these days of absolute idleness . . . when one looks back to the long years of unceasing labour and hustle through wh[ich] I have passed. It does not fret me. In war one takes everything as it comes, & I seem to have quite different standards to measure by. As one's fortunes are reduced, one's spirit must expand to fill the void.
>
> I think of all the things that are being left undone & of my own energies & capacities to do them & drive them along all wasted—without any real pain. I watch & as far as I can—the weak irresolute & incompetent drift of Government policy and turn over what

ought to be done in my mind, & then let all slide away without a wrench.

I shall be profoundly absorbed in the tremendous little tasks wh[ich] my new work will give me. I hope to come to these men like a breeze. I hope they will rejoice to be led by me & fall back with real confidence into my hands. I shall give them my v[er]y best.[124]

While Churchill may have been writing both to reassure himself and to possibly publish in the future, this letter does reveal his genuine sense of frustration, isolation, and desire to win redemption through frontline service. He craved action, and waiting with nothing to do was extremely difficult.

Since he was awaiting orders, Churchill was permitted to leave the divisional reserve and return to London for a few days to visit his family. This trip was a true luxury as it allowed him to rest and relax in a much more comfortable setting. He was able to spend Christmas with the family and escape the boredom and isolation that had plagued him as he waited for word of his next assignment.[125] Only a year before, he had been First Lord of the Admiralty, planning the ill-fated Dardanelles Campaign. Now, he did his best to live in the present and enjoy the comforts of home and family. Clementine was particularly happy to see her husband, and they savored every moment of their time together. Indeed, Churchill was so immersed in family life that he nearly missed his return train and had to run to catch it as it was pulling away from the station.[126]

On December 27, Churchill was back in France and still waiting.[127] Rather than remain idle, he took a trip with his friend Captain Spears to visit French positions. On December 29, they traveled to Neuve Chapelle and Vimy Ridge to observe the fighting.[128] At Vimy Ridge, he witnessed combat that was much more intense than what he had seen while serving with the Grenadier Guards.[129] This was both an exciting and enlightening moment, and he did his best to glean useful insights on modern combat from this experience.[130] In his December 30 letter to Clementine, he noted:

> The Germans obligingly stopped shelling it [Neuve Chapelle] as we arrived & I was able without much risk to see this part of the line, wh[ich] fills in a gap in my now extensive examination of the front. . . . I was able to go to the very farthest point we hold at Vimy Ridge. . . . I believe that Spiers & I are the only Englishmen who have ever been

on this battle-torn ground. . . . These men who have suffered the whole terrible experience of these vain attacks, repeated almost word for word the arguments wh[ich] I so unsuccessfully addressed to that weak & foolish Cabinet.[131]

While observing the fighting at Vimy Ridge, Churchill nearly lost his life when his Colt pistol, which he was wearing around his neck on a lanyard, began to fire rounds at his feet. Spears ducked behind the nearest traverse in their trench while Churchill, according to Spears, "danced like a cat on hot bricks in his attempts to get out of the unpredictable line of fire as the barrel pointed this way and that. I collapsed on the duckboards laughing until I could laugh no longer."[132] The cause of this accidental discharge is a mystery, but Churchill was lucky to have escaped unharmed as the slugs from his .45-caliber pistol would have inflicted life-threatening wounds had they struck him at such a short range.[133] During a tense moment in June 1940, Churchill reminded his friend of this incident when Spears was nervously fumbling with a pistol and pointed it in his direction. In both cases, Spears described Churchill as "half amused" but noted that his friend had a gift for humor and storytelling in life's darkest times.[134]

On this trip, Churchill also met with several French generals and dignitaries to discuss the conditions at the front. His former position as First Lord of the Admiralty provided access for the curious major far in excess of what was typically available to an officer of his rank. He was eager to learn as much as possible and compared notes with the French generals. Near the conclusion of this meeting, Churchill, Spears, and the French delegation posed for a photo. Churchill is seen in the center wearing his newly acquired French poilu-style helmet, a piece of equipment that had already become his trademark.[135]

Churchill had adopted this new headgear a few weeks earlier as he quickly recognized that the French helmet design was superior to the British tin-hat pattern. This equipment was clearly nonregulation, but he believed that it not only provided enhanced protection but also distinguished him from his men. He remarked, "My steel helmet is the cause of much envy. I look most martial in it—like a Cromwellian. I always intend to wear it under fire—but chiefly for appearance."[136] True to his word, the newly acquired helmet and Churchill became almost inseparable for the remainder of his time at the front. This desire to accept nothing but the best for himself was typical of

Churchill and could be seen as selfishly breaking the rules or attempting to stand out from his men. However, it also speaks to a mind that was active in pursuit of military superiority and a willingness to adapt to the realities of modern warfare. Indeed, after Churchill returned from his time in the trenches, he would make multiple speeches in Parliament and write a series of pamphlets arguing for better equipment, including helmets, for the British troops. This is clear evidence that, whatever his initial motives, he clearly saw the need for improved equipment and was willing to expend political capital on behalf of the frontline troops.

In addition to fulfilling his desire for superior equipment, Churchill's willingness to adopt the French helmet also had the explicit purpose of distinguishing him from others. This could also be seen as a willful break with regulations, but for those who understand Churchill, it was something far more calculated. Churchill had a dramatic flair, understood the power of image, and had played up various trademark looks, particularly hats and headgear. This bit of the Churchill image occurred by accident in the early days of his political career. While walking with Clementine on a beach in Southport, he was photographed wearing a tattered hat from his childhood that was comically small. Almost immediately, political cartoonists began to portray him as having a bloated face and head that was too large for his hats. Initially, this was a source of annoyance, but Churchill quickly embraced the fact that he had a distinctive appearance and for the remainder of his career was rarely seen without some form of headgear.[137] Like his Victorian dress and trademark cigars, this French helmet defined the man and made him stand out from the crowd. In the damp, cold, drab mud of the trenches, this was a spark of humanity and leadership. Like many great commanders, Churchill was vain, but with a purpose of showing his men that they were following somebody different, somebody who would be part of history.

On December 30, Churchill was officially transferred out of the Grenadier Guards.[138] Although he still did not know what battalion he would receive, he was certain that his time with his old unit was well spent. He had learned much about the realities of modern trench warfare and made friends of the skeptics who believed that he was not a serious soldier. These fond memories would remain with Churchill for the rest of his life. He kept up correspondences with many of the officers, wrote multiple articles and told many stories about his brief time with the unit, and even dedicated his monumental biography of his uncle the Duke of Marlborough to the Grenadier Guards. High praise indeed.[139]

6th Battalion of the Royal Scots Fusiliers

On New Year's Day 1916, Churchill learned that he was being assigned to the 6th Battalion of the Royal Scots Fusiliers.[140] This pleased him as the Royal Scots Fusiliers were an old division with a proud combat history that included serving under his ancestor, the Duke of Marlborough, during the War of Spanish Succession.[141] The fact that the unit was recruited primarily from the Scottish Lowlands also appealed to Churchill as his seat in Parliament was from Dundee. While this was a relatively safe seat for a Liberal, Churchill was always happy to win over potential voters, and given his recent political fortunes, he could not afford to take anything for granted.[142] In a typical Churchillian quip, which he repeated often in the coming weeks, he said he owed to Scotland "his wife, his constituency, and his regiment."[143] Even though his transfer was not finalized, Churchill wasted no time acquainting himself with his new unit and arranged for dinner at the 9th Scottish Division officers' mess that very night. There, he had a pleasant dinner with the divisional commander, General William T. Furse, and the assembled staff officers. Churchill was already acquainted with several of the staff members, and the New Year's dinner had a warm and convivial atmosphere.[144]

Despite this auspicious beginning, Churchill knew he had much to do before assuming command. On a personal level, he needed to finalize his own staff and arrange to move himself and his belongings to the new unit. While packing was never easy for Churchill, this task was complicated by the fact that he now needed the uniform of a lieutenant colonel, not a brigadier general as he had planned. In addition to these personal details, Churchill also wanted to learn as much as he could about the battalion. He soon discovered that the unit was not in top fighting condition as it had suffered extremely high casualties in September and October 1915 at the Battle of Loos.[145] Approximately three-quarters of the officers and men had been killed or wounded in this battle, and the ranks had not been brought up to full strength.[146] The new men who had arrived were of generally lesser quality and experience than the veterans they had replaced, and they had yet to prove themselves to the grizzled and skeptical soldiers who remained. Even with these new troops, the battalion, which had an authorized strength of 1,050 officers and men, was down to approximately 700 personnel present and fit for duty.[147] Given this drain on the battalion's quality and quantity, Churchill knew that he would need to use his personal leadership and charisma to ensure that these men were ready to fight.

On January 3, Churchill wrote to Clementine and requested a volume of collected works by Robert Burns, the Scottish poet known for popularizing and preserving the unique Scottish dialect and sense of tragic romance.[148] He believed that by reading the Scottish bard's verse aloud to his men, he would be able to lift their spirits and show that he shared a love for and understanding of their native land. While this may strike modern readers as a comically naive combination of upper-class Victorian foppishness and cultural appropriation, it was a genuine attempt to understand and bond with his men. In the harsh realities of the trenches, it seems likely that he gave up on the notion of dramatic readings, as there is no written record that he ever did one. However, before departing for the trenches, Churchill arranged for a bagpiper to play during dinner with his fellow officers. In honor of his home constituency, he asked the piper to play *Bonnie Dundee*, but he privately complained to Clementine that the tunes were "doleful dirges."[149] It is clear that Churchill wanted to be a dynamic leader and was willing to think creatively to find ways to inspire his men.

In addition to his request for a copy of Burns's poems, Churchill also asked Clementine for a more practical item—a lieutenant colonel's uniform. For a man who had recently ordered the uniform of a brigadier general, this was indeed a blow to the ego, but Churchill knew the value of uniforms and symbols of rank. His promotion to the temporary rank was dated effective January 5, 1916, the day he was to officially take command of the battalion, and would ultimately be the highest rank he ever attained.[150]

The uniform of the Royal Scots Fusiliers was in most ways identical to the khaki service dress that Churchill had been wearing with the Grenadier Guards. All he needed to add was the insignia of his new rank, a four-pointed star called a pip, which was worn on the sleeve of the service tunic. What set the Scottish Fusiliers off from their English brothers in arms was the distinctive Glengarry cap. This hat was black and similar in shape to the standard-issue service cap, but it distinguished itself with a red-and-white checkered pattern around the bottom edge and two long ribbons flowing from the back. In addition, each of the Scottish units took pride in affixing their own unit insignia to the left front of the cap and to the lapels of their field uniforms.

Despite his desire to fit into his new unit, Churchill never fully embraced this distinctive headgear in which his troops took so much pride.[151] While in the field, he preferred to wear his French helmet because it made him easily recognizable while offering better protection for his head than wool and ribbon.[152] Churchill did affix the unit insignia to his tunic and would, on occasion, wear his Glengarry cap to boost morale and show solidarity in official photos.[153]

Now that he knew which battalion he was to command, Churchill set about finalizing his staff. Because the battalion had suffered disproportionate losses in the officer ranks and because Haig felt he owed Churchill the courtesy of selecting his deputy, he would have unusual latitude in selecting a second-in-command.[154] Anticipating a brigade command, he had initially requested that both Edward Spears and Archibald Sinclair serve under him. However, since he was only commanding a battalion, he could not get both. Spears was currently serving in a critical position as a liaison officer to the French, while Sinclair was bored and underutilized in a staff position. Sensing that Spears would be difficult to pry loose, Churchill picked Sinclair.[155]

Spears understood why Churchill could not have him as his deputy and bore him no ill will for his decision. He continued to serve as a liaison officer and would enjoy a long and successful military and political career, in which he became an MP, became a major general, and wrote several books about his adventures. He and Churchill remained close friends for the reminder of their lives. During the interwar period, Churchill wrote the foreword to Spears's World War I memoirs, *Liaison 1914* (1930) and *Prelude to Victory* (1939).[156] After Churchill became prime minister, Spears was appointed as his personal envoy to the French government.[157] Spears had a remarkable inside view of the war, first witnessing the crumbling of the French government in June 1940 and afterward serving as an envoy to Charles de Gaulle and the Free French.[158] Although they sometimes disagreed on matters of policy, Spears and Churchill trusted each other intimately and relied on each other's unique combination of military and political knowledge.[159]

For now, Churchill had only Sinclair, but this was an inspired choice. The two had formed a close friendship in the years before the war, and Sinclair viewed Churchill as a personal and political mentor. They respected each other's character and looked forward to an adventure together. The idea that fighting in the trenches would be something akin to a schoolboy's adventure may strike modern readers as anachronistic, even vulgar; however, this is a true reflection of the broader attitudes of upper-class Britons and of both men's views of the war and their friendship. Throughout his life, Churchill chose his friends for their character and their willingness to seek out adventure, and Sinclair fit both criteria perfectly.[160]

Churchill knew that Sinclair wanted to see active service and had been frustrated by a series of staff jobs that were safe but far removed from any action. Indeed, almost a year before, on February 17, 1915, Sinclair had written to complain, "I am an utter fraud. I've never been near the trenches or even left the peaceful inglorious seclusion of the one-housed village. . . . To be kept away from London to go to live in a ditch for ten days was bad enough but to be left behind in this backwater of desolation was the limit."[161] Now Churchill was offering his friend the opportunity to escape the boredom of his present circumstances and to serve as his assistant. While this position would require a large amount of paperwork, it was much closer to the front, and Sinclair found it impossible to resist his friend's magnetic charm. In the weeks that followed, this friendship and enthusiasm would be subjected to the hardest of tests, the audit of battle, but it would emerge even stronger than before.

Preparing the Battalion for Battle

Now that he had chosen his deputy, Churchill needed to prepare his new battalion for combat. This would be an extremely difficult task on multiple levels. Except for Sinclair, the officers of the 6th Battalion were unknown to Churchill, and by any account, they were shockingly young and inexperienced. In fact, the forty-one-year-old Churchill frequently referred to them as "quite young boys" and estimated that their average age was twenty-three.[162] Perhaps more worrying than their age was their lack of training and service time. Among the officers, only Lieutenant Edmund Hakewill-Smith was a professional soldier, and he was a young and relatively inexperienced subaltern, having just received his commission in June 1915. As was common in the British Army during this period, most of the remaining officers had been civilians just a few months before. They had been rushed through training and were now doing their best to replace more experienced officers who had been lost in the bloody battles around Loos.

Despite this lack of experience, a cadre of brave and dedicated officers were waiting for Churchill. In the coming weeks, they would prove their worth and win the undying admiration of their commanding officer.[163] Hakewill-Smith, for example, was mature and experienced far beyond his years. Like Churchill, he had attended Sandhurst and had been commissioned a second lieutenant in 1915. The lessons he learned there were still fresh and were supplemented by his experiences at Loos. Churchill would lean heavily on Hakewill-Smith in the coming weeks, particularly on his ability as an instructor. This role as a trainer would quickly earn Hakewill-Smith the admiring moniker of "Bomb Boy," as one of the first tasks Churchill would assign him was to familiarize the replacement troops with the proper use of hand grenades. "Bomb Boy" would excel at this role and many others, earning Churchill's trust as a reliable and professional member of the unit. Hakewill-Smith would be wounded twice, win multiple decorations for bravery, and rise to the rank of major general in World War II, an impressive set of achievements indeed.[164]

While not a professional soldier by vocation or inclination, Captain Andrew Dewar Gibb was a similarly impressive officer whom Churchill would quickly learn to depend on in the coming weeks. A barrister in his civilian life, Gibb had passed the Scottish bar in 1914, only to have his legal career interrupted before it started by the outbreak of war. He volunteered to join the army, and despite his sometimes sour and bookish disposition, he became a reliable and well-regarded officer. When Churchill assumed command, Gibb was in command of B Company but would soon be named the battalion adjutant.[165] Gibb was not a flamboyant leader and often kept his own council, yet this quiet nature belied an active mind and a dedication to his men. After the war, Gibb flourished in a broad array of vocations, working as a lawyer, a university professor, an author of multiple books, an MP, and the leader of the Scottish Nationalist Party.

All told, a solid group of men who were representative of the British Army during the period awaited Churchill. The ranks were understrength and had been filled with untrained replacements, but there was a core of capable officers and veterans to build around. In the coming days, Churchill would struggle with one of the most difficult tasks he ever attempted: winning the trust and respect of these men, forging them into a cohesive unit, and leading them into battle.

Admiral John "Jackie" Fisher was a legendary figure in the British Admiralty. His relationship with Churchill was tumultuous in the extreme. (Library of Congress, George Grantham Bain Collection.)

The most famous living soldier in the British Army at that time, Kitchener had clashed repeatedly with Churchill during their careers. Yet despite their differences, he was the only high-ranking official to visit Churchill after his resignation from the Admiralty, and his kind words helped sustain Churchill during the difficult months ahead. (Library of Congress, George Grantham Bain Collection.)

Violet Asquith (later Mrs. Bonham Carter) was one of Churchill's closest friends and confidants during this difficult period. She had an impressive intellect and wit, was a social butterfly, and, as the daughter of Prime Minister H. H. Asquith, had access to the inner workings of the British government. (Library of Congress, George Grantham Bain Collection.)

The predreadnought battleship HMS *Irresistible* sinking at the Dardanelles, March 18, 1915. While Churchill considered the loss of obsolete ships such as this acceptable, their destruction was a shock to the British Admiralty and public. After the loss of the *Bouvet*, *Ocean*, and *Irresistible* on March 18, plans quickly shifted to an amphibious assault on the Gallipoli Peninsula. (Library of Congress, George Grantham Bain Collection.)

CHURCHILL S'EN VA-T-EN GUERRE.

WINSTON (*through force of nautical habit, to Sir JOHN FRENCH*). "COME ABOARD, SIR!"

This satirical image of Churchill at General French's headquarters depicts the commonly held view that the former First Lord of the Admiralty was a political insider who was not entirely serious about his role as a soldier. (Punch Cartoon Library / TopFoto.)

Churchill visited the front with his friend Captain Edward Spears (*third from the left*) on December 29, 1915. During his visit, he received the latest updates on the conditions at the front and stopped to take this photo with a group of French generals. Note that Churchill had already adopted the French poilu-style helmet. (© IWM Q 49305.)

Churchill painted this bleak scene of Plugstreet under German artillery fire during one of his short periods of rest. (Painting C4 *Plugstreet under Shell Fire* by Winston S. Churchill, 1916 © Churchill Heritage. Reproduced with permission of Curtis Brown, London on behalf of Churchill Heritage Ltd © Churchill Heritage Ltd.; image courtesy of Marina Brounger.)

This contemporary photo of Plugstreet shows the grim aftermath of the German artillery bombardment. (Australian War Memorial, Reference Number E01516.)

Second view of Plugstreet. (Australian War Memorial, Reference Number P01835.066.)

This unfinished portrait of Archibald Sinclair, painted by Churchill during their time at the front, reveals their close friendship and Churchill's artistic talent. (Painting C16 *Unfinished Portrait of Archibald Sinclair* by Winston S. Churchill, 1916 © Churchill Heritage. Reproduced with permission of Curtis Brown, London on behalf of Churchill Heritage Ltd © Churchill Heritage Ltd.; image courtesy of Marina Brounger.)

Before leaving his unit, Churchill stopped to take the following photo. He is seated in the center wearing the Scottish-style bonnet. Archibald Sinclair is wearing a British Army officer's cap and is seated on Churchill's right. Andrew Gibb is seated immediately on Churchill's left, and Edmund "Bomb Boy" Hakewill-Smith is second from the left in the front row, looking away from the camera. (Wikimedia / Samleighton87, CC BY-SA 4.0, https://creativecommons.org/licenses/by-sa/4.0/legalcode.)

4

The Passionate Warrior
Churchill Takes Command

When Churchill assumed command of the 6th Battalion of Royal Scots Fusiliers on January 5, 1916, he was stepping into a challenging situation that would test his leadership to the fullest. The unit was in a depleted state from its losses at the Battle of Loos, he was replacing a popular commanding officer, and his status as a controversial politician was seen as an unwelcome distraction.[1] Andrew Gibb, one of the few surviving officers from the Battle of Loos, described the unit's mood as "mutinous" and wished that Churchill would go to the Argyles if his heart was set on wearing a kilt and commanding a Scottish battalion.[2] The unit was in need of rest and refitting, and the thought of a new, high-profile commanding officer was especially dispiriting to the veterans. Despite his enthusiasm, almost nothing went right for Churchill that day.

Hoping to inspire his new command, Churchill prepared a dramatic scene and cast himself at the center. He ordered the men to assemble in an open field that had a small hill on the edge. Once the troops were ready, Churchill and Archibald Sinclair rode over the crest of the hill and appeared seemingly from nowhere. To top off the scene, both men were riding black horses, in an almost apocalyptic manner.[3] Although this was an impressive way to introduce himself to his troops, it was not wise. Churchill's reputation as a dangerous schemer, political showman, meddler, and dilettante preceded him, and such a dramatic entrance had the effect of exacerbating these prejudices. As one officer, F. G. Scott, described the scene: "Just before noon an imposing cavalcade arrived. Churchill on a black charger, Archie Sinclair on a black charger, two grooms on black chargers followed by a limber filled with Churchill's luggage—much more than the 35 pounds allowed weight. In the rear we saw a curious contraption: a long bath and boiler for heating bath water."[4] For a man who was concerned about his image and making a strong first impression, Churchill could have hardly done worse than this histrionic display.

After his overly dramatic entrance, Churchill continued to make things worse over the next few hours. To instill discipline and loyalty among his officers, he met with them at lunch and told them, "Gentlemen, I am now your Commanding Officer. Those who support me I will look after. Those who go against me I will break."[5] According to Lieutenant Hakewill-Smith, this had the unintended effect of harming the officers' morale: "It was quite the most uncomfortable lunch I had ever been at. . . . Everyone was agreed that we were in for a pretty rotten time."[6]

In addition to these ill-chosen words that opened him up to charges of favoritism, Churchill had repeated the mistake he made on joining the Grenadier Guards a few weeks before and yet again brought too much equipment and luggage.[7] This exacerbated the beliefs that Churchill was not serious about his military service, was oblivious to the realities of life at the front, and was an effete poser. Of particular interest was a strange metal item, the purpose of which was a mystery to the men. It turned out to be a bathtub, which Churchill brought so that he could relax and clean himself while at the front.[8] While this particular item was initially the cause of much scorn and disbelief, it would quickly become a source of much enjoyment and relief as Churchill allowed his fellow officers to use his tub and clean themselves while remaining near their positions.[9] For the time being, however, the bathtub seemed to prove that the battalion's new commanding officer was not to be trusted.

An afternoon inspection and parade went even worse. While Churchill hoped that an inspection followed by close-order drill would reinforce unit cohesiveness and pride, he again appeared like a dilettante in front of his men. As a cavalryman, Churchill had not used infantry commands since his days as a cadet at Sandhurst, a deficiency that quickly became glaringly obvious. Despite his authority as commanding officer and his zeal for command, he simply could not remember the correct words. According to Hakewill-Smith:

> The after lunch parade was a farce. The men were at the slope when Churchill appeared on his charger. Captain Gibb reported that all

were present. While the troops were still at the slope, Churchill called out: "Royal Scots Fusiliers! Fix Bayonets!" The command could not possibly be carried out from the slope position. A couple of chaps put their rifles on the ground and pulled out their bayonets; the rest were merely mystified. Eventually, Gibb persuaded Churchill to call "Order Arms" and to fix their bayonets in the normal way.

Winston then inspected the men. Having done so, he gave a cavalry order: "Sections Right!" This meant nothing to the Jocks, who had the sense to stand still and do nothing.[10]

The assembled men did their best to interpret these orders and muddle through, but Churchill had made yet another misstep in front of his already-skeptical unit.[11] First impressions are powerful things, soldiers are suspicious creatures, and Churchill's time was running out.

Winning the War on Lice

Churchill understood that he had failed, and he quickly changed tactics. Now, rather than being a melodramatic petty tyrant with too much kit, he decided to play the role of a humble and concerned officer. In his second meeting with his officers, he addressed the issue of sanitation. While this was not a glamorous topic, it was something that Churchill took seriously. As a student of history, he had read about the impact of disease on British troops in Crimea and elsewhere, and as a young subaltern, he had witnessed firsthand the debilitating impact of tropical diseases in Cuba, India, Sudan, and South Africa. This was his opening to not only improve the welfare and fighting abilities of his men but also demonstrate that he was, in fact, a caring and enlightened commanding officer.

Churchill focused his energy on lice, a tiny insect that was a big problem for men in the trenches.[12] Viewed skeptically by some, this was a good-faith effort to improve the unit's morale, hygiene, health, and fighting abilities.[13] Lice were not only irritating spreaders of pestilence but also the mark of a unit that did not take hygiene seriously. If a unit could not care for its own basic needs, Churchill reasoned, they clearly could not be expected to accomplish more complex and dangerous tasks such as engaging the enemy.

With an eye toward inspiring his officers to take the issue of lice more seriously, Churchill gave a speech that made a powerful impression on the skeptical Gibb: "War is declared, gentlemen. On the lice. With these words, did the great scion of Marlborough first address his Scottish Captains assembled in council. And with these words was inaugurated such a discourse on *pulex Europaeus* [*sic*], its origin, growth, and nature, its habitat and its importance as a factor in wars ancient and modern, as left one agape with wonder at the erudition and force of its author."[14]

In this, his second meeting with his officers, Churchill had set the tone for his new command by focusing on something seemingly small—personal hygiene. By forgoing the opportunity to talk about himself, indulge in his famous oratory, or make another dramatic entrance, he demonstrated that he could be a servant leader. This was a particularly important message to send to his new battalion as morale was low and many of the officers and senior enlisted were dead or missing.[15]

While it would take weeks to properly train the men and replace their equipment, the war on lice could begin immediately. There was an abandoned brewery near the Fusiliers' position, and in an ingenious bit of fieldcraft, the men converted some of the vats into boilers to sanitize clothing. Much like the sock-exchange service that Churchill had witnessed with the Grenadier Guards, these makeshift boilers were put into near-constant use keeping the men's clothing and bedding sanitized and lice-free.[16] Churchill also ensured that the battalion doctor coordinated with the officers on the best way of maintaining sanitary conditions in the field, and "after three or four days spent in toil as unsavory as any I [Gibb] have ever devoted myself to . . . we were certainly a liceless battalion."[17] This seemingly small victory had a definite effect on the unit. The now lice-free battalion's health and morale quickly improved, and it was able to focus its attention on more complex tasks.

Winning the Officers

Over the next three weeks, Churchill was a whirlwind of energy and ideas. He seemed to be everywhere, inspecting the unit's preparation for its move to the front, encouraging singing, organizing football teams, learning men's names, adopting Scottish slang, and making personal connections with nearly every man in the unit.[18] As Violet Bonham Carter described this period, "He flung himself into the task with the zest and concentration with which he invested the smallest as well as the greatest things in life. Nothing that he touched was ever done by halves."¹⁹ Captain Gibb, who had been skeptical of Churchill, described the impact of these efforts:

> From day to day the C.O. introduced particular little innovations which he liked and by the end of ten days he had produced a manifest smartening up on every side . . . it is only just to admit he improved us greatly. Meantime he improved on us. All the company commanders were invited to dine in the H. Q. mess and there they learnt a little of the charm and courtesy of the man as distinct from the Colonel. No doubt he sought to win us, but for that he is only to be admired, and his capacity for coaxing and charming the best out of even the most boorish is a gift which I never ceased to wonder at. He materially altered the feelings of the officers towards him by this kindness . . . the wonderful genius of the man. And so he began a conquest achieved in two or three short months and over men of a race not easily moved or won over.²⁰

In fact, despite his negative first impression, Churchill had won over the officers and become a commanding officer who was trusted and loved rather than feared and despised. Churchill helped his own cause by being particularly generous with alcohol and his trademark cigars. Even at this stage of his career, he was identified with a fondness for drink and cigars, and since alcohol and tobacco were perpetually in short supply at the front, these items were particularly prized. Indeed, as Gibb described the mess, "Nobody who was entertained there ever forgot it . . . and if he left without a large cigar lighting up his mollified countenance that was because he was a non-smoker and through no fault of Colonel Churchill."²¹

As the officers became more comfortable around their famous commander, they eventually began to discuss politics. Over the coming months, Churchill would frequently talk about the Dardanelles and other political scandals of the day. While skeptical of the wisdom of the Dardanelles, many were eventually converted to Churchill's belief that it was a brilliant campaign that could have shortened the war and saved them from their present uncomfortable surroundings. In these stories, Churchill frequently mentioned his former First Sea Lord, Jackie Fisher. Churchill's glowing descriptions of the admiral's brilliance and warmth made it clear that despite the strain placed on their friendship by Fisher's resignation and erratic behavior, Churchill still loved him dearly. Churchill was significantly less charitable about Kitchener, and it was clear that he was still very bitter about Asquith's betrayal.[22] While some of the men may have had political differences with their commanding officer, they all seemed to genuinely enjoy his vivid storytelling and no longer resented the fact that they had a celebrity within their ranks.

Winning the Men

After winning buy-in from his officers, Churchill quickly focused his attention on the rank and file of the battalion. To ensure that his men were ready for their upcoming move to the front, he focused his energies on training the inexperienced members of the unit in the rudiments of modern warfare and fieldcraft. He was particularly fervent about trenches and improvised defenses as he understood that they were difficult to properly construct and maintain, and they could easily mean the difference between life and death.

According to Gibb, "To see Winston giving a dissertation on the laying of sandbags, with practical illustrations, was to come inevitably to the conclusion that his life study had been purely of poliorketics and the corresponding countermeasures. You felt sure from his grasp of the practice that he must have served apprentice to a bricklayer and a master mason, while his theoretical knowledge rendered you certain that [Christopher] Wren would have been proud to sit at his feet."[23]

Churchill personally supervised many of these training evolutions, but he relied on Lieutenant Hakewill-Smith to provide the majority of the hands-on instruction. Despite his tender age, Hakewill-Smith was a combat veteran and had attended Sandhurst within the past year. He was, therefore, familiar with the realities of trench warfare as well as the official methods of instruction. This allowed him to combine experiences from both the field and the classroom to provide the best of both the practical and the theoretical.

One of the tasks that Hakewill-Smith focused on was instruction in the proper throwing of hand grenades. Small grenades had proved very useful in trench warfare, yet many of the new replacements were ignorant of their use.[24] Hakewill-Smith created a practice grenade range and a training curriculum and took it upon himself to ensure that the entire unit was proficient in the use of grenades. This zeal and initiative quickly earned Churchill's respect, as well as his loving nickname, Bomb Boy.[25] Unable to contain his boyish enthusiasm for weapons, Churchill even took part in the grenade training and described it in a letter to Clementine:

> In the morning Archie & I practiced bomb-throwing. It is a job to be approached gingerly. You pull out the safety pin, & . . . then 5 seconds afterwards there is [a] real good bang & splinters fly all over the place. . . . As soon as you have thrown it, you bob down behind the parapet until the explosion has occurred. Sometimes the men are stupid—drop the bomb in the trench or close to it—then the bombing officer [Hakewill-Smith]—a young Sandhurst kid—deftly picks it up and throws it away with perhaps 2 seconds to spare. . . . It is perfectly safe so long as you do it right.[26]

Churchill also wanted to learn from fellow officers about their experiences as commanding soldiers at the front. In early January, he traveled to Hazebrouck, France, to attend a lecture about the recent Battle of Loos. The fact that the Scottish Division, of which his battalion was a part, had suffered 60 percent casualties in the recent battle had left a strong impression on Churchill, and he hoped that he would learn something valuable.[27] The lecture was given by Colonel Arthur Holland, an officer who outranked Churchill and was a respected authority on military operations. Despite Holland's rank and credentials, Churchill believed that the lecture was a wasted opportunity to reassess British tactics and strategy. He was upset that this failure had not inspired more critical analysis, and as he described in a letter to Clementine, "Afterwards they asked what was the lesson of the lecture. I restrained an impulse to reply 'Don't do it again.' But they will—I have no doubt."[28]

On January 13, Churchill learned that the British had finally completed their evacuation from Gallipoli. The withdrawal had been an unprecedented success as the Ottomans did little to oppose it and the Allies suffered extremely light casualties.[29] Churchill was glad that his brother, Jack, was safe and that the apocalyptic predictions of the Allied planners had not come true, but he also realized, as he would quip after Dunkirk, that "wars are not won by evacuations."[30] On a more personal level, Churchill was sad but defiant, noting, "History will vindicate the conception, & the errors in execution will on the whole leave me clear."[31] Instead of overseeing such great campaigns, Churchill complained about his relatively humble position, where "the days slip away quickly in the transaction of small things."[32]

While Churchill insisted on rigorous training, he also understood the need for leisure, even in wartime. To this end, he organized a football team, which played matches against several of the neighboring units.[33] He took great pride in the team, and the Fusiliers responded by winning every match they played.[34] Churchill's efforts culminated in a field day and concert for the men on January 16. The explicit purpose was to boost the men's morale, and Churchill took great pleasure in describing the games in his letter to Clementine:

> The sports were highly successful & the men were really delighted. They were the most amusing sports—mule races, pillow fights, obstacle races etc. All well organized & supported by g[rea]t keenness & interest. After dark we had our first concert in a big barn. Such singing you never heard. People sang with the greatest courage who had no idea either of words or tune. Jack Seely and other officers came & Jack presented prizes for the sports & called for three cheers for me & an extra one for you, all which were most heartily given. . . . Quite a cheery day. The men enjoyed themselves immensely. Poor fellows—nothing like this had ever been done for them before. They do not get much to brighten their lives—short though they may be.[35]

Churchill's field day clearly improved the morale of his men, but it did not alter the grim fact that the unit would soon be put on the line and tested in battle.

Preparing to Move to the Front

On January 20, Churchill and Sinclair traveled to inspect the sector of the line where the battalion would be inserted in one week. Churchill had long understood the importance of topography in military affairs and wanted to form a mental image of the physical space he would be asked to defend.[36] The position centered on the tiny Belgian village of Ploegsteert. Thanks to the marshy terrain, which made mass movements difficult, this was a relatively quiet sector of the front, and no major action was anticipated.[37] Despite the tranquil setting, the two men were careful to inspect the forward positions and were happy to find them in a satisfactory condition. Churchill remarked that the trenches were relatively dry and would drain well in the event of rain, were lined with duckboards, had parapets that were sufficiently thick to stop bullets, had adequate communication trenches and dugouts, and were protected by a satisfactory amount of barbed wire. He also inspected the battalion headquarters, which was in an old brick farmhouse known as Laurence Farm, located some five hundred yards behind the trench lines. Here, the small mess and working spaces for the staff were Spartan but clean and orderly. In addition to the main battalion headquarters, there was an additional reserve position some three-quarters of a mile behind the front line. This would provide some additional safety from small-arms fire, but it was still well within range of German field artillery and offered little protection from plunging shellfire. While Churchill would work to maintain and improve these positions for the entire time he was stationed there, he was pleased with what he saw on his first visit to Ploegsteert.[38]

Despite this brief diversion, training continued at a frenzied pace. Churchill worked incredibly long hours in these final days before deploying to the front, doing everything in his power to prepare his men for the trial that lay ahead. On January 24, the battalion moved closer to the front, to the village of La Crèche.[39] Rather than let the troops become anxious in this holding area, Churchill did his best to keep the mood light and encourage them. While he believed that he had done all he could to prepare his men for battle, the wait was difficult. On January 26, the battalion moved into reserve positions and awaited orders to move into the trenches.

Sensing that this was his final time to speak with his officers before they entered battle, Churchill addressed them in a wise and almost fatherly manner, which he later compared to that of Polonius in Shakespeare's *Hamlet*: "Don't be careless about yourselves—on the other hand not too careful. Keep a special pair of boots to sleep in and only get them muddy in a real emergency. Use alcohol in moderation but don't have a great parade of bottles in y[ou]r dugouts. Live well but do not flaunt it. Laugh a little, & teach your men to laugh—g[e]t good humor under fire—war is a game that is played with a smile. If you can't smile grin. If you can't grin keep out of the way till you can."[40]

This excellent speech effectively summed up Churchill's new approach to war:[41] take care of your men and yourselves, take courage, and keep a positive disposition even when things are difficult.[42] While this was not as pithy as "keep buggering on," "action this day," "we shall never surrender," or many of his later and more famous quotes, it was inspirational and effective, nonetheless. In fact, during his time in the trenches, Churchill truly waged war with a smile that, even in difficult times, made others believe that things would be better.[43]

A Fascination with Airpower

Despite his bravado, Churchill became increasingly concerned about the German domination of the skies above his Fusiliers' positions. Starting in January, he had noticed that the Germans commanded the air and that Allied fliers were almost never seen. Churchill feared that this deficiency was having a detrimental effect on his troops' morale, and he became increasingly agitated about the seeming lack of urgency in regaining the aerial high ground. On January 23 (just days before he led his men to the front lines for the first time), he complained to Clementine about the inefficiency of the Naval Air Service. Churchill believed that he should have been allowed to serve as air minister, and that if he had been in this position, the skies would be swept free of German aircraft. He regrettably understood that his place was at the front and that "it is better to go on simply here for a while."[44]

Despite this understanding, Churchill continued to lament the German command of the skies and closely followed the debates in Parliament about airpower over the ensuing days. On January 25, he wrote David Lloyd George, the minister of munitions, a pointed letter that was critical on a broad range of defense issues and stated, "Even in the air, where at least the defensive has no advantage, we have lost our ascendancy. How long ago was it you wrote, 'We are slouching to disaster?'"[45] On January 26, he wrote to Clementine about the recent debate about airpower in Parliament and took direct issue with the assertion of the undersecretary of state for war, Harold Tennant, that "nearly every fight in the air takes place on the German side of the trenches."

He scoffed at this claim and provided a personal anecdote: "Tennant's answer in the H of C about German aeroplanes never coming over our lines reads amusingly here. I saw one flaunting himself 20 miles behind the line yesterday; & 4 of them threw bombs within 50 yards of the party of men I sent on to prepare these billets for our reception. The flying officers tell me a sad tale of their difficulties, & the utter want of knowledge & drive that characterizes present War Office administration."[46]

Even after his unit moved into their positions at the front, Churchill continued to obsess over airpower. His letters during this period are filled with complaints and observations about zeppelin raids and the powerful effect that airplanes had on him and the troops below. On February 13, he wrote to Clementine, "This afternoon many aeroplanes overhead, & much shooting at them. I was disgusted to watch 1 German aeroplane sailing above scornfully in the midst of 14 British—none of wh[ich] c[oul]d or worse still perhaps—*w[oul]d* bring him to action. Ours seemed to sheer off time after time, & he went where he pleased for at least an hour & a half. As for our guns they fired hundreds of shells without lifting a feather of this hostile bird."[47]

While Churchill had been an early advocate for airpower, these experiences only strengthened his determination to win control of the sky. For the remainder of his life, Churchill would be a proponent of airpower. Indeed, when he became minister of munitions in 1917, he dedicated increased resources toward building new and more powerful flying machines. Similarly, during the Wilderness Years, he repeatedly warned of the growth of German airpower and demanded more funding for British air forces. Finally, when he became prime minister in May 1940, he was immediately thrust into massive air battles in France and then Britain, and he made command of the sky a top priority. But for now, all Churchill could do was to try to focus on defending a sector of ground in an obscure part of Flanders and hopefully win the glory and redemption he craved.

In the Lines at Last

Late in the evening of January 26, the battalion began, at last, to march toward the front. They arrived before daybreak and were in position to hold a portion of the front approximately one thousand yards across.[48] The Scots relieved the 8th Border Regiment, and few recognized Churchill in the darkness as he kept the French helmet pulled low over his face and concentrated his efforts on getting his men in place. According to Gibb, this did provide a moment of levity: "My guide said to me: 'Excuse me, Sir, but your commanding officer is very like Mr. Winston Churchill.' I agreed and said that the resemblance had often been remarked."[49]

While this was an insignificant occurrence in the broader context of World War I, it was an exciting moment for Churchill. Decades before, as a child commanding nothing more than toy soldiers on his nursery room floor, he had dreamed of the moment when he would command a large unit in battle.[50] Now he was about to live out these childhood visions of glory, and as an increasingly confident Gibb noted, "Winston was in his element."[51] He shared his feeling with Clementine: "Rest assured that there will be no part of the line from the Alps to the sea better guarded. It will be watched with the vigilance that mobalised [sic] the fleet."[52]

On the first night in the lines, Churchill was perhaps too energetic, and he passed a message to his officers at 4:00 a.m. stating that the wind conditions were ideal for a German gas attack. This message was ignored by Gibb and the other officers, who did not appreciate being woken up by an excitable commanding officer whom they suspected was "daft." The next day, Churchill passed a similarly questionable warning to his officers, noting that the kaiser's birthday was approaching and that an attack or increased artillery fire might mark the occasion.[53] These attacks never materialized, and Churchill quickly ceased issuing such warnings to his men.

A mere eighty yards from the Germans, life at the front quickly developed its own routine. The unit spent six days in the trenches followed by six days in a reserve capacity. While it would have been easy to slip into complacency and neglect his duties, Churchill was an active leader for the entirety of his time at the front. On January 27, he wrote about his awesome sense of responsibility: "One has to keep on thinking—so many directly dependent on one being right; & the German army heavy on our front. You know a Colonel's day in the line is almost the greatest demand on a man's qualities—v[er]y like being the captain of a v[er]y big ship in submarine infested waters."[54]

In addition to his powerful sense of duty and desire to prove his doubters wrong, Churchill was driven by his sense of justice. As he would do so often in his famous speeches during World War II, Churchill cast the war as a moral contest between good and evil. He called the eighty-yard strip of no-man's-land between the two armies "the frontier between right and wrong."[55] Although he was aware of the horrors of war and the moral dilemmas of killing, Churchill was proud to be fighting for the cause of liberty. This sense of purpose seemed to sustain him through the difficult days and provide him with an almost missionary drive.

Churchill's Active Leadership

As a battalion commander, Churchill was an exceptionally active leader. While he was considered something of a nuisance, he took personal ownership and responsibility for the success and well-being of his men. He seemed to always be visiting some part of the front lines, supervising the officers and men, and giving them encouragement as they faced the hardships of modern war.[56] In the words of Gibb: "From the very day of our arrival in the line, it was apparent to all that Winston's motto was going to be 'work,' in the sense of trench building and trench repairing and improvements."[57]

Since his days at Sandhurst, Churchill had taken a particular interest in fortifications, and now he was eager to put his knowledge to use and hopefully save the lives of his men.[58] If an attack was not expected, Churchill would typically wait until after dark to repair damaged trenches so as not to alert the Germans to their efforts or unnecessarily expose his men.[59] Despite the fact that it deprived men of sleep, this clever fieldcraft won Churchill the respect of his troops. Gibb described Churchill's routine:

> Early and late he was in the line. On average he went round three times a day, which was no mean task in itself, as he had plenty of other work to do. At least one of these visits was after dark, usually about 1 a.m. . . . He was always in the closest touch with every piece of work that was going on, and, while at times his demands were a little extravagant, his kindness and the humour that never failed to flash out made everybody only too keen to get on with the work, whether the ideal he pointed out to them was an unattainable one or not.[60]

These extraordinary efforts were quickly noticed by the officers and men. Jock McDavid recalled the impact of Churchill's presence on the unit, noting, "It was sheer personality. . . . He had a unique approach which did wonders to us. He let everyone under his command see that he was responsible, from the very moment he arrived, that they understood not only what they were supposed to do, but why they had to do it."[61]

As part of his approach to war, Churchill also made extraordinary efforts to bond with his men. Unlike most officers during this period, Churchill interacted with his enlisted men. He learned their names, did his best to remember personal details, and soon adopted the slang and jokes of the Scottish working class. Churchill's immersion in Scottish culture became so thorough that he had to remind himself not to drop into too deep a Scottish accent as it would be seen as patronizing.[62] This behavior was dangerously close to crossing the line of fraternization, but Churchill erred on the side of kindness and approachability. As a member of both the officer and upper classes, Churchill retained many of his paternalistic prejudices, but he adored his men. This was by far the most time he ever spent with the working classes, and he truly enjoyed the lack of pomp and pretense that army life provided.[63]

Churchill went to great lengths to demonstrate to his men that he cared about them, and he became known as rather soft on discipline. For example, sleeping on guard duty was an offense that was severely punished in all armies of the period. In the British Army, it was punishable by death during time of war, and although capital punishments were rare, terms of penal servitude lasting up to ten years were common.[64] Instead of resorting to such draconian measures, Churchill adopted a more pragmatic approach. He preferred a mixture of shame, empathy, intimidation, and humor with little actual punishment. He believed that his psychological method was more appropriate for his men, who were predominantly citizen soldiers. They had only been in the army for a few months, lacked the discipline and toughness of veterans, and would respond better to kindness than harsh discipline.

For the veterans in the unit, Churchill was also willing to be surprisingly lenient. Because the unit had suffered devastating losses at Loos a few months before, he made it a policy to forgive most infractions for men who had survived that bloody battle. Word of this policy quickly spread through the ranks, and soon nearly every man in the unit had become a veteran of Loos.[65] Churchill eventually realized that he was being manipulated but chose to neither reverse his policy nor verify whether men had been with the unit during the battle. Ever the politician, Churchill chose to flatter and reward rather than to apply draconian military punishments.

While the average enlisted man appreciated Churchill's pragmatism and approachability, some of his fellow officers believed that he was too lenient.[66] The class prejudices and social stratification of the Victorian-era professional army were alive and well, and Gibb and other officers feared that Churchill's kindness would result in a lack of discipline and a breakdown of authority within the ranks. They feared that men would refuse to follow orders and "indulge themselves in the luxury of telling their sergeants to go to hell!"[67]

Word of Churchill's unconventional methods eventually spread outside the unit and resulted in a written reprimand from his brigade commander in mid-March. The brigade commander cited Churchill's "undue leniency" in enforcing discipline and punishing delinquent soldiers.[68] Churchill acknowledged this admonishment but appears to have done little to alter his approach, and the brigade commander made no further inquiries. While Churchill believed that his methods were necessary to restore flagging morale, the battalion's cohesiveness and discipline were never truly tested in a major battle. However, for the next few months, the battalion rank and file appreciated the willingness of their nonconformist commanding officer to flaunt the regulations and allow them a comparatively easy time.[69]

In the Lines at "Plugstreet"

Churchill and his men held a relatively unimportant and quiet sector of the front near the Belgian village of Ploegsteert. Perhaps inevitably, the town was given the nickname Plugstreet by the men, who found their new name significantly easier to pronounce.[70] Churchill described this humble location with his typically vivid language: "'Plugstreet' Village consisted in the main of a long row of well-built brick houses, some of them four storeys high, looking blankly towards the enemy across flat, soppy fields . . . except for its church, it had been very little injured by artillery fire. Many of the houses had holes in them, but all were perfectly weatherproof and comfortable, and in most windows the glass was not broken."[71]

Sadly, the village soon suffered almost complete destruction. The commander of the Scottish Division was "most energetic" in his use of artillery, and "the Germans replied to [their] bombardments by continual retaliation which eventually reduced the countryside to a pockmarked wilderness scarred with shapeless ruins."[72] Despite the bleak landscape, Churchill was glad for his time at the front because it offered him purpose and distraction. He expressed these feelings in a February 13 letter: "I never expected to be so completely involved in the military machine. It almost seems to me as if my life in the g[rea]t world [of London politics] was a dream, & I have been moving slowly forward in the army all these years from subaltern to Colonel."[73]

Because it held a relatively quiet sector of the front, the battalion quickly established a routine where it "moved in and out of the trenches on six-day spells. . . . Our so-called rest billets when out of the line were separated by scarcely a mile and a half of flat country from our front trenches, at this point about three hundred yards from those of the Germans. In this situation, living on a little more than a square mile of ground, we were destined to remain for over three months."[74] While there were no major battles, there was no shortage of risk. As Churchill described it, the front was "comparatively calm

... with only the usual experiences of local bombardments, sniping and trench raids and counterraids."[75]

Despite this cavalier attitude in his writings, Churchill understood that the front was still a dangerous place. Because of the rules of combined probability, even low daily-casualty figures added up to a very high percentage over time. Death or wounds would find nearly everyone who remained in the lines for enough time.[76] Indeed, during the few months in which Churchill commanded the 6th Battalion, it suffered a casualty rate of approximately 20 percent (15 killed and 123 wounded), a rate that was comparable to those of other units in similarly quiet sectors of the front.[77]

This brutal law of averages sapped morale and initiative and made many soldiers fatalistic and superstitious. To combat dread and complacency, Churchill relied on his famous energy and optimism. He made a special effort to be upbeat and sympathetic around the wounded and was often one of the first men on the scene when a man was hit. This presence and care had a powerful effect on the men, and it was remarked that "no commanding officer ever was more attentive to his wounded," and he typically provided "comfort and cheer" to those in peril.[78] As he admonished his officers on the eve of first entering the lines together, Churchill waged war with a smile and a positive attitude. He seemed to always make the best of the situation and tried to make those around him see the best, not the worst. While Churchill always was a romantic adventurer, this was more than simple naivety. This ability to remain upbeat even in times of uncertainty and gloom was Churchill's secret to being an effective wartime leader, both in uniform and out.

The biggest danger to Churchill and his men was artillery fire. Artillery was the greatest battlefield killer of the war, even in a quiet sector of the front.[79] In addition to the German artillery, which was so accurate that Churchill sometimes believed it was specifically targeting him, there was a significant danger of British short rounds.[80] These short rounds were particularly frustrating because of their fratricidal and wasteful nature.[81] Whatever their origin, shells were a near-constant danger accounting for several casualties per day on average.[82]

Churchill had four significant near misses from German shells on February 3, 12, 16, and 19. Each of these could have easily killed or incapacitated him, but he escaped them all shaken but unharmed. In later years, he would provide them as "proof" that he had been saved to fulfill some great destiny. The February 3 incident occurred when he and the members of his staff were concluding their lunch at Laurence Farm. As the officers were about to end their meal and return to work, a German shell crashed through the roof of the building and exploded in the adjoining room. It sent metal fragments through the wall and into the room with the assembled officers, wounding Lieutenant Jock McDavid in the finger and destroying a lantern that Churchill was holding.[83] McDavid later said, "Winston had been toying around with his lamp . . . when the shell came along. A piece of shrapnel almost split the battery holder in two—it lodged in the metal of the battery holder."[84] Had he not been holding the lantern in this exact location, history might have been very different as it embedded in the lamp and missed hitting him by mere inches. Churchill, however, believed that this "lucky escape" confirmed that he was being saved for some greater purpose.[85] Thanks to his exceptional good fortune, it provided little more than excitement, an amusing story, and a curious artifact from his time in the trenches; the lamp can still be viewed at Chartwell as part of the National Trust Collections.[86]

Churchill's next near miss occurred on February 12 when he was observing British artillery positions with a friend from his subaltern days, General Henry H. Tudor, who was now serving as the divisional artillery commander. As the British guns attempted to strafe the German positions, they provoked rapid and accurate counterbattery. Shells from German field artillery and trench mortars landed all around Churchill and Tudor and forced them to huddle against a parapet for protection. Both men escaped unharmed but were covered in dirt from the near misses.[87] Churchill was impressed that the parapets withstood the pounding, and he noted his sense of relief to Clementine: "I found my nerves in excellent order. . . . But after it was over I felt strangely tired; as if I had done a hard day's work at a speech or article."[88] Interestingly, Churchill and Tudor would have another near miss from artillery fire in 1918 when he was visiting the front in his capacity as minister of munitions. The two men witnessed the opening phases of the German Spring Offensive, and they were again forced to take shelter as "the shells upon our trenches seemed almost to touch each other, with hardly an interval in space or time . . . the weight and intensity of the bombardment surpassed anything which anyone had ever known before."[89]

After they renewed their bond in the trenches, Tudor's and Churchill's paths would cross multiple times. Tudor remained in the army after the war, and thanks to his political connections, he was promoted to lieutenant general and appointed to lead the British police forces in Ireland. In this capacity, he worked with the secretary of state for the colonies, Churchill, and commanded the controversial paramilitary unit the Royal Irish Constabulary, better known as the "Black and Tans." Tudor was a divisive figure during his tenure, in large part because of the violence perpetrated by the Black and Tans.[90] In 1922, this force was disbanded, and thanks to Churchill's intervention, Tudor was reassigned to command British police forces in Palestine. Again, controversy followed Tudor as he attempted to recruit gendarmes from the recently disbanded Black and Tans and was seen as neglecting his civil duties. Tudor ultimately resigned and retired to Newfoundland, where he survived an assassination plot by the Irish Republican Army and died of natural causes in 1965.[91]

Churchill survived another near miss from artillery fire on February 16. As he and Sinclair were sitting down to breakfast at their headquarters, the building was again rocked by German fire. A shell penetrated the building and landed in the adjacent room, sending fragments into the dining room, where Churchill was eating. While Churchill and Sinclair were uninjured, the signals room where the shell hit was destroyed; the signal officer who was on duty at the time, Lieutenant Laurence Kemp, suffered five wounds, and another man nearby was also struck.[92]

Churchill's fourth near miss, on February 19, provided an opportunity for self-deprecating humor that he would recall countless times over the coming decades. In early February, he had received comments on his paper from December titled "Variants of the Offensive." This memo was originally presented to General French but subsequently passed to his replacement, General Haig. Haig saw the merits in the document and forwarded it to the general staff for comments.[93] As the author, Churchill was given the opportunity to address the concerns of the general staff and make further revisions. Churchill was happy to potentially influence the war, but he was less pleased when the copy for revisions was sent to him in an insecure manner:

> A proof of this vital document was forwarded to me in France, reaching me through the post office while I was actually at my headquarters in the line. The rule against taking secret documents into the front line was strict and as I gazed at the print in my sandbagged, half-demolished farm the feeling that the enemy was scarcely a thousand yards away became strangely accentuated in my mind. However, we were to go into our "rest billets" a mile farther back at daybreak.

> I would then make such revisions in the proof as were necessary, and send it in by an officer for transmission to London though the Army Headquarters at Bailleul.[94]

When Churchill arrived back at his headquarters, he began to "tackle [his] correspondence, which had accumulated during [their] spell in the trenches, and in particular to address [himself] to 'Variants of the Offensive.'"[95] He worked for approximately thirty minutes before being "distracted by two or three shell-bursts about 300 yards away in the field immediately beyond that in front of [their] house. Farther away . . . little white puffs of shrapnel showed an unwonted liveliness."[96] Churchill gazed at the terrible beauty "as if from a box at the theatre." The shells came closer, first two hundred yards away.

> After a minute or so, came another. There is no shell more unpleasant to the experienced ear than the one which comes straight towards you and bursts short. You hear the whine growing to a whistle, ever more intense in note and pregnant with the menace of approach, and it is only when you see a cartload of earth leap into the air in front of you that you are quite sure that no harm is done. This particular shell (a 4.2) burst with a disagreeable bang [on] the other side of the road, about 40 or 50 yards away. It occurred to me that our house . . . might very likely be the enemy's target, and that the next shell might comfortably hit the bull's-eye. At the same time more distant crashes in other parts of the village seemed to show that "Plugstreet" was about to receive special attention at the enemy's hands.[97]

Churchill was defenseless and scrambled out of the room and into a small underground cellar with a brick roof. Here, he joined an elderly lady and her daughter who had refused to be evacuated from the village as well as two typists from the battalion staff. Despite the illusion of protection, Churchill "did not like the cellar. The vaulted roof looked strong but was actually only two bricks thick. The place was so crowded that there was barely room for anyone else, so [he] got up . . . [and] went into the adjoining building, which was used as [their] battalion office."[98] While the office did have large windows facing the Germans, it had "a back room where at any rate two brick walls stood between [Churchill] and the fire . . . a barrier of two walls is a fair defense: the first explodes the shell, the second probably stops the pieces."⁹⁹

As Churchill sat down in the back room to wait out the artillery barrage, he realized that in his haste to find shelter, he had left his letter and papers behind, including the secret draft of "Variants of the Offensive." This breach of operational security was the least of his worries, however:

> "Plugstreet" Village began to endure one of the first of those methodical bombardments which gradually reduced it to ruins. Every minute or two came shells, some bursting on the fronts of houses, some piercing their roofs, others exploding in the courtyards and offices behind. The shriek of the exploding projectiles, their explosions and the crash and rattle of falling brickwork, became almost continuous. My Adjutant [Gibb] soon joined me in our back room, and here we sat and smoked, at first not unpleasantly excited, but gradually becoming silent and sulky. From time to time tremendous explosions close at hand told us that neighbouring buildings were struck. The soot came down the chimney in clouds, and the yard at the back, on which we now looked, was strewn with fragments of brick and masonry. One shell burst on the face of the opposite building before our eyes, making a gaping hole. We continued to sit in our chairs, putting our faith rather doubtfully in our two brick walls. When one has been under shell fire every day for a month, one does not exaggerate these experiences. They were the commonplaces of the life of millions in those strange times. The bombardment lasted about an hour and a half. The intervals between the shells grew longer, and presently all was silent again.¹⁰⁰

Shortly after the barrage finally lifted, Archibald Sinclair appeared "in the highest spirits. He had been making a tour of the men's billets when the enemy began to fire on the village and had remained a serene spectator a few hundred yards away, waiting as he put it, 'until the rain stopped.'"¹⁰¹

Churchill, Sinclair, and Gibb returned to the headquarters to survey the damage and faced a scene of devastation. The room where Churchill had been working before the bombardment was "wrecked and shattered. Daylight streamed through a large hole in the brickwork above the bay-window. The table, the furniture, papers, objects of all kinds, had been hurled into confusion. Everything was covered with thick, fine, red brick dust."[102] As Churchill's cohort surveyed the destruction, the two French women who had sheltered with him in the cellar burst in with frenzied excitement. "'Oh mon Commandant,' said the girl, 'come and look at the cellar where we were; it came into the midst of us.' We followed: the brickwork which formed the roof of the cellar had been shattered, and there on the floor lay a long 30-lb. shell, unexploded." Although one of the signal-room personnel had sustained a minor injury, none were seriously hurt.

Churchill ordered the two women to evacuate their home at once and returned to his office to search for the secret memo he had been working on before the attack. He located everything of importance, except the secret document: "Nothing was missing but that, and nothing mattered but that. It had gone; it had vanished completely."[103]

Understanding the potentially grave security implications if the document fell into enemy hands, Churchill's mind raced: "How and by what agency could it have been spirited away? Certainly not by the shell. If the room had been blasted by an explosion, the explanation would have been complete; but if this document alone among my papers was not found in the litter of the room, it must have been taken by someone . . . who comprehended its immense significance."[104]

Next, his mind jumped to thoughts of espionage or foul play: "The frontier line was but a few hundred yards away. Our Intelligence reports had warned us of the probability of spies among the inhabitants who still remained. Suspicion filled every breast, and every possible precaution was always to be taken. My imagination began to construct half a dozen sinister explanations. . . . Every sort of terrifying possibility crowded in upon my mind, and no remedy of any kind suggested itself."[105]

While Churchill did not report the missing document, he "passed the next three days in helpless anxiety," cursing himself for not returning it when it was improperly sent to him via military post and for letting it out of his possession, even under the stress of an artillery barrage.[106]

The tension was relieved in an anticlimactic manner, which Churchill joked about for years afterward.[107] "On the third day, I happened to put my hand into my right inner breast-pocket, which I hardly ever used. There I found, safe and secure, the paper I had been so feverishly seeking." Apparently, Churchill had acted instinctively and secured the document as he sought shelter from the barrage, but neither in the stress of the moment nor afterward had he remembered this quick thinking. Churchill now gave a "gasp of delight and relief, and the precarious, battered abodes of 'Plugstreet' under rainy skies and bitter winds seemed as safe and comfortable as home."[108]

While Churchill did his best to maintain a brave public face, these four near misses in a little over two weeks caused him to be considerably more fatalistic in his private letters. He wrote to Clementine, "One lives calmly on the brink of the abyss. But I can understand how tired people get of it if it goes on month after month. All the excitement dies away and there is only a dull resentment."[109] Despite the strain of these incidents, Churchill understood that as the ranking officer, he was a symbol of bravery and courage for the entire battalion. Ever the actor, he would choose to play the part of a bold and determined leader. As an actor, Churchill was so successful that he convinced Gibb that "there [was] no such thing as fear in him."[110] This skill would prove just as effective in the dark days of World War II as it did here in the trenches of the first.

Painting at the Front

Despite the danger and exhaustion of battalion command, Churchill still found time to paint. The reason was simple: painting restored him mentally and physically. Especially during trying times such as these, he used painting as a means of personal succor and revival. Indeed, Churchill's ability to find beauty and inspiration amid chaos was remarkable. In the first few weeks of February, he had several close encounters with German shellfire, and his graphic descriptions of the bombardment of Plugstreet clearly attest to the shock and sorrow he felt. However, on February 10 he took great joy in composing a painting of Plugstreet's shattered and destroyed buildings.

Over the next few weeks, Churchill painted frequently when he was not busy with his frontline duties.[111] He painted at least four different views of Plugstreet, each from a different angle and each showing increasing damage to the buildings.[112] Three of these are similar views of Laurence Farm, with minor variations in battle damage, framing, and figures. One of these he gave to the battalion on his departure from the unit. Another, which showed a man who is believed to be Archibald Sinclair sitting in a chair and reading a newspaper in the damaged courtyard of Laurence Farm, he gave as a gift to Sinclair.[113] The painting would soon become a treasured possession for Sinclair, and it has remained in the family to the present day. In addition to this landscape painting, Churchill began a close-up portrait of Sinclair but only finished a roughly painted outline of his facial features and an outline of his torso in pencil. Despite the unfinished nature of this work, it provides a good likeness of Sinclair's rugged and handsome features and reflects significant skill and care on the part of Churchill.[114]

It has been noted that Churchill's style loosened up and became more primitive during this period, likely because he was both hurried and away from the professional influence of his friend Sir John Lavery.[115] This does not mean that Churchill did not take extreme care in his paintings; he was simply developing his own style. At times his thoughts were so consumed by art that he could think of little else. Hakewill-Smith noted this obsession:

> Winston started painting the second or third time he went up to the farm. Each time we were in the line he spent some time on his paintings. Gradually, too, the courtyard became more pitted with shellholes. As his painting came nearer to completion, he became morose, angry, and exceedingly difficult to talk to. After five or six days in this mood, he suddenly appeared cheerful and delighted, like a small boy at school. I asked him what had happened, and he said[,] "I have been worried because I couldn't get the shell-hole right in the painting. However I did it, it looked like a mountain, but yesterday I discovered that if I put a little bit of white in it, it looked like a hole after all."[116]

This ability to focus on something different and all-consuming was critical for Churchill. He described this means of escape and renewal in a February 22 letter to Clementine: "I think it will be a great pleasure & resource to me if I come through all right."[117]

In expectation of leave in early March, Churchill wrote to Clementine insisting that she "must parcel out the days as well as possible," instructing her on the dinners he wanted and the plays he wished to see, and insisting that he be given an entire day to paint at Lavery's studio.[118] Winston also insisted that Clementine have her portrait made by the famous artist. While he was away, Lavery had been very kind to Clementine, and she frequently visited his studio after making the rounds on the London social scene. Like her husband, Clementine valued Lavery's generous and unassuming nature and used these visits for escape and relaxation.[119] Thinking about art provided both Churchill and Clementine much-needed distraction from the stress and loneliness they faced during this period. Churchill looked forward to seeing Clementine's portrait, and when he finally did, he was not disappointed. He treasured the work and would keep it close by when he was working so that he could gaze at it and find a muse whenever he needed. The portrait has remained in the Churchill family and is a permanent fixture of the Chartwell study to this day.[120]

Churchill clearly wanted to paint more, but he understood that he could not neglect his duties and that his battalion needed a commanding officer, not a painter. To this end, he forced himself to paint only when it did not affect his duties. This was a wise choice, as approximately ten miles away, a young Austrian dispatch runner serving in the German Army was also dreaming of being an artist, sketching a deserted church, and pondering a future in politics.[121] His name was Adolf Hitler, and, like Churchill's, his future would forever be changed by his passion for art and his experiences in the trenches.[122]

Leading from the Front

Rather than sit idly by and await the next barrage, Churchill wanted to take the fight to the enemy.[123] To this end, he chose to court danger by leading thirty-six separate patrols into no-man's-land.[124] This was a task not typically expected of a battalion commander, yet Churchill felt as if he needed to show that he was willing to lead by example.[125] In a letter dated February 15, he described the purpose of one raid as "prowling about looking at our wire and visiting our listening posts." This dangerous task was necessary to ensure that the battalion's defenses were in proper condition and that they were not susceptible to a German night attack. He remarked with some understatement that such raids were "always exciting."[126]

Others, including Hakewill-Smith, noticed Churchill's gallantry and were happy to boast about their commanding officer's atypical valor: "He never ducked when a bullet went past with its loud crack. He used to say after watching me duck: 'It's no damn use ducking; the bullet has gone a long way past you by now.'"[127]

Churchill understood that his participation in these night patrols distinguished him from other field-grade officers and won him the respect of his fellow soldiers.

In a moment of self-congratulatory bravado, he noted, "I do not mind noise [of bullets and shells] as some v[er]y brave people do." Yet, after another near miss while on a trench raid, he wrote Clementine and privately admitted to the strain, speculating what it would have been like if he had been killed by this shell rather than spared: "I felt—20 yards more to the left & no more tangles [of wire] to unravel, no more anxieties to face, no more hatreds & injustices to encounter; the joy of all my foes, relief of that old rogue, a good ending to a chequered life, a final gift—unvalued—to an ungrateful country—an impoverishment of the war-making power of Britain wh[ich] no one w[oul]d ever know measure or mourn."[128] While melodramatic, this passage is revealing. Churchill enjoyed the excitement and diversion of frontline service, but he believed that he had been wronged and worried that he may never achieve the fame and prominence he passionately desired.

False Hope

Although Churchill frequently claimed that he thought of nothing other than the duties of being a battalion commander, this was at best a self-serving half-truth. True, Churchill was involved in the minutiae of command and repeatedly showed his dedication to his men; he also did his best to stay informed about the politics and the partisan machinations of the day. He devoured newspapers and reports of speeches, acquired gossip from Clementine and his friends, and even received visits from several high-ranking political figures while serving on the front lines. This, of course, did not substitute for physically being in Parliament and the clubs of London, but Churchill nevertheless eagerly plotted his return to power. As a distraction from the dull realities of the trenches, he dreamed of leading the opposition against Asquith and toppling his old mentor. While the prime minister had many political enemies and his political situation was tenuous, this daydream was clearly driven by Churchill's hurt feelings and escapism, not by political realities. Just how misguided Churchill was would be revealed in early March.[129]

On March 2, Churchill left the battalion in the temporary command of Sinclair and returned to London to attend secret sessions of Parliament on the conduct of the war.[130] While Churchill was blessed with a mind that was usually flexible and adaptable, he failed to correctly understand the political climate he was reentering. He expected to be welcomed back into the upper strata of British politics as something of a prodigal son. Clearly, he had paid his debts through military service and would be forgiven. There was important work to be done, and Churchill believed that everyone would recognize his talents and allow him to again apply his gifts. Although he honestly believed these fanciful notions, the sentiments were not shared by anyone with power or influence in the British government.

Throughout the day on March 3, Churchill worked to prepare a speech for the naval estimates debate scheduled for March 7. He worked with a fury, planning his masterstroke against Asquith and all who had opposed him. He canceled his planned social engagements, including the unveiling of his portrait at the National Liberal Club, and poured all his energy into this speech, which he believed would propel him to the top of British politics.[131] The belief that he could take leave from his unit, attend a few closed-door meetings, give a single speech, and then be made prime minister is simply ridiculous—even for a man as dynamic as Winston Churchill.

As part of his attack on Asquith, Churchill had originally planned to publicly denounce his old friend Jackie Fisher. Churchill revealed this plan to Sir Francis Hopwood, claiming that he would "teach that d[amne]d old Oriental scoundrel F[isher] what it meant to quarrel with him."[132] While there is little doubt that Churchill intended to blame Fisher, fate intervened in an unexpected way. Some of Fisher's friends learned of Churchill's plan to denounce the admiral and hastily arranged a luncheon meeting between the two. Ever the political operator and gracious host, Churchill agreed to hold the meeting at his home on 41 Cromwell Road. Churchill may have decided to host the meeting out of politeness and a sense of obligation but soon found himself yet again enraptured by his old friend's charisma and passion for naval affairs. The two quickly appeared to mend their tattered friendship and enjoyed the conviviality and bonhomie of the old times.

Although Churchill was happy to have reconciled with his old friend, Clementine could immediately sense danger.[133] She understood that her husband was a poor judge of character in general and was particularly gullible with regard to Fisher.[134] Clementine had detested Fisher for nearly a year because, while eating lunch at the Churchill home, he had said that her husband was visiting his "French whore." Churchill was away in France, and this was likely little more than an inartful double entendre referring to General John French, but it so angered Clementine that she told the First Sea Lord, "Be quiet you silly old man and get out."[135] After kicking the admiral out of her home, Clementine forced herself to be civil to Fisher over the intervening months, but she correctly saw him as having a dangerous influence over Churchill.

Now, with her husband refusing to listen to her commonsense protests, Clementine decided to take matters into her own hands. At the March 4 luncheon she hosted at her home, she shocked F. E. Smith, who witnessed her violently confronting Fisher, saying, "Keep your hands off my husband. You have all but ruined him once. Leave him alone now."[136] This extraordinary breach of etiquette became a subject of rumor and scandal among his friends but did not change Churchill's mind. Against Clementine's advice, he met with Fisher again on the evening of March 5.[137] Eager for approval, Churchill read his planned speech to Fisher. Sometime since their lunch the previous day, he had made a critical addition to the speech. Near the conclusion of the work, he added a section demanding Fisher's immediate return to the Admiralty. This was a rapid reversal indeed. Now, Churchill was willing not only to be friends with Fisher but to tie their political fortunes together.

This dramatic reconciliation was only the latest in a melodramatic relationship. Despite their egos and explosive personalities, Churchill and Fisher adored one another and were forever feuding and making amends. Once Fisher became First Sea Lord, he and Churchill soon discovered that they could not stand working with each other. They feuded constantly. Churchill perpetually went behind Fisher's back to achieve his policies. They had opposite work and sleep schedules. Each suspected the other of trying to undermine his position. They exchanged frequent histrionic outbursts. Fisher was perpetually resigning, and Churchill was perpetually begging him to stay. When Fisher finally did resign, he engaged in a whisper campaign to discredit Churchill while Churchill spread rumors that Fisher was mad. Yet, despite this melodrama, they adored each other, they recognized each other's brilliance, and even when they were feuding, they spoke of each other in almost loving terms.[138]

Now, both men thought that they could use the other to regain power. Churchill believed he could orchestrate the collapse of the Asquith coalition while also demonstrating that he was willing to forgive Fisher and act in the best interests of the nation. Fisher believed that if he could force Asquith out as prime minister or Arthur Balfour out as First Lord of the Admiralty, he would again be the logical choice to lead the Royal Navy.[139] Both men knew the power of Churchill's rhetoric and believed that a few critical words on the conduct of the war could sway public opinion and force Asquith out of office.

In retrospect, it is clear that both men were letting their active and immature imaginations get the better of them and that each was trying to use the other for his own ends.[140] Fisher was particularly craven and manipulative, playing to Churchill's vanity and deflated sense of self-worth. Churchill needed little convincing that a glorious return to power was within his grasp, and he easily fell into Fisher's trap. Now, Churchill's good nature and his desperate desire to return to politics made him oblivious to the fact that Fisher was manipulating him.[141] Fisher could not believe his good fortune. Churchill was willing not only to be a political ally but to make a speech demanding his return to office. On the morning of March 6, Fisher wrote to Churchill to provide advice and ensure that he would not have a change of heart:

> *4:00 a.m.!! The Early Bird!*
> YOU are the *late one!!*
> My dear Winston,
> I've slept over what you said to me last night—It's THE epoch of your Life!—
> I am going to be the humble instrument! So magnificent a proof OF YOUR SOLE OBJECT BEING THE WAR will have (justly) an *immense* effect on your popularity. Ride in on the crest of that Popularity! THE WAR—THE WHOLE WAR—AND NOTHING BUT THE WAR! Do you imagine that if you got up and said "*What are over* half a million of our men doing *now* in an unattackable Egypt and in Solonika where we are being fooled by a few Austrians—*when these half a million men in France are of vital consequence?* Do you imagine you would not topple over the whole present gang? and also ask what a big British Fleet is NOW doing in the Mediterranean? *When the grand Fleet is in danger!!!*" . . .
> The Reason why the Government are strong is THERE IS NO OPPOSITION LEADER! *Get up every night and batter the box from the Opposition Bench!* No use your sending up one Rocket and then going to have your head "*bashed in*" at the Trenches! Go the whole Hog! *Totus Porcus! Salvation—Here and Now!* I repeat what I have said behind

your back. *There is no one in it with you to conduct the War—and you can be Prime Minister if you like!*

"THE NAVY IS IN DANGER" IS THE CRY! TAKE YOUR OATH, if I ONCE GET IN THERE *WILL BE HELL TILL YOU GET IN!*

I say this from *PURE* belief that the present mob are absolutely effete! *Audacity* and *Imagination* are the requirements of a successful war—*THEY DON'T NOW EXIST!* Its *NOT "Wait and See"* we want but *"Push and Go!"* Not *"Asquith and Balfour,"* but *Winston and—*

Fisher then gave a series of suggestions on how to sharpen Churchill's attacks on Asquith before finishing with a final dramatic flurry:

To *win the War and with no other heartfeeling do we two coalesce! We can do it! Come on!*
Yours as heretofore,
Fisher
I am at Berkley Square the *WHOLE* day if you want me.
I am not going to leave the house.
My telephone number is Gerrard 8795.[142]

With over a century of hindsight, this bizarre letter is genuinely disturbing. Yet for Churchill, who had worked with Fisher and who saw true genius in his unorthodox style, it strengthened his resolve.[143]

Churchill received further encouragement on March 6 from three Liberal MPs, Sir Henry Dalziel, Sir Arthur Markham, and Sir Alfred Mond. Each of these men had broken with Asquith and now backed his rival David Lloyd George. Each of these backbenchers encouraged Churchill to attack Asquith and happily enabled his visions of grandeur. Later that afternoon, Churchill met with his friend C. P. Scott, the famous journalist. Scott also encouraged Churchill to attack Asquith and told him that he should resign his army command and return to politics permanently. Churchill was happy to receive this advice as it seemed to confirm his own opinion of the situation and himself. What Churchill did not consider was that these men had their own agendas. The three Liberal MPs were working to make Lloyd George, not Churchill, the next prime minister, and Scott had been sent by Fisher with the express purpose of ensuring that he would follow through with his promise to speak against the government.[144] These meetings strengthened Churchill's resolve by making him vastly overestimate the support he enjoyed and by playing into his fantasy that his speech would orchestrate the collapse of the Asquith government.

To further goad Churchill into attacking Asquith, Fisher wrote a second letter on March 6:

> Dear Winston,
> If you dont follow my advice *then* your Future is RUINED!
> DON'T GO BACK! *Stick to* THE BOX OF THE LEADER OF THE OPPOSITION—your last words are splendid!!
> *"I feel events are so grave in the Navy that my duty is HERE with HEALTHY not HOSTILE criticism!"*
> IT IS NOT TOO LATE!! THEREFORE I SPEAK!! Otherwise I would have held my tongue. Let me as First Sea Lord be a subsidiary matter—the one to see NOT ONLY the old programme completed but to take fresh gigantic steps for fresh gigantic doings with Big Conceptions that will end the War! *You Winston Churchill yourself ask nothing! Simply you are there to help!* and feel more use at the opposition leaders box than the unwilling partner of an effete conduct of the war!!!
> Yours
> F
> STICK TO THIS!
> Don't let Asquith know.[145]

Despite Fisher's almost childish demand to not let Asquith know about the planned speech, Churchill did just that! The prime minister attended a dinner party at Churchill's house that evening and was surprised to hear about his host's plans to attack his administration the very next day.[146] Asquith knew that Churchill was ambitious and had been hurt by his exclusion from power, so in some ways this awkward revelation was expected. The prime minister's wife, Margot, tried to change Churchill's mind through flattery, noting that he had made a brave decision and was well on the path to redemption, but he risked ruining this goodwill by speaking out against the government's conduct of the war.[147] Despite this excellent advice, Churchill was unmoved. If anything, it had the opposite effect on the obstinate former First Lord.

While he needed no further encouragement, C. P. Scott again visited Churchill on the morning of March 7. Churchill assured Scott that he would in fact carry out his attack on Asquith but noted that the speech needed even greater bravery than service in the trenches.[148] Scott and Fisher were pleased that Churchill had not wavered, but the admiral nevertheless sent one final letter of encouragement:

> My Dear Winston—
> Please forgive my d——d reiteration but I am terribly afraid of the Asquithian cajolery! (*am I already too late?*)
> Providence has placed the Plum in your mouth, *Certain Prime Minister!*
> You have no Rival as Leader of the Opposition and Such a Cry for assuming the position!!! SO PATRIOTIC!!!!
> *"The Navy in Danger"*
> *"But not 'TOO LATE' FOR Safety"* . . .
> *There is seething and wide-spread discontent at the conduct of the War!*
> But the People see no one as a new Leader!
> There is a Cave of Adullam but no David has come along!
> See the 1st Book of Samuel Chap 22 Verse 2
> "He became a Captain over them"
> "And there with him about 400 Men!"
> AINT THAT A GOOD MAJORITY FOR YOU?
> SO DONT GO BACK!
> Never leave that Box—once you have banged it as you will this afternoon—As meek as Mosese you'll say your mission is to help!
> YES! Help the War!
> YES! "BIG CONCEPTIONS! QUICK DECISIONS!"
> That will be our War Cry!
> "THINK IN OCEANS!"
> SHOOT AT SIGHT!
> That will be our action!

Go in and Win!
Dont Falter
"Aut Caesar Aut Nullus"
Accept no post in this Government
They are doomed!
Fate has you in it's Grasp!
Dont wriggle out of it!
D——n Fisher!—You get
Prime Minister!
That will end the War!
Nothing else will!
The Country wants a Man!
Every War always wants a Man!
Dont go back—accept nothing!
Yours
F[149]

This third unhinged letter from Fisher did nothing to change Churchill's plans. Rather, he believed that he was on the verge of achieving a great political coup. He was, in reality, about to demonstrate the impetuousness and dangerous lack of judgment that his critics had long alleged.[150]

The Fateful Speech

On March 7, 1916, Winston Churchill did something he had not done in twelve years—he rose to speak against the government.[151] Rumors about his speech had spread over the previous days, and the House of Commons was crowded with members who sat in nervous anticipation. Churchill did not disappoint. He grabbed his audience's attention with a dramatic turn of echoing oratory: "I shall have to strike a jarring note . . . a note not of reproach, nor of censure nor of panic, but a note in some respects of warning."[152] While Churchill was quick to praise the courage and dedication of the officers and men of the Royal Navy, he argued that their sacrifices were being undermined by uninspired and lethargic efforts from the current First Lord of the Admiralty, Arthur Balfour.[153]

According to Churchill, Balfour's uninspired leadership had put Great Britain at risk. Now, he demanded boldness:

> You cannot afford to indulge even for the shortest period of time in resting on your oars. You must constantly drive the vast machine forward at its utmost speed. To lose momentum is not merely to stop but to fall.
>
> We have survived, and we are recovering from a shortage of munitions for the Army. At a hideous cost in life and treasure we have regained control, and ascendency lies before us at no great distance. A shortage in naval material, if it were to occur from any cause, would give no chance for future recovery. Blood and money, however lavishly poured out, would never repair the consequences of what might be even an unconscious relaxation of effort.[154]

Churchill's criticisms were severe and were designed to imply that Britain faced disaster if his demands for a more aggressive conduct of the war were not implemented.[155]

After offering this menacing vision of defeat, Churchill then claimed that he could be the instrument of salvation if he were given the opportunity to enact his bold strategy:

> I have come down here this afternoon to say these things with the deepest sense of responsibility. I say them because I am sure there is time to avoid all these dangers, because I am sure that it is not too late. If it were too late, silence would be vital. It is not; there is time; and I am anxious that the warning and exhortation which I am going to use, and am using, which may possibly excite resentment, but which must, nevertheless, be said, should be spoken while it is quite certain they may produce a useful effect. But I say advisedly that, though there is time, the Admiralty must not think the battle over. They must forthwith hurl themselves with renewed energy to their task, and press it forward without a loss of a day.[156]

Churchill then discussed at length the menace posed by German submarines and zeppelins and his proposal for combating these dangers.

For almost the entire speech, Churchill's stark criticisms were well argued and well reasoned. He exposed failures of the Asquith government, detailed the threats posed by the Germans, and promised that a more active prosecution of the war could still result in victory. Had Churchill simply stopped a few paragraphs before the end of his speech, it very well may have jump-started his political career. As Lloyd George confided to Lord George Riddell, "He should have stopped after criticizing the Administration."[157]

Yet in the conclusion he snatched defeat from the jaws of victory by demanding the return of Jackie Fisher to the Admiralty. In a few disastrous paragraphs, Churchill threw away all the goodwill and advantage his speech had won:

> But I have not spoken to-day without intending to lead up to a conclusion. I have not used words of warning without being sure first that they are spoken in time to be fruitful, and secondly, without having a definite and practical proposal to make.
>
> When in November, 1914, Prince Louis of Battenberg told me he felt it his duty to retire . . . I was certain that there was only one man who could succeed him. I knew personally all the high officers of the Navy, and I was sure that there was no one who possessed the power, the insight, and energy of Lord Fisher. I therefore made it plain that I would work with no other First Sea Lord. . . . He returned to his old place, and the six months of war administration which followed will, I believe, rank as one of the remarkable periods in the history of the Royal Navy. . . .
>
> I have no doubt whatever what it is my duty to say now. There is a time when I did not think that I could have brought myself to say it, but I have been away for some months, and my mind is now clear. The times are crucial. The issues are momentous. The great War deepens and widens and expands around us. The existence of our country and of our cause depend upon the Fleet. We cannot afford to deprive ourselves or the Navy of the strongest and most vigorous forces that are available. No personal consideration must stand in between the country and those who can serve her best.
>
> I feel that there is in the present Admiralty administration, for all their competence, loyalty and zeal, a lack of driving force and mental energy which cannot be allowed to continue, which must be rectified in one way. I am sure the nation and the Navy expect that the necessary step will be taken. . . .
>
> I urge the First Lord of the Admiralty without delay to fortify himself, to vitalise and animate his Board of Admiralty by recalling Lord Fisher to his post as First Sea Lord.[158]

This was certainly a dramatic way to conclude the speech, but the effect was not what Churchill had intended.[159]

The House of Commons was stunned into silence.[160] Churchill's well-reasoned criticisms of the government and his brilliant oratorical flourishes were almost completely forgotten. Instead, the members focused on the concluding paragraphs and the bizarre demand to recall Fisher to active duty. Violet Bonham Carter, who was watching from the gallery, was shocked by the inexplicable conduct of her friend.[161] She recorded the thoughts of many who witnessed the speech: "Had I gone mad? Had Winston?"[162] Violet left the House of Commons gallery and soon encountered her stepmother, Margot; Eddie Marsh; and her husband. The universal reaction was one of amazement and shock. Everybody believed that the speech was a disaster. When Marsh asked, "Do you think he has done for himself?" he was comforted by Margot Asquith, who wisely noted Churchill's youth and predicted, "If he goes back and fights like a hero it will all be forgotten."[163] Again, the words of the politically astute wife of the prime minister were prophetic, but the path forward for Churchill seemed as formidable as ever.[164]

In the parliamentary debate that followed, Churchill was savagely attacked by members of both parties. His demand to recall Fisher was openly mocked and his sanity questioned. On March 8, Arthur Balfour spoke in defense of his conduct at the Admiralty and delivered a devastating blow.[165] Balfour claimed that the Royal Navy was "stronger than it has ever been in its history" but made no efforts to address Churchill's specific criticisms.[166] Rather, he attacked Churchill's judgment. Balfour claimed to be "astonished" and suggested that Churchill lacked the Duke of Marlborough's ability to master his emotions. He dismissed the speech as illogical, noting, "I cannot follow the workings of the right hon Gentleman's mind." In a final twist of the rhetorical knife, Balfour concluded, "I should regard myself as contemptible beyond the power of expression if I were to yield an inch to a demand of such a kind, made in such a way."[167] Churchill was stunned by the personal nature of these attacks. Balfour had not addressed his points but had instead tried to discredit the messenger.[168]

Over the next few days, the press relentlessly attacked Churchill and his speech. This was not the rhetorical success that would sweep him to power; rather, it was a public failure that compounded his troubles. This latest misstep only seemed to prove the long-standing criticism that Churchill was reckless, untrustworthy, and dangerous. While Churchill attempted to clarify his remarks and defend his character, the press and Parliament had already made up their minds, and the damage was done.[169]

Increasingly desperate and divorced from reality, Fisher sent numerous letters of encouragement to Churchill. The admiral implored him to continue his attacks and to devote his full efforts to leading the overthrow of the government.[170] Rumors circulated that Churchill would not be returning to his battalion in Flanders and would instead remain in London to resume his political activities full-time.[171] Even though he was suffering from a self-inflicted wound from his recent speech, Churchill still believed that he was better prepared to conduct the war than any other British politician. He was frustrated by the resistance and animosity his recent speech had provoked and believed that his criticisms of Balfour and Asquith were still unaddressed and remained valid. Despite these feelings, the simple fact was that Churchill had damaged his reputation and could not easily resume his once-brilliant political career.

Desperate for friendship and consolation, Churchill paid a visit to the home of Violet Bonham Carter.[172] This was the first time they had met since his going-away party in November, and in the meantime, she had married her father's private secretary, Maurice Bonham Carter. While Violet expressed joy at seeing him, Churchill's mind was clearly preoccupied. Perhaps seeking flattery and reassurance, he even gruffly insulted her, suggesting that she had betrayed him as well.[173] Violet had good reason to be angry since Churchill had just attacked her father on the floor of Parliament, but instead she repeatedly assured him of her loyalty and continued friendship. With this much-needed reassurance, he slowly began to open up to her again. They talked as they so often did—about politics and as equals. Violet questioned why Churchill would ask for the recall of Fisher after Fisher had done so much to undermine his own cause. He responded that he had heard rumors of internal friction and malaise within the Admiralty and believed that Fisher's dynamism would reinvigorate the war effort. This was a questionable judgment from Violet's perspective, but she chose not to press the issue as it had already caused him so much grief.[174]

Violet then asked if the rumors that he wanted to remain in London were true. Churchill confessed that he believed that it was "right for him to remain here and exercise what influence he had at the heart of affairs." This revelation surprised Violet and made Churchill defensive, and he insisted that many friends and supporters wanted him to return to politics immediately.[175]

Although Violet had feared for Churchill's life while he was at the front, she counseled her friend to return to his unit. She softened the blow by admitting that he would ultimately play an important role in the conduct of the war by returning to politics, but for his own sake, he must return to France. Despite this wise counsel, Violet was unsure which path her friend would choose and was haunted by the thought that she may be ordering Churchill to his death.[176]

Desperate for guidance, Churchill made two visits to his former mentor H. H. Asquith at 10 Downing Street, on March 9 and 11. This was an unusual decision as he was still deeply hurt by the knowledge that the prime minister had cast him aside for political reasons, and he had attacked Asquith's policies just days before in his now-infamous speech. Nevertheless, Churchill seemed to desire Asquith's advice and reassurance. While neither man kept a record of the first meeting, the prime minister confided in Violet about the pathetic state of her friend and his former protégé. Violet kept this conversation a secret for fifty years until after Churchill's death, when she published her memoir about their friendship.[177]

In the first meeting, Asquith did his best to reassure Churchill that he could again be a key figure in British politics while warning that he needed to moderate his self-destructive impulses. Asquith made an already-uncomfortable situation worse by reminding Churchill that his late father, Randolph, had similarly thrown away a promising political career in a dispute about the budget. He warned, "If I can, I want to save you from doing the same thing. You know nothing but affection prompts me. It is because I care for you that I shall save you."[178] While this was true enough, his father's political failures were a touchy subject for Churchill. He believed that, like his father, he was a misunderstood genius who had been betrayed by the jealousy and lack of vision of less talented but more powerful politicians.[179]

With tears in his eyes, Churchill argued that he was ready to return to politics and insisted that he had many friends who would support him. Asquith dismissed this quickly: "At the moment you have none who count at all." Despite the curtness of this observation, it was correct. Churchill lacked any influential friends who were willing to provide him an office or political patronage, and a return at that moment would be seen as rash. Instead, Asquith advised that Churchill return to his unit, at least for the moment, "to do what I am sure is right—right above all for his own sake." This blunt political advice was clearly not what Churchill had sought, but when they parted, Asquith was convinced that he would return to France and resume his military duties.[180]

Apparently, Churchill was unconvinced; he returned to 10 Downing Street and again met with his former mentor. He once more pleaded that he was ready to return to politics, and once more Asquith did his best to provide comfort and wise council. According to Asquith, he "wrestled with Satan for his [Churchill's] soul" in such a manner that "rarely has any missionary exerted himself in more up-hill work of salvation."[181] After about an hour of begging, Asquith believed that he had succeeded in convincing Churchill that his political future was best served by returning to the front and continuing to serve honorably. Asquith believed that he "had got an uncertain but restraining grip on the shoulder of a would-be suicide."[182] While he desperately wanted to return to politics, Churchill knew that his former mentor was correct and that his motivations were pure. He thanked Asquith for this second meeting and sent a letter the next day informing the prime minister that he would leave for the front.[183]

Churchill Returns to the Front

Churchill arrived at Plugstreet dejected. His great plans for a dramatic return to power had backfired and made him the laughingstock of both parties.[184] He felt so depressed that on his way back to Plugstreet he wrote a message to Asquith resigning his command. He quickly realized that this was folly and then sent another message taking back the resignation. Asquith clearly felt pity for Churchill and chose to neither accept the first resignation nor publicize this bizarre series of events.[185] Churchill recognized that Asquith had done him a favor and later wrote him a short note from "in the field," thanking him for "more time in which to consider [his] course."[186] Despite this reflection, Churchill was "eaten up" with frustration after being out of power for nearly a year.[187] He described his feelings in a candid manner in his March 13 letter to Clementine: "Across the troubled waters one can only steer by compass—not to do anything that is not honourable & manly, & subject to that to use my vital force to the utmost effect to win the war—there is the test I am going to try my decision by. Dual obligations, both honourable, both weighty have rent me. But I am sure my true war station is in the H[ouse] of C[ommons]. There I can help the movements of events."[188]

Churchill was correct that his talents could be better employed elsewhere, but as long as Asquith remained in power, his path to office was blocked, and he was best served by remaining a dutiful soldier.[189]

Churchill still held out hope for promotion to brigade command. He knew that several brigades needed new commanders and believed that he had proved his worth, but on March 19 he received news that one of the brigade commands he had been hoping for had been given to a more experienced officer.[190] From the perspective of the hierarchical British Army, this was the correct decision. However, Churchill had used the possibility of a brigade command as a motivation and believed that it should be his. He was now more determined than ever to leave the army as soon as he could do so without appearing to be running from his duties as a battalion commander.

On the same day Churchill received this news, his second-in-command, Archibald Sinclair, was preparing to return to England for a brief leave. Churchill was so concerned for his friend's well-being that he delayed his own departure to allow his deputy some much-needed rest. He also insisted that Sinclair stay with Clementine and his sister-in-law, Goonie Churchill, and sent explicit instructions to his wife about caring for his friend.[191] This was more than a friendly gesture or reward for an old friend. Rather, Churchill felt guilty. The two friends had privately discussed Churchill's desire to leave the army. Sinclair understood that Churchill wanted to reenter politics but stated he intended to remain with the unit. Churchill advised Sinclair to reconsider this choice, but his friend felt honor bound to remain.

While Churchill always claimed to enjoy the military life, he understood that his friend did not: "Archie is burdened by the war, and he has got so much older and duller. Poor little man he has got a twenty month dose. . . . [Archie] hunch[es] . . . himself up under the weight and weariness of the war like a very sick hen in a very large puddle on a cold day. He is most courageous, conscientious, and hard-working, but he hates every hour of it with a profound loathing."[192]

Despite these feelings of guilt, Churchill's mind was set on leaving the army the first good chance he had. He elaborated on this decision in a March 22 letter to Clementine: "I do not think any reason is needed beyond the general reason—wh[ich] is the true one—that I think it right to resume political & Parl[iamen]t. Duties wh[ich] are incompatible with holding a military command. . . . I shall have served for nearly five months at the front, almost always in the front line, certainty without discredit—discharging arduous &

difficult duties to the satisfaction of my superiors & to the advantage of my officers and men."[193]

In her typically wise and understanding way, Clementine tried to calm her husband and ensure that his departure was not too hasty. While she feared for her husband's safety and passionately desired his return, she repeatedly counseled him to remain at the front.[194] She noted that his frontline service created a "military halo" around her husband where neither the press nor his political rivals were willing to criticize him.[195] While Churchill had apparently made up his mind to leave the unit by late March, he heeded Clementine's wise counsel that he must be careful about the manner of his departure.[196]

The Honorable Path Home

On April 19, Churchill was informed that his 6th Scottish Battalion would be consolidated with the 7th Scottish Battalion in early May.[197] This reorganization was necessitated by the combination of high casualties, a declining stream of volunteers, and a desire to keep the unit entirely Scottish.[198] The practice of combining depleted units was common at the time as a response to the near-constant drain on manpower and was in no way a reflection on Churchill's leadership.[199] Rather, the manpower shortage was due in large part to the failures of the government to institute an effective conscription policy in a timely manner, an issue that Churchill had warned about for months.

Now, the army's manpower shortage presented an opportunity for Churchill. Since the 7th Battalion was commanded by a more senior officer, Churchill would be forced to relinquish command.[200] Afterward, he would have to wait to be reassigned. This reorganization would provide the perfect cover for a return to politics. Now, Churchill could claim that he had served with his unit until the very end and that he had been forced out and left with little choice but to return to London as a battle-hardened hero. Years later, when writing *The World Crisis*, he would be careful to highlight that the unit had been so depleted by men that it was consolidated and that he was lower on the seniority list than his replacement.[201] However, Churchill was barely able to hide his pleasure when he shared this news with Clementine: "It is really a most fortunate and natural conclusion and well worth having waited for."[202]

After the battalion left the front line for the last time on May 3, Churchill wasted no time in securing official permission from his chain of command to return to London and reenter politics on a full-time basis.[203] His request was granted, and he would be allowed to leave as soon as he officially handed over command of the battalion on May 7.[204] During this brief interlude, Churchill was a flurry of activity. In particular, he wanted to ensure that his fellow officers would not have their careers placed in limbo by the consolidation of the unit. As Gibb noted, this extraordinary effort was appreciated:

> He was anxious to find employment—congenial employment—for those who were to be thrown out into the cold when the battalions amalgamated. He took endless trouble; he borrowed motor cars and scoured France, interviewing Generals and staff officers great and small, in his efforts to do something to help those who had served under him. . . . No man was ever kinder to his subordinates, and no commanding officer I have ever known was half so kind. . . . The early months of 1916 are by far my most treasured war memory. It was my happiest time, and it was my most interesting time. For work in intimate association with Winston Churchill was the last experience in the world any of us expected—our course did not lie that way.[205]

Thanks in no small part to his dedication, Churchill's fellow officers were genuinely sorry to see him depart. While he was always something of a prima donna, Churchill gradually won them over with his energy and kindness. Now, as a final act, Churchill worked assiduously to ensure that his staff had meaningful work to do after his departure. This not only left an enduring impression on officers like Gibb and Hakewill-Smith but also ensured that their careers would continue to prosper so that they could later be influential allies for Churchill.

In his final days in the battalion, Churchill tried particularly hard to convince Sinclair to return to London with him. Sinclair hated war and life in the trenches, yet he decided to remain with the unit, much to Churchill's dismay. For the remainder of the war, Churchill would write to his friend and frequently try to tempt him into quitting, but Sinclair remained unflinchingly loyal.[206] Late in the war, Churchill even tried to use his position as minister of munitions to order Sinclair to return and work under him as a special liaison at the ministry. Sinclair declined as he felt bound by his duty and feared that his fellow officers would see him as seeking "the softest of soft jobs," so he had his regimental commander refuse to release him from frontline duty.

Churchill fumed but begrudgingly accepted the fact that his friend had a powerful sense of duty to remain in a position he so despised.[207]

Bound by his unusual sense of obligation, Sinclair served honorably for the remainder of the war. He was promoted to major and served in the Guards Machine Gun Regiment, and he repeatedly refused Churchill's siren songs. Shortly after the conclusion of the war, he finally left the army and took Churchill up on his offer of employment. Starting in 1919, he served first as his personal military secretary at the War Office and then as his private secretary in 1921 when Churchill became the colonial secretary. In both these roles, Sinclair was efficient and loyal and could tolerate his boss's unusual management style.[208]

In 1922, Sinclair finally stood as a candidate for Caithness and Sutherland, and with the help of Churchill and Lloyd George, he won. He became more closely aligned with Llyod George politically but was always a trusted confidant of Churchill's, even when he chose to "re-rat" and return to the Tories. Sinclair would remain a devoted Liberal for the remainder of his life. He worked for and against Churchill on numerous policies, including school and agricultural reforms, free trade, and urban planning.[209] Before the outbreak of World War II, Sinclair was one of the few prominent politicians who joined Churchill to oppose the appeasement of Hitler. While both men paid a short-term political cost for this principled stance, they would ultimately be vindicated. Upon assuming the office of prime minister in 1940, Churchill asked Sinclair to serve as his secretary of state for air, a role he fulfilled dutifully for the remainder of the war. As the head of the Liberals, Sinclair was able to convince his party not to openly challenge Churchill's role as head of the government. He did this in part out of loyalty to Churchill but also because he believed that the unprecedented times required national unity.[210]

Churchill's Final Meeting with His Battalion

Churchill held a final meeting with the officers on May 7. He was introduced by Gibb, who noted that he had been "devilish decent to [them]." Then Churchill told the officers "that he had come to regard the young Scot as a 'formidable fighting animal,' and he touched on his other connections with Scotland [Clementine and his seat in Dundee] in the most appreciative fashion."[211] These accolades had the desired effect of stirring the patriotism of the Scottish officers and left them with a kind impression of Churchill.

As Gibb described his tenure as their commanding officer: "No more popular officer ever commanded troops . . . he was hard working, persevering, and thorough. . . . We came to realize, to realize at first hand, his tremendous ability. . . . And much more, he became our friend. He is a man who is apparently always to have enemies. He has made none in his old regiment, but left behind him there men who will always be his partisans and admirers."[212] Powerful words indeed for a man who had initially doubted Churchill but, despite his quirks, learned to love him.[213]

To document this last meeting, Churchill and his officers posed for a group photo. Churchill is seen seated in the center of the frame wearing the traditional Scottish bonnet of his battalion.[214] While this was the official uniform for the unit, this meeting was one of the few times he was ever seen wearing the headgear.[215] In fact, he was rarely seen without his poilu helmet, which provided superior protection and also made him instantly identifiable. Perhaps this sartorial choice was a simple act of friendship. Perhaps it was a political statement. Perhaps he wanted to better show off his face for history. Whatever his reason, the photo shows Churchill simultaneously looking at ease with his friends and brother officers and looking defiant, perhaps anticipating the political battles that lay ahead.

After formally turning over command of the battalion on May 7, 1916, Churchill departed France and traveled across the channel to England. As part of relinquishing command, Churchill was transferred to the Territorial Force Reserve. This transfer effectively took him out of consideration for future commands and ended his path to further promotions.[216] He would continue to serve as a major in the Queen's Own Oxfordshire Hussars for decades to come, but this was a social appointment, not an active assignment.[217] In fact, as a condition for his release from active-duty service, Lord Kitchener made Churchill promise that he would not apply for another command for the remainder of the war.[218]

It is tantalizing to imagine how Churchill's military career might have progressed had he chosen to remain in the army. Many have suggested that he had so impressed his superiors that he was being considered for a brigade command and would have likely received one in the coming months had he chosen to remain on active duty.[219] The less glamorous fact is that Churchill's departure was well timed, as it helped him avoid the bloody Battle of the Somme, which began in July and cost the Allies over six hundred thousand casualties.[220] Had he participated in the battle, it is entirely possible that he would have felt compelled to again test his luck and courage under fire, perhaps with horrific results.[221] Instead of fighting in this gruesome battle of attrition, Churchill was safe in London, where he could criticize it publicly as further proof that British strategy was deeply flawed and produced little more than a horrendous butcher's bill.

Churchill's return to politics after a brief but honorable time at the front was almost certainly for the best. This sentiment was perfectly captured by his division commander, Lieutenant General Sir Charles Fergusson, who wrote a warm letter of farewell noting, "I am glad that you have come through this experience safely. And there is no doubt that your knowledge of the difficulties and deficiencies out here, obtained first hand, will be of immense use to the service hereafter."[222] Fergusson was perhaps more correct than he knew. Within two days of arriving in England, Churchill was back speaking in the House of Commons.[223] He was eager to make up for lost time and make a name for himself by applying his hard-won experiences regarding modern warfare.

Churchill's months in the trenches had served him well. True, he won no decorations for his actions, nor was he mentioned in dispatches, but he had proved himself to be a brave and humble leader.[224] For the remainder of his life, he would draw from his experiences in modern warfare, tell stories about his exploits, and treasure the friendships he had made in the trenches.[225] Now, it was Churchill's turn to apply these lessons, claw his way back into political relevance, and continue one of the most remarkable comebacks in a life filled with tragedy and triumphs.

5

The Uncertain Future

Churchill Returns to Politics

Churchill's first weekend home from France was a whirlwind of activity that revealed much about his character and plans for rehabilitating his career. He chose to spend this first weekend at Blenheim Palace, his ancestral home. This grand estate was built as a monument to the Duke of Marlborough and had always held a special place in his heart. It was his birthplace as he arrived unexpectedly after his mother had experienced a fall and a bumpy carriage ride while accompanying a shooting party. As a boy, he had roamed the halls on frequent family visits, admiring the grandness and sense of history the place provided. Despite sleeping too late and almost missing the opportunity, he proposed to Clementine in the gardens. He had enjoyed the grand library and scoured the family documents for information about his ancestors, admired the gardens, wandered the hills, and hunted in the estates. Remarking on the importance of the home, Churchill once quipped, "At Blenheim I took two important decisions: to be born and to marry. I am happily content with the decision I took on both those occasions."[1]

Now, Churchill returned to this special place looking for inspiration and renewal, but he brought something new—painting supplies.[2] During that weekend, Churchill painted whenever he had a free moment. He poured out his frustration with a volcanic energy and produced two finished canvases. Churchill's painting caught the attention of his houseguests, Sir Ian Hamilton and his wife, Jean. Hamilton was an old friend of Churchill's and had been the commander of Allied ground forces at the Dardanelles. Like Churchill's, Hamilton's reputation was ruined by the failed campaign, and he believed that they had both been wronged. Churchill had invited Hamilton to Blenheim Palace to discuss coordinating their defense and rehabilitation efforts in the coming months. They agreed to work together toward their common cause, but the exact details of these discussions remain unknown as neither man appears to have kept notes about their plans.

These political machinations could not keep him from indulging in the delicious distraction that painting provided.[3] General Hamilton's wife, Jean, noted Churchill's fascination with painting with a mixture of amusement and pique: "Winston is rather wonderful, very sincere and direct in his work, and paints like lightning; he loves being watched and being told how it is going all the time. He painted two pictures—one of the house which I instantly copied in pastel, and one of the view from the front of the house."[4]

In the months that followed, Churchill and Hamilton would continue to work together to mend their tattered reputations and defend themselves before the newly founded Dardanelles Commission.

After spending a relaxing and productive weekend at Blenheim, Churchill returned to a London political scene still very unsure as to what his future held. Despite this uncertainty, he was confident that he could again ascend to the top of British politics. He was now aided by his newfound love of painting as well as the perspective he had earned by serving at the front, but he had little else. He was desperately short of money. His credibility still suffered from the Dardanelles and his request to recall Fisher. He had no office and no hope of getting one as long as Asquith remained prime minister. Yet he still believed in his own divine destiny.

Shortly after his return to London, Churchill visited John Lavery's studio, not as a friend or fellow painter but as a subject. The officers of the armored car squadrons had collected funds and commissioned a portrait as a thank-you present for his support and enthusiasm for armored warfare.[5] He posed in his military uniform and French helmet and was very pleased with the likeness his friend produced. While Churchill would have preferred to forget much about the period that surrounded this painting, he treasured the artwork for the remainder of his life, and it still hangs at Chartwell to this day.[6]

This was not the only portrait of Churchill painted in the weeks after his return from France. In fact, the artist Sir William Orpen also executed a brilliant likeness of him, which had a special place in his heart and would become a treasured keepsake. Many years later, when discussing the picture with the director of the Tate Gallery, Sir John Richardson, Churchill admitted, "Yes it is good," but then revealed that the context was similarly important, noting, "In fact when he painted it I'd lost pretty well everything."[7]

The Political Path Forward

For the remainder of the war, Churchill applied his talents and energy toward the active prosecution of the conflict. He was glad to be back in the political arena and quickly involved himself in a wide range of issues, including manpower and conscription, war financing, improvements in equipment and munitions, air defense, and the creation of an independent Air Ministry.[8] He was frequently critical of Asquith and his own Liberal Party, but these criticisms were now better informed and less peevish thanks to his experiences at the front.[9]

Two days after his return from the front, Churchill returned to Parliament and gave a speech on the need for expanding the conscription.[10] He had supported the first Military Service Act, which had passed in January while he was at the front.[11] This legislation helped fill part of the manpower shortage but only covered unmarried men between eighteen and forty-one and did not include the Irish. The second bill, which was now up for debate, would expand the draft to include married men as well as Irishmen. In the weeks immediately following the failed Easter Rising, tensions with Ireland were reaching a breaking point.[12] The possibility of conscription seemed to lend credence to the claims of Irish Nationalists who declared that Great Britain cared only for empire and would happily order the sons of Éire to their deaths.[13]

While he was not unsympathetic to the Irish cause, he believed that the needs of the empire took precedence during this time of existential crisis.[14] Churchill had long supported expanding conscription, and witnessing firsthand the depleted ranks of his Scottish battalion only strengthened this conviction. Therefore, Churchill argued passionately for the new conscription legislation, including the expansion of the draft to Ireland. This was unacceptable to the Irish Nationalist MPs and led to the first known use of the heckle "What about the Dardanelles?" during Churchill's speech on the expansion of the conscription legislation. This ad hominem attack on a seemingly unrelated matter genuinely surprised Churchill, and he struggled to regain his composure.[15] His enemies quickly seized on the taunt's ability to disturb the otherwise unflappable speaker and would continue to employ this tactic for decades.[16] While the second conscription bill would pass with Churchill's support, this was something of a Pyrrhic victory. It made new enemies among the Irish Nationalists and gave rise to a brutally effective, if unfair, catchphrase: "What about the Dardanelles?"

The effectiveness of this quip revealed that Churchill was a long way from achieving the political comeback he desired. On May 14, Churchill sent a letter to Fisher. The admiral had resigned on May 15 of the previous year, setting off the chain of events that had ultimately derailed Churchill's career. Now, both men were political castoffs, and Churchill struck a reflective and conciliatory tone: "This accursed year has now come to an end & please God there will be better luck for you & me in the next, & some chance of helping our country to save itself & all dependent on it. Don't lose heart. I am convinced destiny has not done with you."[17] It is unclear if Churchill believed that Fisher could ever return to power, but he was certain that he himself would.

Careful to avoid further controversy, Churchill shifted his focus toward a series of issues designed to improve the conditions of troops serving on the front lines. His time in the trenches had opened his eyes to the needs of common soldiers, and now he was determined to do something for them.[18] One of the first issues he focused on was the importance of air superiority. During his time at the front, he had witnessed the emerging technology of airpower and the powerful impact it could have on frontline troops.[19] His diary entries made repeated references to the German air superiority and his belief that it was unacceptable.[20] In his May 17 speech on air defenses, Churchill demanded greater efforts and attention for the air war, claiming, "Nothing stands in the way of our obtaining the aerial supremacy in the war but yourselves."[21]

Churchill continued to advocate for a better understanding of the plight of frontline troops and for their lives to not be carelessly wasted. In his May 23 speech on army estimates, he pleaded for a wholesale reconsideration of British strategy:

> I say to myself every day, What is going on while we sit here, while we go away to dinner and home to bed? Nearly 1,000 men— Englishmen, Britishers, men of our race—are knocked into bundles of bloody rags every twenty-four hours, and carried away to hasty graves or to field ambulances. . . . Do not let us be drawn into any course of action not justified by purely military considerations [a criticism of the Somme offensive, which was about to be launched

after several delays and alterations for political reasons]. The argument which is used that "it is now our turn now" has no place in military thought.²²

These powerful words struck a chord with the British public. The beginning of the Somme offensive in July seemed to confirm that British troops were being sacrificed needlessly on behalf of their French allies.²³

In the weeks that followed this speech, it began to take on a life of its own. It was quoted and commented on widely and was in such demand that it was published in the popular penny pamphlet *The Fighting Line*.²⁴ Soldiers and their wives began to write with examples of government waste and abuse, asking for help and support. Churchill was now something of a populist reformer.²⁵ In many ways this was nothing new as Churchill had long championed military reforms with gusto. As a young politician, he had espoused numerous reforms for the British Army in the wake of the Boer War, and in 1901, he was the only Tory to oppose a bill to greatly increase spending on the army. Even after he switched parties and joined the Liberals, he would take a keen interest in military matters, simultaneously arguing for the betterment of the common British soldier and voting against a series of spending increases that he viewed as unnecessary and wasteful. While many of Churchill's contemporaries saw his actions as political theater reminiscent of his father, Randolph, who had resigned as chancellor of the exchequer over the issue of military spending, this decision reveals that he did have a deeply held if seemingly contradictory core of beliefs.²⁶

Building on the momentum from his May 23 speech, Churchill gave a similarly ambitious and provocative speech on July 24. Here, he advocated for a fairer system of frontline service time, quicker promotions for enlisted soldiers, and greater recognition for bravery among enlisted troops.²⁷ Churchill, who had been accused of being a medal hunter earlier in his career, understood that awards were tangible rewards for service and that men often valued them highly.²⁸ Thus, he specifically argued for more awards for enlisted personnel to improve morale and fighting spirit within the ranks.

In this speech, he displayed a compassionate view of the common man who faced death in an anonymous fashion: "It is the privates, non-commissioned officers, and the regimental officers whose case requires the sympathetic attention of the House and the Secretary of State. Honours should go where death and danger go, and these are the men who pay all the penalties in the terrible business that is now proceeding."²⁹ While Churchill was always a kindhearted man, it is difficult to imagine this level of concern for the working-class soldiers or a willingness to make a speech on their behalf before his time in the trenches.³⁰

For the remainder of the war, Churchill tried to apply his experiences in the trenches to politics. In early September, he pleaded unsuccessfully with Asquith to delay the introduction of tanks until there were enough to guarantee success and not squander the surprise. Churchill thought he had convinced Asquith and was surprised when the prime minister ignored his excellent advice.³¹

While the initial tank attacks were successful in achieving limited objectives, Churchill later bemoaned the fact that they could have done more: "The first twenty tanks, in spite of my protests . . . were improvidently exposed to the enemy at the Battle of the Somme. The immense advantage of novelty and surprise was thus squandered . . . the certainty of a great and brilliant victory, was revealed to the Germans for the mere petty purpose of taking a few ruined villages."³² While he would apply this and countless other insights during World War II, Churchill was largely marginalized on matters of strategy for the remainder of World War I.

The fact that he was ignored when he was so often correct reminded Churchill just how far his political fortunes had fallen.³³ He believed that his talents and millions of lives were being wasted. While he would have to wait to better apply his talents in the political and military spheres, he soon returned to writing as a means of making his views known. The result was ultimately beneficial as Churchill carefully documented his dissenting views for the record and also gained a significant financial benefit from his pen.

Frustrated in Politics, Rewarded in Writing

As a backbencher, Churchill was a long way from being at the center of politics, and his attacks on his own party made it unthinkable that he would receive a cabinet position under Asquith. Yet, despite his desire to hold office, wield power, and earn a cabinet minister's pay, this reduced role was a blessing in disguise. Freed from the responsibilities and censorship of the cabinet, Churchill was able to be more critical of the government. This willingness to attack the government combined with his extraordinary skill as a writer made Churchill an attractive commodity for various publishing outlets and created something of a bidding war for his work. This allowed him both a path out of his desperate financial situation and a means for exposing his views to a much broader audience, two things that were essential for his rehabilitation.

From both a pecuniary and publicity standpoint, Churchill's writings were an outstanding success. Despite his reduced political status, he quickly found that there was still a strong interest in his writings. The *Sunday Pictorial* and the *Strand* commissioned a series of four and six articles, respectively, at the generous rate of £250 per article, and the *London Magazine* paid £500 each for a series of six.[34] In addition to producing publicity, these articles had the more practical effect of relieving Churchill from yet another personal financial crisis. In fact, when he left the army and returned to politics, his salary as an MP was entirely consumed by debt service, and he had a mere £123 in his bank accounts.

The rapid influx of cash from publications prevented what would have been a humiliating bankruptcy and instead allowed him to boast to his brother, Jack: "Money worries need not weigh with you. I find myself able quite easily to earn ten or twelve thousand pounds in the next six months. So that Cromwell [their shared home] and all in it will be well supplied. Mind you let me know of anything that wants paying. I get 4 or 5 shillings a word for everything I write: and apparently even at this price the newspaper is a gainer."[35]

While Churchill was a far too optimistic about his newly improved financial circumstances, he clearly profited from his skill with the pen, an avenue to redemption that would have been closed to him had he immediately stepped into an office upon his return.

Churchill's four articles for the *Sunday Pictorial* were particularly successful. The *Sunday Pictorial*, the predecessor to the *Sunday Mirror*, was founded in 1915 and rapidly rose in popularity because of its vivid images of the war and its willingness to directly challenge the policies of the Asquith government. In its first year of production, it had become one of the best-selling papers in the world, with a circulation of over one million copies.[36] The paper's editor, F. R. Sanderson, wagered that Churchill's dramatic writing style and willingness to criticize the conduct of the war would appeal to his readers and was willing to pay handsomely. Sanderson's instincts were correct. Sales of the paper rose by as many as four hundred thousand copies on days when Churchill's articles appeared, a truly outstanding number that pleased both the editor and the author alike.

In these articles, Churchill elucidated his own ideas about warfare, in particular the need to stop wasteful frontal assaults.[37] These articles were well written to be sure, but they were also impeccably timed as their publication coincided with the opening of the British offensive at the Somme. This bloody battle of attrition gained little and seemed to prove Churchill's point that a wholesale reconsideration of British strategy was in order.[38] As an alternative to these fruitless assaults, he argued that sea power was an untapped advantage for Britain. With a flair for the dramatic, he dubbed Great Britain "the Great Amphibian" whose natural habitat was, "in the broad seas."[39] Sea power could help them maintain the initiative, strike where they wanted, and keep the enemy guessing rather than be forced to rely on land campaigns such as Gallipoli or the Somme. "If need be, she can crawl or even dart ashore.... Or she can return again to the deep, and strike anew, now here, now there, and no one can guess where the attack will fall."[40]

For those familiar with Churchill's strategic thinking, these arguments were nothing new. In fact, Churchill had been making similar points in speeches, cabinet meetings, and print for decades.[41] What was different about these articles was that they were reaching a mass audience that was increasingly frustrated with the progress of the war. Churchill's clear and bold prose provided a stark contrast to the official statements from the Asquith government, and he proposed a means for victory. Because he was out of power, he could criticize and make suggestions on paper and not have to worry about the messier realities of war and politics.[42] Undoubtably, the articles Churchill wrote in the weeks after his return from the trenches were an unqualified success. They provided critical monetary support, exposed his views to millions, and helped rehabilitate his reputation as a strategist and military expert.

The Dardanelles Commission

In addition to working as an MP and a writer, Churchill spent considerable time in the weeks after his return preparing a defense of his actions for the newly formed Dardanelles Commission.[43] Churchill saw the formation of the commission as both a potential opportunity and a potential trap. If he could convince the commission that his actions were strategically sound and that the subsequent failures were not his fault, then this was an opportunity to officially clear his name and hopefully move past the entire business. If, however, he was officially assigned blame, then, he believed, he would be the scapegoat for the entire fiasco and forever ruined.

Churchill earnestly believed that he was blameless for the Dardanelles and that a fair reading of the evidence would almost make his case for him. To this end, he pushed for the release of classified documents regarding the Dardanelles Campaign. While the commission had access to many of these papers, Churchill wanted full access to prepare his own defense and permission to publish key documents. He did not trust the commission's impartiality and instead wanted to have his case judged in the court of public opinion.[44] He claimed that he had a right to present this evidence in his own defense and that the public had a right to an open inquiry.

Much to Churchill's frustration, his efforts to have the official documents published were repeatedly blocked.[45] While the government refused to release these documents on national security grounds, Churchill believed that they contained little or no damaging information regarding a campaign that had already ended. Instead, he feared that the requests were being thwarted to assign him blame. While Churchill had many enemies, there appears to be no credible evidence of a conspiracy to delay publication of these documents with the goal of destroying his career. Rather, simple bureaucratic conservatism and malaise, not the elaborate plot envisioned by Churchill, seem to be the real culprits.

Ultimately, Churchill would publish many of the relevant documents in his memoir *The World Crisis*. These documents helped Churchill make the case that he had intended to make in his own defense years before. To this end, Churchill was largely successful; the inclusion of these papers added evidence to support his argument, albeit evidence that had been selectively chosen and edited with the express purpose of exonerating its author. By publishing these documents in his memoirs, Churchill unwittingly instigated a new crisis. In response to the publication of the first volume of *The World Crisis*, several Labour MPs claimed that Churchill had leaked national secrets and violated the oath of secrecy he took upon assuming cabinet rank. For a brief period, he was concerned about the prospect of being called to testify, but eventually the controversy died down and was forgotten. However, Churchill was much more careful with his publication of official documents, and he had government censors approve later volumes of *The World Crisis* and received official sanction to publish documents before beginning work on *The Second World War*.[46]

Despite the lack of access to classified materials, Churchill began to prepare his defense for the Dardanelles Commission.[47] On the basis of their previous meeting at Blenheim Palace, he found common cause with his longtime friend Ian Hamilton.[48] As they coordinated their efforts, they settled on a target, the venerable Lord Horatio Kitchener.[49] Despite his legendary status as the victor of campaigns in Sudan and South Africa and the architect of the mass "Kitchener Armies," the once-untouchable soldier now seemed vulnerable.[50] His conduct of the war had come under increasing scrutiny, and his micromanagement, intolerance of perceived disloyalty or ineptitude, and often-gruff manner had made many enemies.[51]

Hamilton sensed the shift in public opinion. He speculated that the true intention of the Dardanelles Commission was not to clear him or Churchill or even to discover the root causes of the Allied failure but to destroy Kitchener.[52] If true, this would provide an opportunity for Hamilton and Churchill to clear their names if they were willing to work against Kitchener. While Churchill had greatly appreciated Kitchener's visit during his final days at the Admiralty, he had a long and troubled relationship with the old general and was willing to betray him if it ensured his own political survival.

Churchill's strategy soon became politically impossible. On June 5, Kitchener was traveling on a secret mission to Russia when his ship, HMS *Hampshire*, struck a mine and sank in the freezing waters off the Orkney Islands.[53] Only twelve sailors were rescued; 727 men, including Kitchener and his entire party, were killed. Ironically, Churchill was preparing his defense with General French when they heard a newspaper boy shouting through their open window that Kitchener had died.[54] Although Churchill was betraying Kitchener at the very moment he heard the news, he was shocked, nevertheless.[55] Churchill immediately realized that his defense strategy was in tatters as it would be politically impossible to place blame on a recently deceased war hero. He now had only a few weeks to alter his strategy and prepare his defense.

On June 23, Churchill wrote to Archibald Sinclair, noting that Parliament was out of session, yet, "I am busy with the Dardanelles Commission, about which I feel hopeful. I write and paint—and ponder."[56] Aided by his painting, he poured his enormous energy into this effort and ultimately decided on a multipronged approach. First, he would rigorously defend the overall strategic concept of an attack on the Dardanelles. Second, he would emphasize that the need to rescue Britain's Russian ally had necessitated urgent actions.

Third, he would prove that he had not interfered with or exerted undue influence on the Admiralty planning process. Fourth, he would insist that the War Council had ample time to examine and question the plan. Fifth, he would point out that, as First Sea Lord, Admiral Fisher had approved all plans for naval operations and had given the order to proceed with the plan. Sixth, he would show that he had no responsibility for the ground operations. Seventh, he would explain that he had conceived the operation as a navy-only option that would risk little and could be easily terminated by simply sailing away. Finally, and more generally, he would claim that the western front had taken priority over the Dardanelles Campaign and that it had ultimately failed because it had never been given the support it needed.[57] This was a logical and complete defense of his strategic thinking and his actions, but would it be enough to clear his name?

Churchill was called to testify before the Dardanelles Commission on September 28 and October 4, 1916.[58] Over these two days, he vehemently defended his conduct at the Admiralty. His prepared opening statement lasted five and a half hours and was an impressive display of logic, rhetoric, and self-serving half-truths. He attempted to simultaneously take the moral high ground by defending his staff at the Admiralty and claim that he was following their advice: "I have no complaint to make in regard to any officer serving under the Board of Admiralty, whether ashore or afloat. On the contrary, I am here to defend those by whose professional advice I was guided."[59] Churchill then presented what he called five distinct truths that were fully supported by evidence:

1. That there was full authority;
2. That there was a reasonable prospect of success;
3. That greater interests were not compromised;
4. That all possible care and forethought were exercised in the preparation;
5. That vigor and determination were shown in the execution.[60]

Churchill's prepared statement was so long that the aging head of the commission, Earl Cromer, became exhausted and was "taken to his bed."[61] In fact, it seemed that Churchill had revived the tactic of exhausting his opponents through the force and length of his debate just as he had with Fisher at the Admiralty.

When the commission recalled Churchill a week later, they questioned him on his and Fisher's roles in planning the operation. The members were clearly skeptical about the First Sea Lord's inconsistent behavior, and Churchill was quick to betray his old friend. Churchill claimed that he had been unaware of Fisher's reservations and that the admiral had multiple opportunities to express these doubts by speaking in a cabinet meeting or drafting a memo for the record detailing his position. According to Churchill, Fisher had not been overruled but had been a key architect of the Dardanelles plan.[62] While Churchill's comments were incredibly self-serving, they were all essentially true and would serve him well.

In the weeks that followed, the commission questioned other key participants, including Fisher, about their roles in the Dardanelles operations. Their evidence was frequently confusing and contradictory, but they did not directly refute Churchill's account. Fisher claimed that he had reservations about the soundness of the plan but supported Churchill out of loyalty. Once the decision to attack through the Dardanelles had been made, the admiral did his best to be a dutiful subordinate and worked "Totus Porcus" to ensure that the plan had the best chance possible for success.[63] Statements such as these made it very difficult for the Dardanelles Commission to reach any firm conclusions about either Churchill's or Fisher's culpability or negligence.

The commission published its initial findings in 1917 and its final report in 1919.[64] The reports highlighted flaws within the planning process but neither explicitly blamed nor exonerated Churchill. As General Hamilton had predicted, the biggest loser was Lord Kitchener. Although Churchill and others chose not to directly criticize Kitchener, the general's reputation was severely damaged. The commission found that Kitchener had failed to exercise proper caution or attention to detail in the planning process and that these initial failures were not promptly corrected and were compounded over time. According to the report, "Lord Kitchener did not sufficiently avail himself of the services of his General Staff, with the result that more work was undertaken by him than was possible for one man to do, and confusion and want of efficiency resulted."[65] The bureaucratic language of the report was an attempt at softening the blow, but the message was clear: Lord Kitchener had failed in his role as the head of the British Army and was responsible for the defeat.[66]

The Dardanelles Commission also concluded that Lord Fisher had not made a strong statement against the operations as he claimed to have done in January 1915.[67] This was a key point for Churchill's defense as he wanted to ensure that he could cast doubt on the entire planning process and show that he had included the Admiralty's professional staff.[68]

In addition, the commission supported Churchill's assertion that the western front had always taken precedence over the Dardanelles, noting, "We are of the opinion that, with the resources then available, success in the Dardanelles, if possible, was only possible upon [the] condition that the Government concentrated their efforts upon the enterprise and limited their expenditure of men and material in the Western theatre of war. This condition was never fulfilled."[69]

Ultimately, the reports of the Dardanelles Commission were deeply flawed and incomplete, and they reflected the fact that they were written under time pressure and political constraints.[70] While the reports clearly blamed the deceased Kitchener, they neither cleared nor convicted Churchill.

This was not the complete exoneration that Churchill had expected but rather a frustrating anticlimax. Press coverage was mixed but generally favored Churchill. His harshest critics would never alter their opinion of him, but when the final report was published in 1919, the war was over and most people simply wanted to move on with their lives.[71] In the words of Lloyd George, "Winston does not come out of it white or black. He comes out grey."[72] Unable to accept that he had not triumphed, Churchill sulked, believing that he had been wronged.[73] He took little comfort from the subsequent Mitchell Report on the operational lessons learned from the Dardanelles Campaign, which concluded that the navy's plan to neutralize Ottoman forts using old battleships was theoretically sound.[74]

To correct these perceived wrongs and tell his side of the story, Churchill did as he had done countless times before: he began to write. He helped his friend, General Hamilton, to edit his massive two-volume memoir *Gallipoli Diary*, which appeared in 1920.[75] For the next twelve years, he also poured much of his literary energy into the massive six-volume history of World War I, *The World Crisis*. Here, he not only told his version of events but finally published many of the official documents the Dardanelles Commission refused to release. While the publication of these documents and his criticism of leaders such as Asquith and Haig created controversy, the overall effect of these books was undeniably positive.[76] Churchill's eloquent prose and manipulation of history ultimately convinced many professional historians and average people alike that he was a critical and underappreciated player in the history of the conflict.[77] As one anonymous colleague aptly described the work, "Winston has written an enormous book about himself, and called it *The World Crisis*." Arthur Balfour was equally terse, claiming that he was impressed by the "autobiography disguised as a history of the universe."[78]

Minister of Munitions

Another hidden benefit of Churchill's role as a backbencher was that he did not have to tie his fortunes to the moribund Asquith government. Instead, he could be something of a free agent. He correctly guessed that David Lloyd George would be the Liberal successor to Asquith and increasingly ingratiated himself with that wing of the party. While playing the part of a patriot and a loyal Liberal, he was increasingly critical of what he, and the British public, saw as a series of failed war policies. In his disastrous speech in March, he had erred by demanding the return of Fisher to the Admiralty. Now Churchill was more patient, if only because he had no other option if he wanted any future with Lloyd George's faction of the Liberal Party.

In December 1916, the end finally came for Asquith and his coalition. While Asquith had been under pressure from both Tory and Liberal MPs, he had stubbornly held on to power and rejected various compromises by Bonar Law and Lloyd George to accept a reduced role in exchange for remaining prime minister. As Asquith's support rapidly eroded, Lloyd George's ascended. Lloyd George's promise to prosecute the war with greater energy won Unionist, Liberal, Labour, and Tory support and signaled the end for Asquith. Churchill believed that the prime minister was broken down and lacked the energy and will to properly defend himself from Lloyd George's assault, noting, "A fierce, resolute Asquith, fighting with all his powers would have conquered easily. But the whole trouble arose from the fact that there was no fierce resolute A. to win this war or any other."[79]

When Lloyd George became prime minister on December 6, his political position was uncertain. He had risen to power by betraying a colossal figure within his own party and now had to rely on the support of a diverse coalition representing the panoply of political parties. To survive, he needed to simultaneously make good on his promise to prosecute the war with greater urgency and avoid controversy that might erode his fragile coalition. While Lloyd George wanted to include Churchill in his cabinet, for the time being he could not take that risk. After six more months of waiting, Churchill finally returned to office as minister of munitions in July 1917. In this capacity, he was indispensable as his energy and enthusiasm provided a much-needed shake-up for the ministry. This efficient administration won him respect from many of the domestic critics who believed that he was little more than a reckless adventurer.

In addition to winning him praise at home, his efforts earned him accolades in the United States as American soldiers were often armed with munitions supplied by British factories. On May 10, 1919, the US War Department officially recognized Churchill with General Order 10, which formally thanked and awarded him the Army Distinguished Service Medal. The citation noted his "exceptionally meritorious and distinguished services" and observed that when "he was confronted with a task of great magnitude," he responded to the challenge: "With ability of a high order, energy, and marked devotion to duty, he handled with great success the trying problems which he was constantly confronted." These were more than empty accolades. In fact, the commander of the American Expeditionary Force, General John Pershing, traveled to the War Office in London to personally present the award to Churchill. Pershing's visit was widely reported, a fact that pleased Churchill and helped solidify his reputation as an architect of victory.[80]

A Final Scene

One day in early June 1916, Churchill arranged to meet his friend Violet Bonham Carter in a garden so that he could show her his newfound love of painting. Violet arrived on time, but as was often his fashion, Churchill arrived late.[81] Always keen to make a grand entrance, he did not disappoint. He was proceeded by several gardeners who were carrying his easel, a large canvas, his chair, and an assortment of painting supplies. Churchill followed behind attired in a white coat and a broad-brimmed hat. He dramatically observed the play of light in the garden, then instructed his men to erect his makeshift studio in his preferred location. Without another word, he began to paint.[82] This was the first time Violet ever saw her friend paint, but she quickly understood that this was much more than a passing fancy: it was something special. She realized that Churchill had found his muse and "was as happy as a child with his new toys."[83]

The sharp-witted daughter of the prime minister also noted something truly atypical about her verbose friend: it was the only thing he had ever done in silence. "When golfing, bathing, rock climbing, building sand castles on the beach, even when playing bezique or bridge he talked. . . . But he painted silently, rapt in the intense appraisal, observation, assessment of the scene."[84]

For months, Violet had worried about the mental health of her friend. She had seen him grapple with frustration and depression before, but nothing compared to the past year.

That year had put an enormous strain on their relationship. Churchill's break with her father and his self-imposed exile to the trenches made Violet question her ability to help her friend in his time of need. Now, seeing him paint, she relaxed.[85] As Churchill painted, he seemed oblivious to the world around him. The only interruption was the occasional rumble of shellfire echoing from across the English Channel. This briefly broke the trance that Churchill had fallen into, and he bitterly complained about his difficulties over the past year.[86]

Violet understood her friend's anguish and did her best to calm his mood. She repeated her belief that Churchill had a star and that he would still achieve greatness. Her words did little, but she was relieved when he returned to his painting, and "[the] tension eased and the clouds lifted."[87] While Violet would later point to this painting expedition as the moment when she realized that her relationship with Churchill had permanently changed, the two would remain friends for the reminder of their lives. Violet's prediction would come true: Churchill did have a star, and the wheel of fate would ultimately turn back to his favor.

Churchill had survived his year of blood, mud, and oil paint. It was his greatest failure and his finest hour.

Conclusion

Churchill's Greatest Failure

This book has examined the worst year of Churchill's life. It has not tried to hide his impetuousness, arrogance, naivety, entitlement, anger, depression, and many other unsavory characteristics. Rather, it has argued that Churchill was a complex, deeply flawed man and that many of his failures were self-inflicted. Despite the heartbreaks during this year, he not only survived but became stronger, wiser, and more resilient. In many ways, Churchill's year of blood, mud, and oil paint was his personal finest hour. This tumultuous year had many more defeats than victories, but it ultimately helped make him the man who would endure countless more sorrows and lead his nation to victory in World War II.

Painting

In this turbulent year, Churchill discovered his love of painting almost completely by accident. This passion grew and would sustain him through some of his darkest times, but before the summer of 1915, he had had little apparent interest in fine art whatsoever. In fact, it was not until after he first experimented with painting as a forty-year-old man that Churchill visited an art museum or ever looked closely at a painting. This is surprising for a man of his social status, especially since he was born in the ancestral home of Blenheim Palace and grew up surrounded by works of art. Despite this fact, it apparently never occurred to Churchill to take art seriously until he experimented with painting in a moment of desperation and weakness, as he would later describe in almost prophetic terms:

> When I left the Admiralty at the end of May, 1915, I still remained a member of the Cabinet and of the War Council. In this position I knew everything and could do nothing. The change from the intense executive activities of each day's work at the Admiralty to the narrowly measured duties of a counsellor left me gasping. Like a sea-beast fished up from the depths, or a diver too suddenly hoisted, my veins threatened to burst from the fall in pressure. I had great anxiety and no means of relieving it; I had vehement convictions and small power to give effect to them. I had to watch the unhappy casting-away of great opportunities, and the feeble execution of plans which I had launched and in which I heartily believed. I had long hours of utterly unwonted leisure in which to contemplate the frightful unfolding of the War. At a moment when every fibre of my being was inflamed to action, I was forced to remain a spectator of the tragedy, placed cruelly in a front seat. And then it was that the Muse of Painting came to my rescue—out of charity and out of chivalry, because after all she had nothing to do with me—and said, "Are these toys any good to you? They amuse some people."[1]

While Churchill's discovery of painting may have been an unlikely happenstance, there is no doubt that it quickly become a lifelong obsession.

Painting for Churchill was similar to fighting a battle. He painted with a flamboyant and energetic style, using large brushes and brushstrokes and vibrant colors. In times of uncertainty, he could rely on painting to provide an almost complete and all-consuming outlet for his energies. During the previous months, he had dwelled on his failures, but now he could channel his thoughts and energies into attacking canvases with his big, bold, and passionate brushstrokes. Now, almost completely by accident and in the middle of the most difficult period of his life, Churchill found a creative outlet that would be a lifelong source of inspiration and diversion.

For the remainder of Churchill's life, painting would pay remarkable dividends. The Muse of Painting helped him not only through this year but through other difficult times. During these moments, Churchill relied on painting because it allowed him to rest and forget the stress of writing, politics, finances, or personal tragedy. When Churchill despaired, he painted. For example, after the death of his mother, Jennie, and daughter Marigold in 1921, Churchill turned to painting to help him grieve.[2] Similarly, his Wilderness Years constituted the single most prolific period for Churchill as an artist as he was out of office and in desperate need of comfort and relaxation.[3] In the wilderness, Churchill was struck by a car, lost almost his entire fortune in the stock market crash, was angered by Mussolini's invasion of Ethiopia and the rise of Hitler, and misplayed the Abdication Crisis. Yet, despite his many political setbacks, he almost always turned to painting as a means of finding his inner peace.[4]

After his surprise electoral defeat in July 1945, Churchill suffered from shock and depression and returned to painting with his almost fanatical energy. He retreated to Lake Como and the French Riviera, and according to his physician, Lord Moran, "he confessed tonight, he had found the solution of his troubles in his paint-box just as he had thirty years ago when he was thrown out over the Dardanelles."[5] In the immediate aftermath of this electoral defeat, he completed fifteen canvases and also began to seriously consider writing his memoirs on World War II.[6] This artistic indulgence, combined with heavier than normal smoking and idyllic surroundings, restored his spirits and provided a path for him to reengage with politics and public life.[7]

During the summer of 1939, Churchill traveled to France with his friend Paul Maze, the famous artist. They painted happily together, but Churchill understood that war clouds were gathering. Just a few days before the outbreak of the war, Churchill said to his friend, "This is the last picture we shall paint in peace for a very long time."[8] Much to his regret, Churchill was correct. He drew numerous sketches, including one of a crocodile for Stalin to demonstrate the vulnerability of the Axis forces in the Mediterranean, but only painted one canvas during World War II.[9] The war placed constant demands on Churchill, but he took pleasure in having his own paintings hung in the situation room. If he could not paint, at least he could enjoy the vivid colors of his own work and dream about happier days ahead.[10]

While not as prominent as his speeches, books, or cigars, it is hard to imagine Churchill without painting. He put enormous pressure on himself and frequently despaired when his self-imposed goals went unmet. Had he not enjoyed this outlet, it is entirely possible he never would have achieved the greatness he so passionately desired and would be a minor footnote in British history today. Instead, painting helped cure Churchill's depressive "Black

Dog" moods, allowed him to savor the beauty of the world, and helped him keep faith in his own destiny.

Although it would be an overstatement to claim that Churchill won World War II because of his love of painting, it nevertheless played a critical part in his broader success. Painting was necessary because it helped him survive the many difficult years before he became prime minister in 1940. In troubled periods such as 1915 and the Wilderness Years, Churchill had just enough patience and perspective to avoid collapsing under the weight of his own expectations. Viewed in this way, Churchill's later successes were a close-run thing. In 1915, as a forty-year-old man, he discovered an untapped passion that gave him the distraction, energy, and calm to be Winston Churchill.

Friendships

While Churchill was a rebellious child and an obnoxious young man, he was genuinely friendly, compassionate, and empathetic. He was loyal and trusting, almost to a fault, and few doubted the passionate affections in his heart. In many ways, he loved not wisely but well. He often chose friends not because they could help his career but for the simple reason that he enjoyed their company. Because of this desire to be with interesting people, Churchill had friends from across the political spectrum and in a wide range of professions, including writers, soldiers, artists, actors, businessmen, publishers, and socialites. While the importance of friends and friendship was critical to Churchill's success, this simple fact is often lost.[11]

By 1915, Winston Churchill had turned friendship into something of a fine art, but after his fall from the Admiralty, he despaired and questioned whether his friends cared about his fate. He need not have worried as his true friends remained loyal, and he was able to make new ones as well. Indeed, during this period, Churchill either strengthened or began friendships with dozens of people who would not only help him survive this most difficult time but also become essential to his future triumphs.

Churchill's relationship with Archibald Sinclair is an excellent example of how this period of adversity solidified one of his deepest personal and most useful political friendships. While these two men had been friends for over a year, it was Churchill's eventual fall from power and his decision to serve in the trenches that allowed for a reunion that made them inseparable through thick and thin. During the months when Churchill served on the front lines, they worked as a nearly perfect team, understood each other instinctually, and worried about the other's health and well-being. Churchill was the more flamboyant of the two, but he benefited from the steadying presence of the more understated Sinclair. His friend even understood that he wanted to return to politics and encouraged him to do so, although Sinclair continued to serve at the front.

Shortly after the war ended, Sinclair happily accepted Churchill's offer to serve as his secretary, a position he held from 1919 to 1921, first at the War Office and then at the Colonial Office.[12] Sensing that he was holding back his talented understudy, Churchill helped Sinclair win a seat in Parliament as a Liberal in 1922, thus beginning a public career that would continue until his death in 1970. While Churchill would leave the Liberal Party in 1924, Sinclair would remain steadfast, earning the sobriquet of "Liberal Crusader."[13] Ultimately, Sinclair would rise to the position of party leader, and despite their political differences, he and Churchill remained close friends for the rest of their lives.[14] The two men wrote hundreds of letters, borrowed books from each other's libraries, went on hunting trips to Scotland, lent polo ponies, stayed as guests at each other's homes, and exchanged political advice and gossip that could be considered compromising to their own parties.[15]

One of their greatest tests was when Sinclair joined Churchill and encouraged his Liberal followers to oppose Hitler and support rearmament. These policies won them few friends, but their mutual support and encouragement allowed them to know they were not alone and ensured they would ultimately be vindicated by history.[16] Sinclair was a key Liberal voice in opposing Neville Chamberlain's policies during the early months of World War II, and he was careful to insulate Churchill from Liberal criticisms. In May 1940, as Chamberlain became increasingly untenable as the leader of the Tory government, Sinclair helped push him out of office by signaling that he only had half-hearted support from the Liberal Party.[17] While he was careful not to overplay his hand, this behind-the-scenes maneuvering led directly to the collapse of Chamberlain and the ascent of Churchill.

After entering office, Churchill understood that he needed to form a national coalition government to provide unity and reflect the political makeup of the nation. To this end, he happily included his friend, and leader of the Liberal Party, into his government as air minister. Despite his limited knowledge of the Air Ministry, Sinclair was an effective administrator.[18] The two worked closely, and they frequently shared dinner and long evenings together just as they had in the trenches of World War I.[19] Although they faced immense public pressure and had a few disagreements, such as the fate of Air Marshal Hugh Dowding, they maintained a wonderful working relationship.[20] While Churchill often sparred with his air marshals, he always trusted Sinclair to provide candid and timely advice and to defuse tense situations between himself and the service chiefs.[21]

Perhaps Sinclair's greatest single contribution to the war was persuading Churchill not to send additional fighter squadrons to France during the first week of June 1940.[22] Churchill understood that Fighter Command was critically short of modern aircraft, but he also felt duty bound to aid the French as they fought to save their country.[23] Acting on the advice of the air marshals, Sinclair helped persuade his friend not to order additional squadrons to France. This was a difficult decision that would be proved correct in the coming weeks as France capitulated and Great Britain fought on alone. Even with these additional assets, Fighter Command was in pitifully short supply of men and machines and was stretched to the breaking point during the Battle of Britain.[24]

In addition to efficiently running the Air Ministry, Sinclair aided Churchill in his role as head of the Liberal Party. Sinclair not only supported Churchill as a replacement for Chamberlain in May 1940 but also protected his hold on power during the war by ensuring that the majority of Liberal members supported the coalition government.[25] In the early weeks of Churchill's tenure, this support was particularly critical as many insiders believed his government would quickly collapse because of his refusal to consider peace negotiations with Hitler. When the Italian Fascist leader Benito Mussolini offered to serve as a mediator between Nazi Germany and the British, many prominent Tories such as Chamberlain and Lord Halifax wanted to inquire about what terms they could obtain. Sinclair saw this as a trap and convinced Liberals to support Churchill's refusal to consider Mussolini as a fair mediator, stating, "There is no possible chance" of Britain receiving "acceptable terms" from an Axis-brokered peace treaty.[26]

In a similar manner, Sinclair and the Liberal Party refrained from openly challenging Churchill even after disasters in France, Greece, and North Africa made him potentially vulnerable. This support should not be undervalued. At the time, Churchill was not seen as the imposing figure that he is today, and Britain suffered many military defeats in the first years of his prime ministership. Because he served no fixed term, Churchill was always subject to elections and votes of no confidence and relied on support from members outside his own party. Even after the surrender of Germany, Sinclair sought to defer holding an election until after the defeat of Japan but was undermined by Clement Attlee and the Labour Party, who were unwilling to forgo an election in the name of national unity.[27] While Labour would shock the Tories with a landslide victory, Churchill always appreciated the fact that Sinclair had no part in this defeat and had remained loyal to him throughout his tenure in office.

This friendship survived the pressures of World War II, in no small part because of the shared experience serving in the trenches of World War I. During the uncertain days of the Blitz, Sinclair would even use this experience to encourage Churchill to take additional safety precautions: "One thing that worries me these days—that you stay at Downing Street without a proper shelter. This is a sad backsliding since we last made war together, when you insisted on battalion headquarters having the best shelter that was available at Lawrence [sic] Farm! You were right then but you must apply the same principle now and go and live in the War Room or somewhere where reasonable protection exists . . . [the rest of the country] would be angry as well as amazed if they knew you were not sleeping in reasonable safety."[28]

Churchill was truly blessed to have a friend like Archie Sinclair. Their lifelong commitment to each other despite their political differences is a tribute to their character and shared experiences during the uncertain days of two world wars.

In addition to Sinclair, Churchill made other strong friendships at the front, most notably Andrew Gibb and Edmund Hakewill-Smith. In later years, Churchill would happily recall the bonhomie that he shared with his comrades at the front and would continue to have both enjoyable and politically advantageous relationships with each of these men. After the war, Gibb would become something of a renaissance man. He joined the English bar; held academic positions at Edinburgh, Cambridge, and Glasgow Universities; became the outspoken leader of the Scottish Nationalist Party; and wrote over a dozen books.[29] Today, he is most remembered for his 1924 monograph, *With Winston Churchill at the Front*, which he published anonymously.[30] This short work was generally positive in its portrayal of Churchill and provides many amusing anecdotes while also corroborating some of the events mentioned in Churchill's letters and later writings about the period. While the two differed greatly on political matters, their shared experience in the trenches forged a genuine respect and admiration.

"Bomb Boy" Hakewill-Smith would also maintain a friendship with Churchill. After World War I, he remained in the army, and he rose to the rank of major general in World War II. He won many honors, served as the military head of German general Albert Kesselring's postwar trial, and was awarded countless honors, yet he would always remember his time with Churchill fondly.[31] He provided numerous interviews about the experience, and his lively storytelling helped expand the oral history of the 6th Scottish Battalion and embellish the Churchill mythos. As an admirer of Churchill's artwork, he even contacted his old battalion commander and arranged for a reproduction of his painting of Laurence Farm to be commissioned. Even as a retired general, he wrote kind words to Churchill and referred to himself humbly as Bomb Boy.[32]

In addition to making friends while serving at the front, Churchill developed close friendships with several prominent artists during the period. Of these, none were as important as those of John Lavery and his vivacious wife, Hazel, who were neighbors to the Churchills when they rented Hoe Farm during the summer of 1915. As chance would have it, Churchill was struggling with his first attempt at oil painting just as Hazel arrived for an unannounced visit. She recognized that her friend was unable to begin his work, and she encouraged him to attack the canvas and not hold back with his brushstrokes. Her strong personality and confidence were infectious, and Churchill found that, thanks to this fortuitous first lesson, he was able to unlock a lifelong passion for art. Churchill appreciated having interesting and accomplished friends who would not force him to talk about politics and would encourage and shape his burgeoning desire to paint. John welcomed Churchill into his London studio, and this soon became a place of retreat and revival. The two worked together often and even painted each other's portraits. This friendship was critical because it ignited a creative spark in Churchill when he desperately needed inspiration and diversion. This was especially important because little else seemed to be going right for him and he worried about his political future.

Hazel and John would continue to mentor and encourage Churchill until they died in 1935 and 1941, respectively.[33] They continued to shape his technique and style, introduced him to other prominent artists, vacationed together, and provided countless hours of entertainment and enjoyment, especially during Churchill's Wilderness Years.[34] When, late in life, John published his memoirs, he highlighted his experiences with Churchill and even included the portraits they painted of each other during the summer of 1915. While he could have certainly chosen portraits by more famous artists and of more famous subjects, his decision to include these paintings is a beautiful testament to the enduring friendship they shared.

Throughout this trying year, Churchill also relied heavily on the love and support of his family, particularly his wife, Clementine. While the two had always had a strong and trusting relationship, strife seemed to bring them closer together, and this crisis was no different. Interestingly, this troubling year is by far the best-documented period of their marriage. When Churchill was serving in the trenches, he poured his fears and frustrations into his letters, and a true sense of love and respect emerged from them. Clementine was quick to reply, and her letters contained unyielding support and savvy political advice. She also spent significant time and expense responding to his frequent requests for care packages containing extra clothing, equipment, and luxury items such as canned foods, cigars, and alcohol. Indeed, it is difficult to imagine that Churchill would have survived this most difficult year had he not had Clementine.

During difficult times, Winston Churchill relied on his friends. While he was occasionally manipulated by some, such as Jackie Fisher, he generally benefited from the kindness and companionship of others. Churchill was just as passionate about his friends as he was about his art or his approach to war. Much like painting, it is difficult to imagine Churchill without friends. His resilience of character during the Great War, the Wilderness Years, and 1940 were in no small way a product of his friends, who understood his flaws and his genius and were ready to stand with him.

Personal Growth

Despite his fame, success, and middle age, Churchill was still surprisingly immature and selfish as a forty-year-old man. While he had a gift for empathy and kindness, he was often so focused on his own career and thoughts that he neglected others. In the immediate aftermath of his dismissal, Churchill could still not see how and why he had failed, but he slowly gained perspective on his failures. With the help of Clementine, he eventually recognized that some of his mentors, such as Asquith and Fisher, were not to be trusted.

Rather, they were happy to use him, cast him aside, or manipulate him if it suited their purposes. This was quite a shock as he thought that his own natural brilliance had kept them enthralled and could not imagine that they would betray him. For somebody as politically savvy as Churchill to be this naive is surprising. Churchill would always be somewhat too trusting, but these betrayals made him more politically astute and calculating.

In addition, Churchill was forced to care for others in a way he had not previously done. Indeed, before taking command of his battalion, he had never commanded a large body of troops for an extended period. Now, he was responsible for approximately seven hundred souls. He quickly became a father figure to both the officers and the men. He enjoyed interacting with them, sharing hardships and packages from home, and ensuring that they had the training, equipment, provisions, and care they needed to be at their best. Churchill had always had an obsessive attention to detail, but in the trenches, it was intensely personal. He sensed that he was making a powerful connection to the men of his unit and was happy to hone his talents for care, empathy, and servant leadership.

Churchill's self-imposed exile to the trenches of the western front was also a unique opportunity to interact with and better understand the feelings of the common people. Despite being a Liberal MP representing a working-class district, Churchill had very little interaction with his constituents. His time in the trenches would be by far the longest time Churchill ever spent with lower classes, and he made the most of this opportunity.[35] As was the case with much of the political elite, Churchill saw himself as a champion of the common man, but from an appropriate distance. Before his time in the trenches, he had never lived with the working class or experienced their discomforts.[36] The closest he had come to understanding the plight of the lower classes was reading the popular work of sociology *Poverty: A Study of Town Life*, by B. Seebohm Rowntree in 1901. This groundbreaking study of institutional poverty in working-class slums had a powerful impact on the aristocratic and sheltered Churchill. Although he would have a desire to aid the less fortunate members of British society for the remainder of his life, this was no substitute for interacting with members of the working classes.[37] While in the trenches, he quickly developed a love and admiration for his Scottish troops, learning their slang, caring for their personal needs and hygiene, and gaining a fuller appreciation for the true concerns of the less privileged members of British society.

After he returned to politics, Churchill immediately became an outspoken advocate for the needs of the common soldier. Since the early 1900s, Churchill had championed the cause of the people through his support of welfare, health insurance, and public education, but now he had tangible experiences to support his policies. He immediately pushed for a series of reforms, including better equipment and steel helmets, a fairer system of computing service time and leave, and more military decorations to recognize bravery among enlisted troops.[38] All of these positions were informed by his experience of war and were unique among the ruling elite of the day.

After the war, Churchill would continue to support working-class issues such as fairer housing and support for wounded veterans. While some of his later actions, such as the return to the gold standard and the opposition to the General Strike of 1926, were less friendly to workers, Churchill truly saw himself as having unique empathy for and understanding of the common man. While many of his plans for reform were interrupted by World War II, he understood the need for improvement and supported a wide range of social programs, including the National Health Service. Although Churchill never entirely abandoned his class prejudices or foppishness, the desire to help the less fortunate was a consistent part of his character that appears to have been strengthened by his time in the trenches surrounded by working-class Scots.

In addition to this salt-of-the-earth perspective, Churchill had an opportunity to further develop his particular style of humor. In difficult times, he understood that simple acts such as smiling, telling a joke, or making a wry observation could lift his spirits and those of the people around him. Both in the political battles in London and in the mud of the trenches, Churchill did his best to remain outwardly positive and optimistic even when he questioned his own future and feared for the fate of his nation. In his instructions to the officers of his battalion, he explicitly told them to weaponize humor and positivity: "Laugh a little, & teach your men to laugh—g[e]t good humor under fire—war is a game that is played with a smile. If you can't smile grin. If you can't grin keep out of the way till you can."[39] Describing Churchill's response to these and other troubling periods, his friend Violet noted his unique ability to persuade others of his genuineness, noting, "His smile was not a mask."[40] Indeed, humor was more than an act; it was an essential element of Churchill's success, and he had ample time to perfect it during this most turbulent year.

This mix of maturity, humility, empathy for the common man, and humor would pay enormous dividends during the dark days of World War II. Churchill could not stop the bombing or rapidly reverse the flood of Axis victories, but he would rely on his ability to interact with and inspire the British people to keep fighting.[41] Visits to bomb-damaged houses, frontline troops, and factory workers were critical for maintaining fighting spirit and keeping the common people engaged in the war effort. While he could not have known it at the time, Churchill grew as a person and developed his "common touch" during this difficult period. In the tumultuous days of 1940, he had little to offer the people but "blood, toil, tears, and sweat." These direct words about the challenges of war were delivered in a manner that resonated with the people and contrasted with the upper-class politicians of the day.[42] As Churchill described his leadership of the common people, "I never gave them courage, I was able to focus theirs."[43]

Time and Distance

Winston Churchill loved nothing more than wielding power and being in the center of political debates. He adored simply being in the House of Commons, surrounded by history and political intrigue. He took great pleasure in the act of politics: giving speeches, working behind the scenes, studying issues, making deals, and leaving his mark on the history of Great Britain. To take this away from Churchill was to deprive him of something he loved more than painting, writing, or even cigars. Yet, for almost this entire twelve-month period, Churchill was politically irrelevant, and for the last half of it, he was out of office and physically distant.

While Churchill could not have known it at the time, this political irrelevance and physical distance were blessings in disguise. His sudden fall convinced many of his political rivals that he was finished, and they focused their attacks on others. This was particularly true after Churchill departed for the western front as it seemed in poor taste to criticize him while he was risking his life in the trenches. Even as his enemies held back, Churchill was emboldened by his frontline service, which allowed him to prove his bravery and provided a measure of moral superiority over those who remained safely at home.[44]

While he was away, Churchill also avoided several of the most divisive issues of the war, including conscription, the abandonment of the Dardanelles, and the future of the Asquith government. Had he remained in London, he would have certainly tried to insert himself into some of these contentious debates and would quite likely have continued to advocate his unpopular positions. Although Churchill probably would have seen these stances as principled, he could ill afford further damage to his reputation.

For example, Churchill had long favored conscription, yet it was extremely unpopular. It passed without his support because it was increasingly seen as a military necessity, but his involvement may have made passage more difficult or linked his name more closely to this unwelcome policy. Similarly, he opposed the abandonment of the Dardanelles but was consistently outvoted in the cabinet. After Lord Kitchener personally inspected the battlefields, there was no chance of the campaign continuing. Had Churchill remained, it seems likely that he would have fought unsuccessfully to save this foundering campaign and damaged his political credibility further. Finally, Churchill's departure allowed him to break with Asquith. While Churchill had long been an admirer of Asquith, over the course of the year, he increasingly felt betrayed and ultimately broke with his political mentor.[45] This was a benefit for Churchill's political future as it allowed him to switch his allegiance to the rising star of the Liberal Party, David Lloyd George, who would soon become prime minister and would eventually bring Churchill back into office as minister of munitions.

Had Churchill remained in the center of London political circles, he would have certainly tried to insert himself into the debates of the day. In doing so, he would have been forced to choose between defending Liberal policies he did not believe in or taking the risky and unpopular position of attacking his own party during a war. Given these choices, it seems likely that he would have further damaged his reputation at a time when his political fortunes were already at a very low point, and he could ill afford further disgrace. Thus, the physical distance of the western front seems to have saved Churchill from himself. While not sufficient for his later successes, being removed from politics was necessary to allow several critical issues to play out, help rehabilitate his reputation, and permit him to return to politics with increased wisdom and maturity.

Perspective on Modern War

Throughout his life, Winston Churchill had romantic and anachronistic views of war.[46] Since his early childhood, he had adored the military and dreamed of winning fame and glory in battle, and this enthusiasm never fully left him. His early games reflected this desire as he spent countless hours playing with toy soldiers, staging mock battles, giving orders to his younger brother, Jack, and dressing in military uniforms.[47] As a cadet at Sandhurst and a young junior officer, he continued to approach war with a sense of adventure and a strong desire to win fame for his exploits. His bravery and desire to see combat and prove himself were unquestioned, and he sought out opportunities for action and adventure. As a result, he had ample opportunity to test his courage, and he deserved the glory he won during campaigns in India, Sudan, and South Africa.

Even though Churchill had considerably more military experience than most members of Parliament, his views on warfare were somewhat outdated and immature by the start of World War I. Like most military experts in Great Britain, he was disproportionately influenced by the Victorian era's small wars on the fringes of the empire.[48] Except for the Boer War, these were typically one-sided affairs where the superior organization and firepower of the British Army proved decisive.[49] This string of easy victories led to arrogance and complacency, and the military bureaucracy adopted an extremely conservative mindset that was resistant to change and innovation.[50]

As First Lord, Churchill had been a technical innovator at the Admiralty, yet his views on warfare had not entirely kept pace with the times. At the outbreak of war, he was particularly poor at understanding the importance of logistics, overestimated the Royal Navy's ability to force decisive action, assumed that the British would naturally dominate the skies, and did not comprehend the extreme difficulties of conducting amphibious operations. Like most of Britain's military leaders, Churchill had much to learn. Because of his flexible mind, impressive work ethic, and passion for military subjects, he was able to quickly adapt his understanding of warfare to fit the new realities. He made many trips to the front, and he even created a scandal by abandoning his post to personally conduct the defense of Antwerp, offering to resign as First Lord and serve as a general. While he enjoyed these experiences, they were more of an impetuous and immature adventure than a serious attempt to learn the arts of war.

What Churchill experienced as a soldier on the western front was fundamentally different. There, in the mud and filth of the trenches, he could see modern war firsthand and learn in ways that would have been impossible had he not served in an active capacity. Churchill's time at the front was critical to his development as a military strategist because he had always learned best by doing. In a November 21 letter to Clementine, Churchill repeatedly referenced how much he was learning, and despite the rigors of military life, he noted, "Altogether I look forward to an extremely profitable spell of education."[51]

While he never fully abandoned his romantic vision of warfare, these experiences made a powerful impression on him and hardened him to the realities of modern conflict.[52] For example, he had seen modern artillery and automatic weapons inflict massive casualties on his Dervish foes at the Battle of Omdurman, but now he learned firsthand what it was like to be on the receiving end of such lethal firepower. He was in awe of the devastating power of modern weapons, the impersonal nature of fighting that these weapons forced upon the men, and the seeming randomness of casualties.[53] The breathtaking destructiveness of modern warfare had a powerful influence on Churchill. He now viewed warfare as something less noble and almost postmodern, noting, "The sombre wars of modern democracy chivalry finds no place. Dull butcheries on a gigantic scale and mass effects overwhelm all detached sentiment."[54]

Although war had lost much of its romantic appeal, he never stopped thinking about modern conflict and engaging in problem-solving. During these few short months, his fertile mind considered an impressive range of topics, from seemingly minor details such as the construction of fortifications and the need to properly recognize the bravery of enlisted soldiers to abstract matters of grand strategy, including the future of armored vehicles and the implications of mass armies and total war on a society.

Of particular note was Churchill's thinking on the future of the airplane and the tank, two emerging technologies that would come of age during World War II. While Churchill was so enthusiastic about airpower that he had taken flying lessons before the war, he had not experienced it as a weapon of war. Now, he could see that the Germans dominated the skies over the trenches. This inspired him to think seriously about the war-winning potential of airpower. He considered the role of strategic and tactical bombing, the need for airpower to support and inspire troops and civilians on the ground, and the ability of airpower to achieve decisive results where other technologies had failed.[55] Despite his positive public demeanor, he frequently complained about German air superiority in his letters and private conversations and could not accept that Great Britain was losing the battle for the skies.[56]

After his time at the front, he would return to London more enthusiastic than ever about airpower. As a politician, and later as minister of munitions, he would make regaining air superiority one of his primary goals, and airpower would play a major role in the Allied victories in both world wars.

Although Churchill had helped fund several early experiments on armored vehicles during his time as First Lord of the Admiralty, his role as the "inventor" of the tank has been greatly exaggerated.[57] Nevertheless, his time in the trenches inspired him to consider technological means for breaking the stalemate. After only a few days in the lines, he could comprehend that new strategies and technologies were needed, and he became an early proponent of armored vehicles. On his own initiative, he drafted a paper proposing a plan to break the stalemate and intended to present this paper to his friend General French, who was the commander of the British Expeditionary Force. When French was replaced by General Haig, Churchill nevertheless persisted, broke the typical chain of command, and presented this original piece of strategy to the new British commander.

Churchill's paper argued for concentrating force at decisive points and using airpower and armored vehicles to achieve a breakthrough, but unfortunately, Haig did not have the technical or political means to implement this bold plan. When the British did start delivering tanks to combat units, Churchill implored Haig and Asquith to not commit them to battle until there were sufficient numbers to achieve decisive results. Churchill's plan was not implemented, and the British wasted the critical element of surprise and squandered another opportunity to achieve victory. Witnessing failures such as these forced Churchill to conclude that many of the top British generals were unimaginative and uninspiring.[58] For example, while attending a briefing about the failed attack on Loos, he quipped that the lesson to be learned was "Don't do it again!"[59] While this was typical of Churchill's brash and presumptuous nature, the fact is that, in a few short months, he had gained a new appreciation for an array of military topics, including mass armies, the increased lethality of modern weapons, the need for mass production, the importance of airpower and armor, and the need for inspired and charismatic leadership.

During the interwar years, Churchill frequently wrote and reflected on the lessons of World War I. While much of this was done for self-serving reasons, he carefully considered the past with an eye toward applying his perspective to future conflicts. As Maurice Ashley noted, this was a significant advantage: "The historical lessons were learned in the second world war; and that they were so learned was due at least in part to the clear, if understandably partial, account of what had happened set out in *The World Crisis*. Seldom do historians fulfill as useful a purpose as that."[60]

During World War II, Churchill's knowledge of modern warfare was imperative to the survival of Britain and the ultimate victory of the Allies. He was able to provide active leadership from his first day as prime minister thanks in no small part to the fact that he had experienced and anticipated many of the problems of modern war. He had more combat experience than many British generals and most American generals at the start of the war, was quick to brag about his experiences, and was not shy about expressing his opinions.[61] While this upset some of the professional soldiers, Churchill believed that his energy and experience were necessary to break the British military out of the complacency and defeatism that had afflicted it during World War I and again in the early months of World War II.[62] As a war leader, Churchill was certainly not perfect.[63] He made his share of mistakes, had fanciful schemes, and often seemed to contradict his own maxims on warfare.[64] Yet, despite these flaws, it is nearly impossible to imagine how any of Britain's alternatives would have been better prepared or could have produced superior results.[65]

Thanks in no small part to his experiences during World War I, Churchill was ready to lead during the second. Churchill understood the all-encompassing reality of total war on an industrial scale. He pushed for conscription, the full incorporation of women into the military and workforce, and the rational management of Britain's human capital.[66] Churchill was an early advocate for airpower and was able to understand and adapt British aerial strategy during the Battle of Britain, the Blitz, and the strategic bombing campaign. Churchill understood the new technology of tanks as a means of breaking the stalemate of the trenches and restoring mobility to the battlefield.[67] Churchill understood the importance of committing all important decisions to writing so that he could force clarity of thought, maintain a paper trail, and avoid mission creep as in the Dardanelles.[68] Churchill possessed an active and flexible mind for military affairs and adapted his thinking to the changing realities of modern war. Despite his flaws, Winston Churchill was the statesman best prepared to lead Great Britain during its "Finest Hour."

Churchill's Finest Hour

In June 1940, Winston Churchill spoke to a nation facing disaster and offered little more than courageous words and his personal reassurance that Britain could still win. At the end of a speech where he candidly discussed the failures of the British and their allies, he concluded with perhaps the most famous sentence he ever crafted: "Let us therefore brace ourselves to our duties, and so bear ourselves that, if the British Empire and its Commonwealth last for a thousand years, men will still say, 'This was their finest hour.'"[69] This sentence not only galvanized a nation but effectively summarizes Churchill's approach to life. Countless times, Churchill faced disaster, defeat, and despair. Yet he doggedly persevered and overcame. His triumphs were greater and sweeter because he had faced failure.

From May 1915 to May 1916, Churchill experienced the most difficult defeat of his entire life. It was a year defined more by its lows than its highs, and he was lucky to simply survive. However, this year gave him painting, friendship, personal growth, time and distance, and a foundational perspective on modern warfare. This was the year that made Winston Churchill the man who kept the spark of freedom alive a quarter century later, in 1940. We would be wise to learn from this story of failure, growth, and redemption.

It was his most difficult year and his finest hour.

Acknowledgments

This book was simultaneously the easiest and the hardest to write of my four to date. It was simple because I had a fantastic story to tell, excellent support from the University Press of Kentucky, and the love and inspiration of my family, most notably our newest addition, Claudia Ann Daniel. It was the most difficult because the COVID-19 pandemic deprived me of the things I like most about writing. I was pained to miss the opportunity to travel, be with friends, peruse libraries and archives, and simply have a sense of routine and normalcy.

Despite physical distance, I could not have completed this work without the following people who loved me and were invested in my success and happiness: Alicia Allison, Dannielle Andrews, Martha Baden, Natalie Baker, Lawson Berry, Mary Berry, Scott Bloom, Jon "Bubba" Ehret, Tom "T-dawg" Foley, Elliott Fullmer, Ty Groh, Leanne Harworth, Michael Jones, Steven Mathena, Bob McKenzie, Sarah Moxey, Natalie O'Neal, Reg Parker, Tom Perkins, Brianna "Gibson" Rade, Brian Smith, and Tatianna Verswyvel. I owe you all a profound debt of gratitude.

I would like to extend special thanks to my wife of over fifteen years, Christina Capacci-Daniel. You truly are my best friend, my one true love, and my raison d'être.

This book is dedicated to my daughter, Claudia, who showed me the true meaning of courage. She was born two months early during the middle of a global pandemic. She was medevaced by helicopter to Phoenix when she was only an hour old. She struggled with life-threatening medical issues and a major surgery. She never stopped fighting, and now she is a beautiful and healthy girl. One day while I was alone in a Phoenix hotel waiting my turn to visit the NICU, I thought of how she was fighting. Churchill's "never surrender" speech entered my mind, and I began pacing around the hotel room, (mis)quoting the speech and thinking of my daughter. I knew then that I would write a book about Churchill and dedicate it to her. In my darkest hour, she inspired me to never surrender.

Notes

Introduction

1. John Lukacs, *Five Days in London: May 1940* (New Haven, CT: Yale University Press, 1999), 82, 102.
2. Martin Gilbert, *Winston Churchill's War Leadership* (New York: Vintage Books, 2003), 37.
3. Winston S. Churchill, *The Gathering Storm* (Boston: Houghton Mifflin, 1948), 599.
4. Ibid., 601.
5. Churchill seems to have been exaggerating this scene for dramatic effect. In addition, he also got the date of this meeting wrong in his memoir, incorrectly stating that it occurred on May 10, when it took place on May 9. Years after Churchill's death, his ghostwriter and fact-checker, William Deakin, told the historian Andrew Roberts that this part of Churchill's narrative should "not be taken seriously." See John Kelly, *Never Surrender: Winston Churchill and Britain's Decision to Fight Nazi Germany in the Fateful Summer of 1940* (New York: Scribner, 2015), 136–37; Jonathan Rose, *The Literary Churchill: Author, Reader, Actor* (New Haven, CT: Yale University Press, 2014), 288.
6. Raymond Callahan, *Churchill and His Generals* (Lawrence: University Press of Kansas, 2007), 7. Interestingly, this was the only time that Churchill's bodyguard, Walter Thompson, ever saw his boss afraid. Tom Hickman, *Churchill's Bodyguard* (London: Headline, 2006), 91. See also Robert Rhodes James, *Churchill: A Study in Failure, 1900–1939* (New York: World Publishing, 1970), 379–80.
7. For the best treatment on this, see James, *Churchill: A Study in Failure*. See also Victor Wallace Germains, *The Tragedy of Winston Churchill* (London: Hurst and Blackett, 1931); Boris Johnson, *The Churchill Factor: How One Man Made History* (New York: Riverhead Books, 2014), 35–38; John Lukacs, *Blood, Toil, Tears, and Sweat: The Dire Warning; Churchill's First Speech as Prime Minister* (New York: Basic Books, 2008), 18–19.
8. Brian Lavery, *Churchill: Warrior, How a Military Life Guided Winston's Finest Hours* (Oxford: Casemate, 2017), 8. Churchill would later claim that he graduated

"eighth in [his] batch of a hundred and fifty," in his 1930 memoir, *My Early Life*. Whether this was a purposeful misstatement or a simple accident remains unknown, but it does not diminish this first major accomplishment. Winston S. Churchill, *My Early Life: A Roving Commission* (London: Thornton Butterworth, 1930), 73.

9. Con Coughlin, *Churchill's First War: Young Winston at War with the Afghans* (New York: Thomas Dunne, 2014); Carlo D'Este, *Warlord: A Life of Winston Churchill at War, 1874–1945* (New York: Harper Collins, 2008), 89–97; Philip Ziegler, *Omdurman* (New York: Alfred Knopf, 1974), 44–45, 55, 86, 93, 100, 115, 149–59.

10. Although Churchill's military exploits were impressive, there is a school of thought that they were largely irrelevant, or even counterproductive, during World War II. According to this view, these experiences were relics from Victorian colonial wars and were from the perspective of a brave but relatively unimportant subaltern. See Callahan, *Churchill and His Generals*, 7; David Reynolds, *In Command of History: Churchill Fighting and Writing the Second World War* (New York: Random House, 2005), 244.

11. On Churchill's early status as a public hero, see Candice Millard, *Hero of the Empire: The Boer War, a Daring Escape, and the Making of Winston Churchill* (New York: Doubleday, 2016). On Churchill as a best-selling author, see Peter Clarke, *Mr. Churchill's Profession: The Statesman as Author and the Book That Defined the "Special Relationship"* (London: Bloomsbury, 2012). On Churchill's remarkable influence over the modern world in just a year and a half as secretary of state for the colonies, see David Stafford, *Oblivion or Glory: 1921 and the Making of Winston Churchill* (New Haven, CT: Yale University Press, 2019). On the question of Ireland, see Paul Bew, *Churchill and Ireland* (Oxford: Oxford University Press, 2016), 95, 97; Mary Cogan Bromage, *Churchill and Ireland* (Notre Dame, IN: University of Notre Dame Press, 1964), 25–100; D. M. Leeson, *The Black and Tans: British Police and Auxiliaries in the Irish War of Independence, 1920–1921* (Oxford: Oxford University Press, 2011), 31–32. On the Middle East, see Christopher Catherwood, *Churchill's Folly: How Winston Churchill Created Modern Iraq* (New York: Carroll and Graf, 2004); David Fromkin, *A Peace to End All Peace: The Fall of the Ottoman Empire and the Creation of the Modern Middle East* (New York: Henry Holt, 1989). On Churchill's unique political résumé, see Martin Gilbert, *Churchill: A Life* (New York: Henry Holt, 1991), xiv.

12. James, *Churchill: A Study in Failure*. According to James, it is too common to focus on the period of Churchill as an untouchable figure in world politics and to forget that he had a rapid and meritorious rise to prominence from 1900 to 1915 and a series of failures, setbacks, and frustrations from 1915 to 1939.

13. See respectively Paul Addison, *Churchill on the Home Front, 1900–1955* (London: Pimlico, 1993), 233–86; James Ashley Morrison, *England's Cross of Gold: Keynes, Churchill, and the Governance of Economic Beliefs* (Ithaca, NY: Cornell University Press, 2021); Arthur Herman, *Gandhi & Churchill: The Epic Rivalry That Destroyed an Empire and Forged Our Age* (New York: Bantam, 2008); Alexander Larman,

The Crown in Crisis: Countdown to the Abdication (New York: St. Martin's, 2021); Robert Paul Shay Jr., *British Rearmament in the Thirties: Politics and Profits* (Princeton, NJ: Princeton University Press, 1977); Tim Bouverie, *Appeasement: Chamberlain, Hitler, Churchill, and the Road to War* (New York: Tim Duggan Books, 2019).

14. On the importance of experience, see Gilbert, *Winston Churchill's War Leadership*, 3.

15. Violet Bonham Carter, *Winston Churchill: An Intimate Portrait* (New York: Harcourt, Brace, and World, 1965), 6–7.

16. Germains, *Tragedy of Winston Churchill*, 11.

17. Paul Johnson, *Churchill* (New York: Viking, 2009), 41.

18. Martin D. Pugh, "Asquith, Bonar Law and the First Coalition," *Historical Journal* 17, no. 4 (December 1974): 813–36.

19. Lavery, *Churchill*, 235; Sonia Purnell, *Clementine: The Life of Mrs. Winston Churchill* (New York: Viking, 2015), 86.

20. Sarah Churchill, *Keep on Dancing: An Autobiography* (New York: Coward, McCann and Geoghegan, 1981), 14.

21. Arthur J. Marder, *From Dreadnought to Scapa Flow* (Oxford: Oxford University Press, 1966), 2:259.

22. Indeed, an early and damning claim that Churchill was dangerous was advanced in 1912 by the influential publicist and essayist A. G. Gardiner, who warned, "You may cast the horoscope of anyone else; his [Churchill's] you cannot cast. You cannot cast it because his orbit is not governed by any known laws, but by attractions that deflect his path hither and thither. . . . 'Keep your eye on Churchill' should be the watchword of these days. . . . He will write his name big on our future. Let us take care he does not write it in blood." James, *Churchill: A Study in Failure*, 61.

23. Gilbert, *Churchill: A Life*, 361.

24. Winston's wife, Clementine, also was a victim of this abuse as she was frequently taunted with shouts of "Gallipoli!" Purnell, *Clementine*, 81.

25. Christopher M. Bell, *Churchill and the Dardanelles* (Oxford: Oxford University Press, 2017), 331; Gilbert, *Churchill: A Life*, 459.

26. Unfortunately, the dichotomy of failure or genius still dominates the popular understanding of the Dardanelles and is unfortunate as both extremes are incorrect caricatures. Bell, *Churchill and the Dardanelles*, 3.

27. Graham T. Clews, *Churchill's Dilemma: The Real Story behind the Origins of the 1915 Dardanelles Campaign* (Santa Barbara, CA: Praeger, 2010).

28. Addison, *Churchill on the Home Front*, 278–79. On the power of analogies and their use and misuse, see Yuen Foong Khong, *Analogies at War: Korea, Munich, Dien Bien Phu, and the Vietnam Decisions of 1965* (Princeton, NJ: Princeton University Press, 1992).

29. Addison, *Churchill on the Home Front*, 278–79.

30. Gilbert, *Churchill: A Life*, 613.

31. Ibid., 290–93.

1. The Dardanelles Disaster

1. Bell, *Churchill and the Dardanelles*, 69.
2. The Allies lost six predreadnought battleships (one French and five British) and the Ottomans two. Lawrence Sondhaus, *The Great War at Sea: A Naval History of the First World War* (Cambridge: Cambridge University Press, 2014), 184. For an excellent overview of the rise of Mustafa Kemal, see Andrew Mango, *Ataturk: The Biography of the Founder of Modern Turkey* (New York: Overlook, 2002), 156–65, 172.
3. Michael Shelden, *Young Titan: The Making of Winston Churchill* (New York: Simon and Schuster, 2013), 319.
4. CHAR 13/46/7-14, CHAR 13/46/24-25, and CHAR 13/46/32-36. See also Clews, *Churchill's Dilemma*; Jeffrey D. Wallin, *By Ships Alone: Churchill and the Dardanelles* (Durham, NC: Carolina Academic Press, 1981), 15, 57, 78, 81.
5. Pritt Buttar, *Collision of Empires: The War on the Eastern Front in 1914* (Oxford: Osprey, 2014); Dennis E. Showalter, *Tannenberg: Clash of Empires, 1914* (London: Brassey's, 2004).
6. Martin Gilbert, *Winston S. Churchill*, vol. 3, *The Challenge of War, 1914–1916* (Boston: Houghton Mifflin, 1971), 143, 159, 170, 177, 184.
7. Stephen Roskill, *Churchill and the Admirals* (New York: William Morrow, 1978), 32–33.
8. Sean McMeekin, *The Ottoman Endgame: War, Revolution, and the Making of the Modern Middle East, 1908–1923* (New York: Penguin, 2015), 163; Marder, *From Dreadnought to Scapa Flow*, 2:203–4.
9. For an intriguing revisionist argument that the Allies' primary objective was to open the Dardanelles to shipments of Russian grain and that Churchill's role in planning the operations has been significantly overstated, see Nicholas A. Lambert, *The War Lords and the Gallipoli Disaster: How Globalized Trade Led Britain to Its Worst Defeat of the First World War* (Oxford: Oxford University Press, 2021).
10. George H. Cassar, *Asquith as War Leader* (London: Hambledon, 1994), 34, 50; Gilbert, *Winston S. Churchill*, 3:231.
11. Andrew Roberts, *Churchill: Walking with Destiny* (New York: Viking, 2018), 196.
12. Gilbert, *Winston S. Churchill*, 3:226; Douglas S. Russell, *Winston Churchill, Soldier: The Military Life of a Gentleman at War* (London: Brassey's, 2005), 354.
13. Sondhaus, *Great War at Sea*, 119.
14. Winston S. Churchill, *The World Crisis, 1915* (London: Thornton Butterworth, 1923), 18–20. Churchill had a long history of opposing frontal assaults; see Lavery, *Churchill*, 19–20, 85. See also Winston S. Churchill, *The Story of the Malakand Field Force: An Episode of the Frontier War* (London: Longman, 1898).
15. In *The World Crisis*, Churchill underscored the moral obligation to aid Russia as a driving force behind the decision to attack the Dardanelles. While this contains an element of truth, it was clearly self-serving. Robin Prior, *Churchill's "World Crisis" as History* (Beckenham: Croom Helm, 1983), 38–40.

16. Robin Prior, *Gallipoli: The End of the Myth* (New Haven, CT: Yale University Press, 2009), 11.

17. This was not the first time Churchill took an interest in the Ottoman Empire. As a young officer serving in India, he had dreamed of traveling to this exotic land, requested to travel to observe the Greco-Turkish War as a newspaper correspondent, and schemed about sending Greek troops to attack the Ottomans earlier in World War I. Gilbert, *Churchill: A Life*, 68–69, 71; Geoffrey Penn, *Fisher, Churchill, and the Dardanelles* (Barnsley: Leo Cooper, 1999), 110.

18. As early as January 2, Kitchener was thinking along these lines. Before the War Council meeting, he had written Churchill that he believed that a naval attack was the best way to relieve pressure on Russia. C. F. Aspinall-Oglander, *Military Operations: Gallipoli* (London: William Heinemann, 1929), 1:52–53.

19. McMeekin, *Ottoman Endgame*, 163

20. Eugene Rogan, *The Fall of the Ottomans: The Great War in the Middle East* (New York: Basic Books, 2015), 130.

21. This fact was even acknowledged in the British official history. Aspinall-Oglander, *Military Operations: Gallipoli*, 1:53.

22. McMeekin, *Ottoman Endgame*, 152–53, 163–66; Rogan, *Fall of the Ottomans*, 128–30; Tim Travers, *Gallipoli 1915* (Stroud: Tempus, 2001), 20.

23. Interestingly, Grand Duke Nicholas did not inform the British of the improved Russian situation. Marder, *From Dreadnought to Scapa Flow*, 2:203.

24. Prior, *Churchill's "World Crisis" as History*, 54–55.

25. Prior, *Gallipoli*, 242.

26. McMeekin, *Ottoman Endgame*, 119, 178, 191. Churchill had already planned a series of strikes using torpedo boats sent rapidly through the Dardanelles to sink the *Goeben* as early as August 1914. These were rejected on the grounds that they were impractical and that Britain was not yet at war with the Ottoman Empire. Christopher M. Bell, *Churchill and Sea Power* (Oxford: Oxford University Press, 2013), 61. Ultimately, repairs to the SMS *Goeben* would be so delayed that many of its guns would be stripped and sent, along with guns from the cruiser SMS *Medjedieh*, to augment the Dardanelles defenses. These guns and additional naval mines were secretly added to the Dardanelles defenses on the evening of March 5–6, 1915. The untimely impact of the *Goeben* on Allied military planning far surpassed its actual importance as a fighting ship. Sondhaus, *Great War at Sea*, 367.

27. Rogan, *Fall of the Ottomans*, 131–32.

28. Ibid., 133.

29. McMeekin, *Ottoman Endgame*, 166–68. On the challenges of airpower facing both sides, see Sterling Michael Pavelec, *Airpower over Gallipoli, 1915–1916* (Annapolis, MD: Naval Institute Press, 2020).

30. On the issue of the Royal Navy not prioritizing mines and minesweeping during the early months of the war, see Marder, *From Dreadnought to Scapa Flow*, 2:70–77.

31. Bell, *Churchill and the Dardanelles*, 69.

32. Bell, *Churchill and Sea Power*, 63–64, 74; Lambert, *War Lords and the Gallipoli Disaster*, 219; Prior, *Gallipoli*, 34.

33. Rogan, *Fall of the Ottomans*, 94. See also Aspinall-Oglander, *Military Operations: Gallipoli*, 1:32–36; Mustafa Aksakal, *The Ottoman Road to War in 1914: The Ottoman Empire and the First World War* (Cambridge: Cambridge University Press, 2008), 136–37.

34. Alan Moorehead, *Gallipoli* (New York: Harper, 1956), 45.

35. Bell, *Churchill and the Dardanelles*, 51–81; Gilbert, *Winston S. Churchill*, 3:234–37, 259–60, 262–65, 268–270.

36. Arthur J. Marder, ed., *Fear God and Dread Nought: The Correspondence of Admiral of the Fleet Lord Fisher of Kilverstone* (London: Johnathan Cape, 1959), 3:117. See also Aspinall-Oglander, *Military Operations: Gallipoli*, 1:54.

37. Marder, *Fear God and Dread Nought*, 3:121.

38. Ibid., 3:132–33

39. Ibid., 3:180–81.

40. Barry Gough, *Churchill and Fisher: Titans at the Admiralty* (Barnsley: Seaforth, 2017), 327.

41. Marder, *Fear God and Dread Nought*, 3:194–95.

42. Moorehead, *Gallipoli*, 51.

43. Gough, *Churchill and Fisher*, 330; Lambert, *War Lords and the Gallipoli Disaster*, 168, 195.

44. Germains, *Tragedy of Winston Churchill*; Penn, *Fisher, Churchill, and the Dardanelles*, 117, 126–27.

45. Prior, *Churchill's "World Crisis" as History*, 60–61, 74–75.

46. Gough, *Churchill and Fisher*, 154–55.

47. Prior, *Churchill's "World Crisis" as History*, 60.

48. Ibid., 71.

49. Churchill, *World Crisis, 1915*, 102.

50. Prior, *Churchill's "World Crisis" as History*, 60.

51. Bell, *Churchill and Sea Power*, 339.

52. For a prominent example of a confidant's candid reflections on the difficulty of working with Churchill, see Arthur Bryant, ed., *The Turn of the Tide: A History of the War Years Based on the Diaries of Field-Marshal Lord Alanbrooke, Chief of the Imperial General Staff* (New York: Doubleday, 1957); Arthur Bryant, ed., *Triumph in the West: A History of the War Years Based on the Diaries of Field-Marshal Lord Alanbrooke, Chief of the Imperial General Staff* (New York: Doubleday, 1959).

53. C. E. W. Beam, *Official History of Australia in the War of 1914–1918*, vol. 1, *The Story of ANZAC: From the Outbreak of the War to the End of the First Phase of the Gallipoli Campaign, May 4, 1915* (Sydney: Angus and Robertson, 1921), 201; Ted Morgan, *Churchill: Young Man in a Hurry, 1874–1915* (New York: Simon and Schuster, 1982), 533. It is also worth noting that the Gallipoli Campaign created a powerful strain on Britain's relations with Australia, New Zealand, and India. See

Richard Toye, *Churchill's Empire: The World That Made Him and the World He Made* (New York: Henry Holt, 2010), 132, 160.

54. Morgan, *Churchill: Young Man in a Hurry*, 533.
55. Bonham Carter, *Winston Churchill*, 8.
56. Marder, *From Dreadnought to Scapa Flow*, 2:201.
57. Prior, *Gallipoli*, 69–70; Wallin, *By Ships Alone*, 33–34.
58. Bell, *Churchill and the Dardanelles*, 73.
59. Gough, *Churchill and Fisher*, 332.
60. Anthony Tucker-Jones, *Churchill, Master and Commander: Winston Churchill at War, 1895–1945* (Oxford: Osprey, 2021), 74.
61. The Australian Official History is particularly critical of Churchill on this point. C. E. W. Beam, *Official History of Australia in the War of 1914–1918*, 1:169–71, 175–76, 200, 392, 604; C. E. W. Beam, *Official History of Australia in the War of 1914–1918*, vol. 2, *The Story of ANZAC: From 4 May to the Evacuation* (Sydney: Angus and Robertson, 1924), 172, 431n1.
62. Gilbert, *Winston S. Churchill*, 3:314–15.
63. Julian S. Corbett, *Naval Operations*, vol. 2, *A History of the Great War Based on Official Documents* (London: Longmans, Green, 1921), 178–83.
64. After the disastrous action of March 18, the British commander, Admiral de Robeck, admitted that the mine threat was greater than anticipated and described this as an impediment to forcing the straits. Penn, *Fisher, Churchill, and the Dardanelles*, 158.
65. Corbett, *Naval Operations*, 2:166–169.
66. Ibid., 2:209.
67. CHAR 2/88/54.
68. Marder, *From Dreadnought to Scapa Flow*, 2:244–46.
69. CHAR 13/65/89; Gough, *Churchill and Fisher*, 335; Marder, *From Dreadnought to Scapa Flow*, 2:244.
70. CHAR 13/65/94.
71. CHAR 13/65/96-97.
72. Pavelec, *Airpower over Gallipoli*, 42–43.
73. See official coded messages to the Admiralty describing the detection of mines on March 14 and a "good aerial record of the minefields today [March] 16th." CHAR 13/65/78; CHAR 13/65/93. See also Aspinall-Oglander, *Military Operations: Gallipoli*, 1:96–100; Marder, *From Dreadnought to Scapa Flow*, 2:247–48. According to General Hamilton, during the planning phase, he asked Kitchener how many modern airplanes he would have at his disposal, and he received the curt reply, "*Not one!*" While this may be an accurate account of their interaction, the documentary record clearly proves that airplanes were available for reconnaissance purposes at an early stage of the campaign. Ian Hamilton, *Gallipoli Diary* (London: Edward Arnold, 1920), 1:8.
74. Corbett, *Naval Operations*, 2:216.

75. Ibid., 217; Marder, *From Dreadnought to Scapa Flow*, 2:246; Sondhaus, *Great War at Sea*, 175.

76. Gilbert, *Winston S. Churchill*, 3:351, 354; Marder, *From Dreadnought to Scapa Flow*, 2:247; Sondhaus, *Great War at Sea*, 176.

77. Marder, *From Dreadnought to Scapa Flow*, 2:246.

78. Corbett, *Naval Operations*, 2:221.

79. Ibid., 2:222.

80. Sondhaus, *Great War at Sea*, 176.

81. The exact time of the sinkings is unknown as the British were not able to see the two mortally wounded ships as they departed, and when the destroyer *Jed* returned to the area to scuttle the ships, they had both sunk. Marder, *From Dreadnought to Scapa Flow*, 2:247.

82. Aspinall-Oglander, *Military Operations: Gallipoli*, 1:91.

83. Despite their limited fighting power, the British had mobilized an incredible forty-one of these obsolete predreadnought battleships by October 1914. Sondhaus, *Great War at Sea*, 119.

84. Marder, *From Dreadnought to Scapa Flow*, 2:237.

85. Rogan, *Fall of the Ottomans*, 141–42.

86. Bell, *Churchill and the Dardanelles*, 164.

87. Rogan, *Fall of the Ottomans*, 142.

88. Bell, *Churchill and the Dardanelles*, 169.

89. Churchill had first met the then colonel Hamilton while on leave from India to attend Queen Victoria's Diamond Jubilee in May 1897. The two met on the boat to England, and despite their twenty-year age difference and gap in rank, they quickly became friends. Churchill enjoyed Hamilton's abilities as a storyteller and was aware that his new friend was the head of musketry training for the British Army in India and a potential future general. The two would maintain their friendship and would cross paths frequently, from the battlefields of the Boer War to the society of London. Morgan, *Churchill: Young Man in a Hurry*, 88; Russell, *Winston Churchill, Soldier*, 155–56.

90. Liman von Sanders, *Five Years in Turkey* (Annapolis, MD: US Naval Institute Press, 1927), 58. See also Rogan, *Fall of the Ottomans*, 143.

91. Prior, *Gallipoli*, 72–128.

92. Sondhaus, *Great War at Sea*, 178–81, 185.

93. Kitchener and Fisher died in 1916 and 1920, respectively. Russell, *Winston Churchill, Soldier*, 355.

94. It has been argued that Churchill's navy-only plan led to the subsequent failures of the ground campaign because he "waited too long before he sought, in any emphatic way, a military force with which to support his naval operations. . . . He allowed the War Council to believe the fleet could achieve much more by itself than it was ever reasonable to expect." Clews, *Churchill's Dilemma*, xviii.

95. Cassar, *Asquith as War Leader*, 21; Pugh, "Asquith, Bonar Law and the First Coalition," 813–36.

96. Cassar, *Asquith as War Leader*, 3–4, 32–33, 208.

97. Michael Brock, ed., *H.H. Asquith: Letters to Venetia Stanley* (Oxford: Oxford University Press, 1983).

98. Pugh, "Asquith, Bonar Law and the First Coalition," 813–36.

99. J. E. Edmonds and G. C. Wynne, *History of the Great War Based on Official Documents: Military Operations France and Belgium, 1915 Winter 1914–1915; Battle of Neuve Chapelle, Battle of Ypres* (London: MacMillan, 1927), 28, 55; George H. Cassar, *The Tragedy of Sir John French* (Newark: University of Delaware Press, 1985), 227–30.

100. Somewhat counterintuitively, artillery finally restored movement in the last year of the war when German planners began to rely on shorter, more accurate barrages, tactics born in large part from resource constraints. See Bruce I. Gudmundsson, *Stormtroop Tactics: Innovation in the German Army, 1914–1918* (New York: Praeger, 1989); David T. Zabecki, *Steel Wind: Colonel Georg Bruchmüller and the Birth of Modern Artillery* (Westport, CT: Praeger, 1994).

101. Cassar, *Asquith as War Leader*, 84–85.

102. Edmonds and Wynne, *History of the Great War: Battle of Neuve Chapelle, Battle of Ypres*, 78, 83–87.

103. Ibid., 151.

104. J. E. Edmonds, *History of the Great War Based on Official Documents: Military Operations France and Belgium, 1915; Battles of Aubers Ridge, Festubert, and Loos* (London: MacMillan, 1928), 52–55.

105. Ibid., 44–82.

106. Stephen E. Koss, *Asquith* (London: Allen Lane, 1976), 188–89.

107. Ibid., 181.

108. Cassar, *Asquith as War Leader*, 87; Koss, *Asquith*, 181–82.

109. Stephen E. Koss, "The Destruction of Britain's Last Liberal Government," *Journal of Modern History* 40, no. 2 (June 1968): 257–77.

110. R. J. Q. Adams, *Arms and the Wizard: Lloyd George and the Ministry of Munitions, 1915–1916* (College Station: Texas A&M University Press, 1978), 32–35.

111. Cassar, *Asquith as War Leader*, 93.

112. Peter Fraser, "British War Policy and the Crisis of Liberalism in May 1915," *Journal of Modern History* 54, no. 1 (March 1982): 1–26.

113. For a range of interpretations of Churchill and French as possible sources for the Shell Crisis story, see Koss, "Destruction of Britain's Last Liberal Government," 257–77; William Manchester, *The Last Lion, Winston Spencer Churchill: Visions of Glory, 1874–1932* (Boston: Little Brown, 1983), 556; Roberts, *Churchill: Walking with Destiny*, 213.

114. Cassar, *Tragedy of Sir John French*, 240–43.

115. Koss, "Destruction of Britain's Last Liberal Government," 257–77.

116. Churchill, *World Crisis, 1915*, 115.

117. Germains, *Tragedy of Winston Churchill*, 225–26; Roskill, *Churchill and the Admirals*, 29.

118. Gough, *Churchill and Fisher*, 510.
119. Marder, *From Dreadnought to Scapa Flow*, 2:278–79.
120. Gough, *Churchill and Fisher*, 278; Marder, *From Dreadnought to Scapa Flow*, 2:267; Moorehead, *Gallipoli*, 45.
121. Marder, *From Dreadnought to Scapa Flow*, 2:267–68, 277–78.
122. Because many of the relevant documents regarding Churchill and the Dardanelles were not declassified until the 1960s, *The World Crisis* dominated the historiography for two generations. Bell, *Churchill and the Dardanelles*, 318, 323, 350.
123. Gilbert, *Winston S. Churchill*, 3:435–36; Jan Morris, *Fisher's Face: Or, Getting to Know the Admiral* (New York: Random House, 1995), 266.
124. Churchill attached a brief cover letter to Fisher informing him that he could still discuss the decision. This indicates that Churchill knew that he was going behind Fisher's back and wanted to appear to be transparent. Gilbert, *Winston S. Churchill*, 3:436.
125. Morris, *Fisher's Face*, 266–67. For the two submarines, see Gough, *Churchill and Fisher*, 377; Marder, *From Dreadnought to Scapa Flow*, 2:277–78; Robert K. Massie, *Castles of Steel: Britain, Germany, and the Winning of the Great War at Sea* (New York: Random House, 2003), 485.
126. CHAR 13/57/27; Marder, *Fear God and Dread Nought*, 3:228.
127. Massie, *Castles of Steel*, 485.
128. Morris, *Fisher's Face*, 267.
129. Ibid.
130. Koss, "Destruction of Britain's Last Liberal Government," 257–77.
131. Bell, *Churchill and the Dardanelles*, 175.
132. Even Fisher's generally sympathetic biographer, Jan Morris, believed that his erratic behavior tarnished his legacy permanently. Morris, *Fisher's Face*, 269.
133. George V, a former navy man, noted, "He [Fisher] should have been hanged at the yardarm for desertion of his post in the face of the enemy," and added, "It really was a most scandalous thing which ought to be punished with dismissal from the service and degradation." Massie, *Castles of Steel*, 489.
134. Marder, *From Dreadnought to Scapa Flow*, 2:283.
135. Gough, *Churchill and Fisher*, 382.
136. Mark Pottle, ed., *Champion Redoubtable: The Diaries and Letters of Violet Bonham Carter, 1914–1945* (London: Weidenfeld and Nicolson, 1998), 50–51 (emphasis in the original).
137. Gough, *Churchill and Fisher*, 378; Lavery, *Churchill*, 235.
138. Cassar, *Asquith as War Leader*, 94; Morris, *Fisher's Face*, 268.
139. Pottle, *Champion Redoubtable: The Diaries and Letters of Violet Bonham Carter, 1914–1945*, 51.
140. Ibid. (emphasis in the original).
141. CHAR 13/57/118-119; Marder, *Fear God and Dread Nought*, 3:228–29.
142. Marder, *Fear God and Dread Nought*, 3:230–31 (emphasis in the original).
143. CHAR 13/57/114-115; Marder, *Fear God and Dread Nought*, 3:233–34.

144. Marder, *Fear God and Dread Nought*, 3:234.
145. Massie, *Castles of Steel*, 487.
146. Pugh, "Asquith, Bonar Law and the First Coalition," 813–36.
147. Pottle, *Champion Redoubtable: The Diaries and Letters of Violet Bonham Carter, 1914–1945*, 52 (emphasis in the original).
148. Bell, *Churchill and the Dardanelles*, 186–87.
149. Marder, *Fear God and Dread Nought*, 3:237–38; Morris, *Fisher's Face*, 268–69.
150. Bell, *Churchill and the Dardanelles*, 178–82.
151. CHAR 2/153/39-41; Marder, *Fear God and Dread Nought*, 3:241–43; Morris, *Fisher's Face*, 270–71.
152. Gough, *Churchill and Fisher*, 390–91.
153. Bell, *Churchill and the Dardanelles*, 181–82.
154. Exacerbating Asquith's difficulties was the fact that the British press was generally pro-Fisher. Penn, *Fisher, Churchill, and the Dardanelles*, 189.
155. For letters of support, see Marder, *Fear God and Dread Nought*, 3:243–47.
156. Penn, *Fisher, Churchill, and the Dardanelles*, 192.
157. Marder, *Fear God and Dread Nought*, 3:247. See also Penn, *Fisher, Churchill, and the Dardanelles*, 193.
158. Bonham Carter, *Winston Churchill*, 8.
159. Cassar, *Asquith as War Leader*, 3–4, 32–33, 208.
160. Adams, *Arms and the Wizard*, 29.
161. Ibid., 28.
162. Koss, *Asquith*, 188–89.
163. Cassar, *Asquith as War Leader*, 95.
164. Ibid., 106–7.
165. Reynolds, *In Command of History*, 38.
166. Morgan, *Churchill: Young Man in a Hurry*, 526.
167. Shelden, *Young Titan*, 315.
168. Cassar, *Asquith as War Leader*, 2.
169. Max Aitken, *Politicians and the War: 1914–1916* (London: Thornton Butterworth, 1928), 32–33.
170. While noting her father's weakness, Violet turns her blame primarily on his rival Bonar Law, claiming that he could have easily ended this political witch hunt. Bonham Carter, *Winston Churchill*, 324.
171. Cassar, *Asquith as War Leader*, 34–36.
172. Brock, *H.H. Asquith: Letters to Venetia Stanley*; Cassar, *Asquith as War Leader*, 99; Koss, *Asquith*, 186.
173. Christopher Bell makes a convincing case that the Tories understood that Asquith was vulnerable and would have demanded the removal of Churchill regardless of the outcome at the Dardanelles. Bell, *Churchill and the Dardanelles*, 2. See also Johnson, *Churchill*, 53.
174. Cassar, *Asquith as War Leader*, 96.

175. Gilbert, *Winston S. Churchill*, 3:459, 464.

176. Pottle, *Champion Redoubtable: The Diaries and Letters of Violet Bonham Carter, 1914–1945*, 53.

177. Ibid.

178. Ibid., 54. In 1911 upon his appointment to First Lord of the Admiralty, Churchill confided to Violet Asquith, "This is a big thing—the biggest thing that has ever come my way—the chance I should have chosen before all others. I shall pour into it everything I've got." Russell, *Winston Churchill, Soldier*, 348. See also Robert K. Massie, *Dreadnought: Britain, Germany, and the Coming of the Great War* (New York: Random House, 1991), 748–49.

179. Bell, *Churchill and the Dardanelles*, 186.

180. Shelden, *Young Titan*, 310, 318. In addition to upsetting the public, Churchill's adventure to Antwerp also caused him to miss the birth of his daughter Sarah, a fact she mentioned with some peevishness in her 1981 autobiography. Churchill, *Keep on Dancing*, 13.

181. Shelden, *Young Titan*, 318.

182. Russell, *Winston Churchill, Soldier*, 357.

183. Roskill, *Churchill and the Admirals*, 50.

184. Prior, *Churchill's "World Crisis" as History*, 132; Addison, *Churchill on the Home Front*, 178.

185. Churchill, *My Early Life*, 176–85; Winston S. Churchill, *The World Crisis, 1911–1914* (London: Thornton Butterworth, 1923), 233–35.

186. Churchill, *My Early Life*, 186–210; Ziegler, *Omdurman*, 86, 93, 115.

187. Winston Churchill, *The River War: An Historical Account of the Reconquest of the Soudan*, vol. 1 (London: Longmans, Green, 1899); Winston Churchill, *The River War: An Historical Account of the Reconquest of the Soudan*, vol. 2 (London: Longmans, Green, 1899); Ziegler, *Omdurman*, 7, 19.

188. Bonham Carter, *Winston Churchill*, 27; Roberts, *Churchill: Walking with Destiny*, 59; Russell, *Winston Churchill, Soldier*, 231–33; Ziegler, *Omdurman*, 186, 215.

189. Trevor Royle, *The Kitchener Enigma: The Life and Death of Lord Kitchener of Khartoum, 1850–1916* (London: Michael Joseph, 1985), 296.

190. Churchill, *World Crisis, 1915*, 374–75.

191. Johnson, *Churchill*, 42–43.

192. Churchill, *World Crisis, 1911–1914*, 234–35; Royle, *Kitchener Enigma*, 296.

193. Writing in 1965, Violet said she believed these were the happiest years of her friend's life, including World War II. Bonham Carter, *Winston Churchill*, 190; Roskill, *Churchill and the Admirals*, 20.

194. Shelden, *Young Titan*, 319.

195. Ibid.

196. Despite being vindicated by Kitchener and history, Churchill had no legal authority to mobilize the fleet before the outbreak of war, a fact that he would later admit to his rival Bonar Law. Bell, *Churchill and the Dardanelles*, 30.

197. Gilbert, *Winston S. Churchill*, 3:468; Morgan, *Churchill: Young Man in a Hurry*, 529; Bonham Carter, *Winston Churchill*, 334.

198. CHAR 14/1, CHAR 14/2; Gilbert, *Winston S. Churchill*, 3:468.
199. Morgan, *Churchill: Young Man in a Hurry*, 535.
200. During much of his career, Churchill was desperately short of cash and deeply in debt. Remaining in the Asquith cabinet was a major boost to his finances as the members pooled their salaries and split them evenly. While the Duchy of Lancaster had an authorized pay of £2,000 per year, the pooled rate was £4,360 per year, a very high income for the period. CHAR 1/120/38; David Lough, *No More Champagne: Churchill and His Money* (New York: Picador, 2015), 109.
201. Royle, *Kitchener Enigma*, 326–33.
202. Churchill, *World Crisis, 1915*, 375–76.
203. Russell, *Winston Churchill, Soldier*, 357.
204. CHAR 14/1.
205. Morgan, *Churchill: Young Man in a Hurry*, 535.
206. Churchill, *My Early Life*, 48, 240, 317, 373, 381.
207. CHAR 13/52/110; Churchill, *World Crisis, 1915*, 379–80.
208. Piers Brendon, *Churchill's Menagerie* (Cambridge: Pegasus Books, 2019), 78.
209. In an unusually personal attack, Churchill vented his frustrations by claiming that his rival owed ascension to the top of British politics entirely to the nepotism of his uncle Lord Salisbury. According to Churchill's peevish prose, "But Mr. Balfour had not felt inclined to begin his reign by an act of abdication, he was still less disposed to have power wrested from his grasp. . . . In this unpleasant situation Mr. Balfour maintained himself for two whole years. Vain the clamor for a general election, vain the taunts of clinging to office, vain the solicitations of friends and the attempts of foes to force a critical issue. The Prime Minister remained immovable, inexhaustible, imperturbable; and he remained Prime Minister." Churchill, *World Crisis, 1911–1914*, 28–29.
210. Gilbert, *Churchill: A Life*, 49.
211. Ibid., 309.
212. Gilbert, *Winston Churchill's War Leadership*, 36–37.

2. The Political Outcast

1. CHAR 14/1; Gilbert, *Winston S. Churchill*, 3:482–85.
2. For an example of this more charitable approach, see Churchill, *World Crisis, 1915*, 384. Here, Churchill claims: "I was treated with much consideration by the new Cabinet. I continued to sit in my old place on Lord Kitchener's left hand. I was nominated to serve on the committee of nine Ministers which, under the title of the Dardanelles Committee, was virtually the old War Council. I was invited to prepare statements on the situation, both naval and general, and every faculty was placed at my disposal by the Admiralty for marshalling and checking the facts." While Churchill may have continued to sit in his old seat and serve on various committees, he was clearly not as powerful as he had

once been. He likely chose to distort the historical record in his memoirs for two reasons: to appear less churlish and to seem more actively involved in the war than he was.

3. Gilbert, *Churchill: A Life*, 319.
4. Bell, *Churchill and the Dardanelles*, 188.
5. Ibid., 187.
6. Gilbert, *Churchill: A Life*, 319.
7. Ibid., 321.
8. Churchill, *World Crisis, 1915*, 378.
9. Ibid., 379.
10. Ibid., 387.
11. Ibid., 389–90.
12. Penn, *Fisher, Churchill, and the Dardanelles*, 207.
13. Rogan, *Fall of the Ottomans*, 189.
14. Churchill, *World Crisis, 1915*, 394.
15. Marder, *From Dreadnought to Scapa Flow*, 2:291–92. For a fascinating account of how Churchill gradually lost touch with the shifting economic and social dynamics of his Dundee constituency, see William M. Walker, *Juteopolis: Dundee and Its Textile Workers, 1885–1923* (Edinburgh: Scottish Academic Press, 1979), 440–44, 483.
16. CHAR 9/52; Robert Rhodes James, ed., *Winston S. Churchill: His Complete Speeches, 1897–1963*, vol. 3, *1914–1922* (New York: Chelsea House, 1974), 2378–84.
17. CHAR 2/66/60; CHAR 2/66/65; CHAR 2/66/67-68; CHAR 2/67/7-8; CHAR 2/67/10-15; CHAR 2/67/18-19; CHAR 2/67/21-22; CHAR 2/67/25; CHAR 13/53/6.
18. Bell, *Churchill and the Dardanelles*, 188–89.
19. Churchill, *World Crisis, 1915*, 394.
20. Gerard J. De Groot, *Liberal Crusader: The Life of Sir Archibald Sinclair* (New York: New York University Press, 1993), 8–9.
21. Ibid., 9.
22. Ibid.
23. Ibid.
24. J. E. B. Seely, *Adventure* (London: William Heinemann, 1930), 220.
25. De Groot, *Liberal Crusader*, 10–12.
26. Ian Hunter, ed., *Winston and Archie: The Letters of Sir Archibald Sinclair and Winston S. Churchill, 1915–1960* (London: Politicos, 2005), 12–13. See also De Groot, *Liberal Crusader*, 12–13.
27. De Groot, *Liberal Crusader*, 13–14.
28. Ibid., 14.
29. McMeekin, *Ottoman Endgame*, 250.
30. Churchill, *World Crisis, 1915*, 396.
31. Ibid., 396–97.

32. Ibid., 399.
33. Ibid., 401–8.
34. Ibid., 407–8.
35. Gilbert, *Churchill: A Life*, 322.
36. Hunter, *Winston and Archie: The Letters of Sir Archibald Sinclair and Winston S. Churchill*, 17–18 (emphasis in the original); De Groot, *Liberal Crusader*, 14.
37. CHAR 1/120/38.
38. Gilbert, *Churchill: A Life*, 322; Lough, *No More Champagne*, 109–10. For her part, Goonie Churchill was also cash-strapped during this period, complaining in an undated letter from 1915 that "to have no money is the devil." CHAR 28/135/13.
39. Gilbert, *Winston S. Churchill*, 3:493–94.
40. Martin Gilbert, ed., *The Churchill Documents*, vol. 7, *"The Escaped Scapegoat": May 1915–December 1916* (Hillsdale: Hillsdale College Press, 2008), 1042; Gilbert, *Winston S. Churchill*, 3:501; Gilbert, *Churchill: A Life*, 322. While peas were rather simple fare, they were one of Winston's favorite foods. Cita Stelzer, *Dinner with Churchill: Policy Making at the Dinner Table* (New York; Pegasus Books, 2013), 172; Lough, *No More Champagne*, 109–10.
41. Mary Soames, *Winston Churchill: His Life as a Painter, a Memoir by His Daughter* (New York: Viking, 1990), 19.
42. David Coombs and Minnie Churchill, *Sir Winston Churchill's Life through His Paintings* (London: Chaucer, 2003), 22; Morgan, *Churchill: Young Man in a Hurry*, 539.
43. Churchill, *My Early Life*, 45–46.
44. Morgan, *Churchill: Young Man in a Hurry*, 539–40.
45. Ibid., 540.
46. Roberts, *Churchill: Walking with Destiny*, 20.
47. Russell, *Winston Churchill, Soldier*, 26.
48. Gilbert, *Churchill: A Life*, 24; Coombs and Churchill, *Sir Winston Churchill's Life through His Paintings*, 15. On Churchill's dislike of school, see Churchill, *My Early Life*, 15–57.
49. Russell, *Winston Churchill, Soldier*, 49.
50. Lavery, *Churchill*, 8.
51. Rose, *Literary Churchill*, 99; Soames, *Winston Churchill: His Life as a Painter*, 17.
52. Roberts, *Churchill: Walking with Destiny*, 13; Russell, *Winston Churchill, Soldier*, 107.
53. Soames, *Winston Churchill: His Life as a Painter*, 17.
54. Winston S. Churchill, *Painting as a Pastime* (New York: Cornerstone Library, 1965), 14.
55. Ibid., 7.
56. Ibid., 8.
57. Coombs and Churchill, *Sir Winston Churchill's Life through His Paintings*, 22.
58. Lough, *No More Champagne*, 110.
59. Churchill, *Painting as a Pastime*, 15.

60. Ibid., 17.

61. Churchill would later say that he believed that God was a genius for making the sky blue and trees green as they would not be as aesthetically pleasing if the colors were reversed. Jonathan Sandys and Wallace Henley, *God & Churchill: How the Great Leader's Sense of Divine Destiny Changed His Troubled World and Offers Hope for Ours* (Carol Stream, IL: Tyndale House, 2015), 208.

62. Churchill, *Painting as a Pastime*, 17.

63. Ibid.

64. Soames, *Winston Churchill: His Life as a Painter*, 20.

65. Sinéad McCoole, *Hazel: A Life of Lady Lavery, 1880–1935* (Dublin: Lilliput, 2015); John Lavery, *The Life of a Painter* (Boston: Little Brown, 1940), 182. Churchill's daughter Mary believed that the Laverys influenced her father's views on Ireland. While the Laverys were passionate about the cause, arguing that fifty years and ten million casualties would not stop the Irish, Churchill argued for compromise. Nevertheless, he "welcomed the unofficial viewpoint," and this political difference did not alter their friendship. In fact, Lavery even opened his London home to an unusual meeting among Churchill, the IRA gunman Michael Collins, and the Unionist leader James Craig, which led to a series of agreements between this trio of statesmen. Soames, *Winston Churchill: His Life as a Painter*, 42–43. See also Bew, *Churchill and Ireland*, 8, 103, 116, 133, 136; CHAR 2/135/106; CHAR 2/136/30-34; CHAR 2/152/93; Stafford, *Oblivion or Glory*, 242–44, 247.

66. Soames, *Winston Churchill: His Life as a Painter*, 17. In the 1920s, Churchill would receive similar advice from one of his many mentors, the postimpressionist painter Walter Sickert. Soames, *Winston Churchill: His Life as a Painter*, 14.

67. Churchill, *Painting as a Pastime*, 17.

68. Coombs and Churchill, *Sir Winston Churchill's Life through His Paintings*, 12.

69. Churchill, *Painting as a Pastime*, 18–19.

70. Ibid., 19; Carl von Clausewitz, *On War*, ed. and trans. Michael Howard and Peter Paret (Princeton, NJ: Princeton University Press, 1976), 101–2, 112, 578, 606, 634. Churchill's friend Violet Bonham Carter also highlighted this comparison in her description of Churchill's passion for painting. Bonham Carter, *Winston Churchill*, 382. For an interesting comparison of Churchill and Clausewitz from a philosophical perspective, see John von Heyking, *Comprehensive Judgment and Absolute Selflessness: Winston Churchill on Politics as Friendship* (South Bend, IN: St. Augustine's Press, 2018), 143–52.

71. Churchill, *Painting as a Pastime*, 20.

72. Ibid., 21.

73. For an art connoisseur's view that the sensitivity of these paintings disproves the warmonger thesis, see Coombs and Churchill, *Sir Winston Churchill's Life through His Paintings*, 12.

74. Churchill, *My Early Life*, 226–27.

75. Coombs and Churchill, *Sir Winston Churchill's Life through His Paintings*, 9.

76. Ibid., 26.

77. Soames, *Winston Churchill: His Life as a Painter*, 46.
78. Ibid.
79. Coombs and Churchill, *Sir Winston Churchill's Life through His Paintings*, 157.
80. Soames, *Winston Churchill: His Life as a Painter*, 46, 48. Despite Montag's and others' efforts, Churchill never liked one of the most notable artists of the era, Pablo Picasso. P. Johnson, *Churchill*, 146; David Reynolds, *The Long Shadow: The Legacies of the Great War in the Twentieth Century* (New York: W. W. Norton, 2014), 344.
81. On the difficulty of security personnel adapting to Churchill's erratic moods and schedule, see Hickman, *Churchill's Bodyguard*.
82. This is something of a contrast to Churchill as a writer and a thinker. In fact, he frequently complained that classic thinkers and inventors were no smarter than he was; they had simply lived first and gotten the credit for their work. While this seems somewhat immature and self-indulgent, it is an excellent example of Churchill's view of himself and the fact that he was largely self-taught. Coombs and Churchill, *Sir Winston Churchill's Life through His Paintings*, 240.
83. Churchill, *Painting as a Pastime*, 19–20.
84. CHAR 1/135/35-37; CHAR 1/138/62-62; CHAR 1/138/79-80; CHAR 1/199/20; CHAR 2/237/33; CHAR 2/237/73-76; CHAR 20/193A/9; CHAR 20/198B/193-198; CHAR 20/198B/204-206. See also Coombs and Churchill, *Sir Winston Churchill's Life through His Paintings*, 27; Soames, *Winston Churchill: His Life as a Painter*, 38–39; Stafford, *Oblivion or Glory*, 49–50.
85. Paul Maze met Churchill while serving as a liaison to the British forces on the western front during World War I. Despite their difference in age, rank, and nationality, they became friends. Maze would indulge Churchill by not only assisting with his paintings but also asking him to write the preface to his memoirs. CHAR 1/256/8-9; Paul Maze, *A Frenchman in Khaki* (London: William Heinemann, 1934). See also Russell, *Winston Churchill, Soldier*, 18; Soames, *Winston Churchill: His Life as a Painter*, 14, 82.
86. Coombs and Churchill, *Sir Winston Churchill's Life through His Paintings*, 240. See also letters between Churchill and Sickert discussing painting techniques: CHAR 1/194/72-73; CHAR 1/194/82-83; CHAR 1/194/92-93.
87. Soames, *Winston Churchill: His Life as a Painter*, 84–86.
88. According to Sarah's autobiography, Nicholson was also the first person to encourage her to dance, and he helped introduce this idea to her parents, stating, "Sarah is looking for something." Churchill, *Keep on Dancing*, 38.
89. Coombs and Churchill, *Sir Winston Churchill's Life through His Paintings*, 242–45. On the concept of dazzle camouflage, see James Taylor, *Dazzle: Disguise and Disruption in War and Art* (Annapolis, MD: Naval Institute Press, 2016).
90. Coombs and Churchill, *Sir Winston Churchill's Life through His Paintings*, 242–45. An electronic search of the official Churchill archive (containing over eight hundred thousand documents) returned no results for Olsson.
91. After the end of the Great War, Professor Kerr sought credit and financial compensation for his work with dazzle painting, and he looked to Churchill for

support and assistance. Perhaps because of his newly discovered love of art or his desire for justice, Churchill was supportive of Kerr's case. It is believed that Churchill used his political influence to create the official Committee of Enquiry on Dazzle Painting to help adjudicate Kerr's and others' claims. While ultimately the committee found against Kerr and for Norman Wilkinson, this was seen by many then and now as a miscarriage of justice. Taylor, *Dazzle*, 72–87.

92. CHAR 20/22A/73.

93. Coombs and Churchill, *Sir Winston Churchill's Life through His Paintings*, 26.

94. Ibid., 26; Soames, *Winston Churchill: His Life as a Painter*, 20.

95. Lavery, *Life of a Painter*, 182.

96. Ibid.

97. Coombs and Churchill, *Sir Winston Churchill's Life through His Paintings*, 26.

98. Ultimately, Lavery chose to include sixty-nine paintings in his autobiography, sixty-seven by his own hand, one by Hazel (a portrait of George Bernard Shaw), and one by Winston Churchill. Lavery, *Life of a Painter*, list of illustrations.

99. This was the first time that one of Churchill's paintings was exhibited. Soames, *Winston Churchill: His Life as a Painter*, 23.

100. Ibid., 57.

101. Coombs and Churchill, *Sir Winston Churchill's Life through His Paintings*, 174. As early as December 1920, Churchill had refused to enter paintings into contests under his own name. CHAR 1/135/36.

102. Despite these honors, Churchill made very little money from his artwork. One minor exception was a series of images he licensed for reproduction on greeting cards. Coombs and Churchill, *Sir Winston Churchill's Life through His Paintings*, 180, 183.

103. Ibid., 150.

104. Ibid., 163; Lord Moran, *Churchill: Taken from the Diaries of Lord Moran; The Struggle for Survival, 1940–1965* (Boston: Houghton Mifflin, 1966), 90.

105. Kelly Crow, "Angelina Jolie Sells Winston Churchill Painting for $11.6 Million," *Wall Street Journal*, March 1, 2021.

106. CHAR 8/19; CHAR 8/23; CHAR 8/26; Warren Dockter, "The Influence of a Poet: Wilfrid S. Blunt and the Churchills," *Journal of Historical Biography* 10, no. 2 (Autumn 2011): 70–102.

107. Elizabeth Longford, *A Pilgrimage of Passion: The Life of Wilfrid Scawen Blunt* (London: Weidenfeld and Nicolson, 1979), 386–88, 410.

108. Ibid., 409; Shelden, *Young Titan*, 318.

109. Morgan, *Churchill: Young Man in a Hurry*, 562–64. In addition to publicly praising Churchill, Blunt would also write to congratulate him for "breaking loose from your official bondage to that gang of incapables which has been making a fool of the British Empire." Longford, *Pilgrimage of Passion*, 409.

110. Churchill, *Painting as a Pastime*, 13. Interestingly, American president George W. Bush decided to paint after reading Churchill's *Painting as a Pastime* on the advice of historian John Lewis Gaddis. In his postpresidential years, painting became a powerful source of refreshment for Bush as he painted hundreds of canvases

and published two books of his works. At the end of his first book on painting, Bush chose to reproduce Churchill's quote, "Happy are the painters, for they shall not be lonely. Light and color, peace and hope, will keep them company to the end." In addition to altering Churchill's spelling of *color*, Bush added his own view: "Churchill was right." George W. Bush, *Portraits of Courage: A Commander in Chief's Tribute to America's Warriors* (New York: Crown, 2017), 12, 190.

111. Churchill, *Keep on Dancing*, 68.

112. For two intriguing works exploring Churchill's unique psychology and its impact on his leadership, see Nassir Ghaemi, *A First-Rate Madness: Uncovering the Links between Leadership and Mental Illness* (New York: Penguin, 2011), 57–67, 119, 133, 136, 197–98, 215–17; Andrew Norman, *Winston Churchill: Portrait of a Unique Mind* (Barnsley: Pen and Sword Military, 2012).

113. See Moran, *Churchill*, 179. For Dr. Wilson's discussion of Churchill's depressive moods more generally, see 149, 151, 180, 195–96, 276, 310, 332, 336, 481, 606, 638, 679–85, 794–95, 803–4, 837.

114. Coombs and Churchill, *Sir Winston Churchill's Life through His Paintings*, 9.

115. Churchill, *Painting as a Pastime*, 31. Churchill was also interested in how memory influenced painting, an insight that inspired Sir Ernst Gombrich to explore this question in his classic work, *Art and Illusion*. Coombs and Churchill, *Sir Winston Churchill's Life through His Paintings*, 13; E. H. Gombrich, *Art and Illusion: A Study in the Psychology of Pictorial Representation*, 2nd ed. (Princeton, NJ: Princeton University Press, 1969), 38–39, 52, 181, 314.

116. Coombs and Churchill, *Sir Winston Churchill's Life through His Paintings*, 30.

117. D'Este, *Warlord*, 259.

118. Johnson, *Churchill*, 91.

119. Coombs and Churchill, *Sir Winston Churchill's Life through His Paintings*, 132.

120. In a July 24, 1945, letter to Brigadier General Raymond Brutinel, Churchill confessed, "I think you know what it meant to me to have a quiet, restful holiday—my first since the War—in such charming surroundings," and noted that he was once again able "to enjoy the relaxation of painting." CHAR 20/194B/199-200.

121. Coombs and Churchill, *Sir Winston Churchill's Life through His Paintings*, 180.

122. As a tribute to her father's love of painting and his stubbornness, after hearing of Winston's stroke, his daughter Sarah claimed, "I have a feeling he could paint with either hand." S. Churchill, *Keep on Dancing*, 234.

123. In addition to painting motions, Churchill also made cigar-smoking gestures on his death bed, much to the amusement of his family. Ibid., 336.

124. Gilbert, *Churchill: A Life*, 324.

125. Morgan, *Churchill: Young Man in a Hurry*, 539.

126. Lavery, *Churchill*, 97–120; Roberts, *Churchill: Walking with Destiny*, 160; Sondhaus, *Great War at Sea*, 47.

127. Gilbert, *Winston S. Churchill*, 3:501, 686, 690; Penn, *Fisher, Churchill, and the Dardanelles*, 219.

128. Morgan, *Churchill: Young Man in a Hurry*, 539.

129. Churchill, *World Crisis, 1915*, 464.

130. Ibid., 465.

131. Both French and Churchill had attended the Harrow school, although it appears that neither man actually enjoyed their time there, and both had an uneven academic record. Morgan, *Churchill: Young Man in a Hurry*, 306; Cassar, *Tragedy of Sir John French*, 138.

132. Gerald French, ed., *Some War Diaries, Addresses, and Correspondence of Field Marshall the Right Honble. The Earl of Ypres* (London: Herbert Jenkins, 1937), 156–58, 164–65, 174–75, 186–87, 190.

133. Churchill, *World Crisis, 1915*, 465.

134. Manfred Weidhorn, *Sword and Pen: A Survey of the Writings of Sir Winston Churchill* (Albuquerque: University of New Mexico Press, 1974), 127, 224.

135. Gilbert, *Churchill: A Life*, 323–24; Russell, *Winston Churchill, Soldier*, 357–59; Lavery, *Churchill*, 236–37.

136. Had the British committed to these assaults earlier, it is possible that they would have succeeded. However, by June, the German commander General Liman von Sanders had already anticipated such a move and was strengthening his defenses in the sector. C. F. Aspinall-Oglander, *Military Operations: Gallipoli* (London: William Heinemann, 1932), 2:158–59.

137. Penn, *Fisher, Churchill, and the Dardanelles*, 207.

138. Russell, *Winston Churchill, Soldier*, 357.

139. CHAR 1/120/28; Lough, *No More Champagne*, 110, 457n17.

140. Churchill, *My Early Life*, 253–312; Millard, *Hero of the Empire*.

141. CHAR 28/142/71; Lough, *No More Champagne*, 110.

142. Lough, *No More Champagne*, 110.

143. Purnell, *Clementine*, 89; Russell, *Winston Churchill, Soldier*, 357–58.

144. Lavery, *Churchill*, 236–37; Travers, *Gallipoli 1915*, 202.

145. Lavery, *Churchill*, 139–52.

146. Bonham Carter, *Winston Churchill*, 341.

147. Ibid.; Ian Hamilton, *Gallipoli Diary* (London: Edward Arnold, 1920), 2:24; Russell, *Winston Churchill, Soldier*, 358.

148. One practical benefit of the canceled trip was that Churchill was able to have his additional life insurance premium of £147 refunded, a development that helped relieve his strained finances. CHAR 28/142/80; CHAR 28/142/86.

149. Bonham Carter, *Winston Churchill*, 341.

150. Ibid.

151. Gilbert, *Winston S. Churchill*, 3:506.

152. Gilbert, *Churchill: A Life*, 323.

153. Prior, *Gallipoli*, 190–209; Russell, *Winston Churchill, Soldier*, 358.

154. Gilbert, *Churchill: A Life*, 324–25.

155. Bell, *Churchill and Sea Power*, 72; De Groot, *Liberal Crusader*, 14.

156. De Groot, *Liberal Crusader*, 14–15.

157. Ibid., 15.

158. Ibid., 16.

159. Maurice Ashley, *Churchill as Historian* (New York: Charles Scribner's Sons, 1968), 88–89; Gough, *Churchill and Fisher*, 410; Rogan, *Fall of the Ottomans*, 189.

160. Bell, *Churchill and Sea Power*, 72; Rogan, *Fall of the Ottomans*, 204.

161. Gilbert, *Churchill: A Life*, 326; Russell, *Winston Churchill, Soldier*, 360.

162. Gilbert, *Winston S. Churchill*, 3:540–41. The Battle of Loos also killed the war poet Charles Sorley and Rudyard Kipling's son, Jack. Reynolds, *Long Shadow*, 179, 339. See also Tonie Holt and Valmai Holt, *My Boy Jack? The Search for Kipling's Only Son* (Barnsley: Leo Cooper 1998).

163. Ultimately, this view was endorsed by the official British history of the campaign. Aspinall-Oglander, *Military Operations: Gallipoli*, 1:354–55.

164. Gilbert, *Churchill: A Life*, 327.

165. Ibid.

166. Churchill, *World Crisis, 1915*, 487.

167. During this time, Churchill also composed a short memo about the possibility of using trench mortars to better target the Ottomans defending the hilly terrain around Cape Hellas and Sari Bair. CHAR 2/74/134.

168. Penn, *Fisher, Churchill, and the Dardanelles*, 214.

169. Russell, *Winston Churchill, Soldier*, 359.

170. Penn, *Fisher, Churchill, and the Dardanelles*, 214; Prior, *Gallipoli*, 214, 217–20. For an overview of Monro's role in the campaign, see C. F. Aspinall-Oglander, *Military Operations: Gallipoli* (London: William Heinemann, 1932), 2:397–412.

171. Churchill, *World Crisis, 1915*, 489. See also Moorehead, *Gallipoli*, 314–15.

172. Bell, *Churchill and the Dardanelles*, 194.

173. Ibid., 195. Churchill's willingness to gamble for political resurrection, while shocking, is entirely consistent with the predictions of prospect theory. Rose McDermott, *Risk-Taking in International Politics: Prospect Theory in American Foreign Policy* (Ann Arbor: University of Michigan Press, 1998).

174. For Monro's official orders, see C. F. Aspinall-Oglander, "Lord Kitchener's Instructions for General Sir C.C. Monro," in *Military Operations: Gallipoli*, 2:69–70.

175. Gilbert, *Winston S. Churchill*, 3:555; Gilbert, *Churchill: A Life*, 327.

176. CHAR 2/74/137; Churchill, *World Crisis, 1915*, 487–88.

177. Churchill would repeatedly demonstrate a willingness to consider the use of gas in various other contexts, including the Russian Civil War, unrest in the Middle East, and thinly held invasion beaches in Great Britain and Ireland. Tucker-Jones, *Churchill, Master and Commander*, 11, 85–86, 93, 100, 183, 245–46; Diana Preston, *A Higher Form of Killing: Six Weeks in World War I That Forever Changed the Nature of Warfare* (New York: Bloomsbury, 2015), 236.

178. Edmonds and Wynne, *History of the Great War: Battle of Neuve Chapelle, Battle of Ypres*, 176–78; Preston, *Higher Form of Killing*, 236, 267, 273.

179. Albert Palazzo, *Seeking Victory on the Western Front: The British Army and Chemical Warfare in World War I* (Lincoln: University of Nebraska Press, 2000), 41–47.

180. See generally ibid.; Preston, *Higher Form of Killing*.

181. For an interesting analogue, Churchill also saw dumdum bullets as a necessary means of killing Britain's enemies. Despite their barbarity, he advocated for their use in several of his early works. Weidhorn, *Sword and Pen*, 29.

182. In the final months of the war, when he was serving as minister of munitions, Churchill enthusiastically expanded the British commitment to chemical weapons. Had the war continued into 1919, he planned to triple the resources dedicated to chemical weapons. Palazzo, *Seeking Victory on the Western Front*, 155–61, 193.

183. Ibid., 489.

184. Ibid., 490.

185. Ibid.

186. Bell, *Churchill and the Dardanelles*, 196.

187. Winston S. Churchill, *The World Crisis, 1916–1918, Part I* (London: Thornton Butterworth, 1927), 235–41.

188. Cassar, *Asquith as War Leader*, 148; Gilbert, *Winston S. Churchill*, 3:57.

189. R. J. Q. Adams and Philip Poirier, *The Conscription Controversy in Great Britain, 1900–18* (Columbus: Ohio State University Press, 1987), 51–61; Reynolds, *Long Shadow*, 414; Denis Winter, *Death's Men: Soldiers of the Great War* (New York: Penguin, 1979), 29.

190. Churchill, *World Crisis, 1916–1918, Part I*, 236.

191. Cassar, *Asquith as War Leader*, 149; Churchill, *World Crisis, 1916–1918, Part I*, 237.

192. Morgan, *Churchill: Young Man in a Hurry*, 549.

193. The intelligence chief, Major General Charles Caldwell, falsified the severity of the manpower shortage and lied under oath to the committee rather than betray his superior, Lord Kitchener. Morgan, *Churchill: Young Man in a Hurry*, 544.

194. Ibid., 544–45.

195. Clausewitz, *On War*, 75–126.

196. Cassar, *Asquith as War Leader*, 151–52.

197. Morgan, *Churchill: Young Man in a Hurry*, 545.

198. Ibid., 546.

199. Ibid., 546–47.

200. Addison, *Churchill on the Home Front*, 181.

201. Ibid., 181–82.

202. Cassar, *Asquith as War Leader*, 131.

203. Bonham Carter, *Winston Churchill*, 348.

204. Aitken, *Politicians and the War*, 185; Bell, *Churchill and the Dardanelles*, 196–97.

205. Bonham Carter, *Winston Churchill*, 349.

206. Morgan, *Churchill: Young Man in a Hurry*, 552.

207. In an August 3 letter to his brother, Jack, Churchill claimed that there were "so many able men in the Cabinet that it is very difficult to get anything settled." Gilbert, *Churchill Documents*, 7:1115. This dislike of large committees would be put

into practice during World War II; he would use it as a reason to keep his War Cabinet as small as possible. This was a double-edged sword that often overworked the smaller staff.

208. Morgan, *Churchill: Young Man in a Hurry*, 553.
209. Gilbert, *Churchill: A Life*, 328.
210. Bell, *Churchill and the Dardanelles*, 197.
211. Churchill, *World Crisis, 1915*, 498.
212. Gilbert, *Winston S. Churchill*, 3:561–62.
213. Bell, *Churchill and the Dardanelles*, 197–98; Gilbert, *Churchill: A Life*, 328.
214. Aspinall-Oglander, *Military Operations: Gallipoli*, 2:413–26.
215. Cassar, *Asquith as War Leader*, 132–33; Royle, *Kitchener Enigma*, 337–38, 342–43.
216. Morgan, *Churchill: Young Man in a Hurry*, 553.
217. Cassar, *Asquith as War Leader*, 134; Byron Farwell, *The Great War in Africa, 1914–1918* (New York: W. W. Norton, 1986), 251; Gilbert, *Winston S. Churchill*, 3:565–67.
218. For an overview of Churchill's attempts at political reforms on the African continent going back to his early days in politics, see Shelden, *Young Titan*, 129–36.
219. Churchill's actions probably delayed the German advance; however, his willingness to abandon his post as First Lord, rush to Belgium, commit the untested Naval Division to battle, and act as a modern warlord angered and upset many, who saw it as proof of his unstable and unreliable nature. Ibid., 310–12.
220. Churchill had first broached the subject of using armored cars in Africa as early as February 1915, but his plan had been politely refused by the minister of finance and defense, Jan Smuts. CHAR 13/69/16; CHAR 13/69/24.
221. Morgan, *Churchill: Young Man in a Hurry*, 553–54.
222. Ibid., 554.
223. Gilbert, *Churchill: A Life*, 328.
224. Farwell, *Great War in Africa*, 251–52; Tucker-Jones, *Churchill, Master and Commander*, 54.
225. James, *Churchill: A Study in Failure*, 97; Morgan, *Churchill: Young Man in a Hurry*, 554.
226. Bell, *Churchill and the Dardanelles*, 203.
227. Bell, *Churchill and the Dardanelles*, 198; Gilbert, *Winston S. Churchill*, 3:563–64; Gilbert, *Churchill: A Life*, 328.
228. Russell, *Winston Churchill, Soldier*, 359.
229. Bonham Carter, *Winston Churchill*, 349.
230. Bell, *Churchill and the Dardanelles*, 198–99.
231. Rose, *Literary Churchill*.
232. Roberts, *Churchill: Walking with Destiny*, 228.
233. CHAR 9/51; James, *Winston S. Churchill: His Complete Speeches, 1897–1963*, 3:2390–2403; Gilbert, *Churchill: A Life*, 329.

234. Gilbert, *Winston S. Churchill*, 3:569; Roberts, *Churchill: Walking with Destiny*, 228.
235. Gilbert, *Churchill: A Life*, 328.
236. James, *Winston S. Churchill: His Complete Speeches, 1897–1963*, 3:2390–2403. On the echoes between World War I and World War II, see Bonham Carter, *Winston Churchill*, 351.
237. Bonham Carter, *Winston Churchill*, 351.
238. Gilbert, *Churchill: A Life*, 329; James, *Churchill: A Study in Failure*, 97.
239. Morgan, *Churchill: Young Man in a Hurry*, 555.
240. Bell, *Churchill and the Dardanelles*, 202–3.
241. Bonham Carter, *Winston Churchill*, 351–52.
242. Ibid., 352.
243. Gilbert, *Churchill: A Life*, 328–29.
244. Gilbert, *Winston S. Churchill*, 3:784; Roskill, *Churchill and the Admirals*, 62; Russell, *Winston Churchill, Soldier*, 360.
245. Hunter, *Winston and Archie: The Letters of Sir Archibald Sinclair and Winston S. Churchill*, 24–25; De Groot, *Liberal Crusader*, 18.
246. De Groot, *Liberal Crusader*, 18.
247. Soames, *Winston Churchill: His Life as a Painter*, 24; Russell, *Winston Churchill, Soldier*, 359.
248. Winston S. Churchill, *Thoughts and Adventures* (London: Thornton Butterworth, 1932), 99; Russell, *Winston Churchill, Soldier*, 360.
249. Shelden, *Young Titan*, 321.
250. Morgan, *Churchill: Young Man in a Hurry*, 556.
251. Lough, *No More Champagne*, 111–12.
252. Ibid., 112.
253. Purnell, *Clementine*, 89.
254. Bonham Carter, *Winston Churchill*, 352.
255. Morgan, *Churchill: Young Man in a Hurry*, 556–57.
256. Ibid., 557.
257. Bonham Carter, *Winston Churchill*, 352; Gilbert, *Churchill: A Life*, 329.
258. In December 1920, Churchill registered the Colt and 150 rounds of .45-caliber ammunition with the London Police Department pursuant to the recently passed Firearms Act of 1920. In addition to this weapon, he also reported a .256 Mannlicher Sporting Rifle, a 9mm Webley automatic pistol, a .32 Webley automatic pistol, and a .450 Wilkinson revolver. CHAR 1/137/102-103.
259. Russell, *Winston Churchill, Soldier*, 361–62.
260. For example, he had previously carried an 1896 pattern "broom-handle" Mauser with soft-tipped ammunition on his campaigns in South Africa. At the time, this pistol had state-of-the-art firepower. Despite the pistol's impressive lethality, it did him little good as he lost it during his famous attempt to free an armored train from a Boer ambush. This may have been a fortunate oversight as he was opposing mounted men with rifles and would have been badly

outgunned if he had been able to fight back rather than surrender. After his capture, he decided to abandon the soft-tipped bullets, believing that they undermined his claim to be a noncombatant. See Churchill, *My Early Life*, 204, 266–67.

261. Bromage, *Churchill and Ireland*, 90.

262. Morgan, *Churchill: Young Man in a Hurry*, 557. Jennie's fear that her son would be out of shape was not unfounded, as Winston himself would frequently mention that he was tired and would occasionally note the difficulty of keeping up with younger and fitter men in his unit.

263. While Churchill budgeted £140 per month in his absence, as was so often the case, he was overly optimistic in his personal expenses. In fact, before his departure, the household expenses were closer to £220 per month, and the household frequently incurred debts of £280 per month during the time he was gone, a figure that was inflated in part by his frequent requests for food, clothing, and luxury items. Lough, *No More Champagne*, 112.

264. Cassar, *Asquith as War Leader*, 8.

265. D'Este, *Warlord*, 199, 232–33, 277, 286, 301.

266. Seely, *Adventure*, 233–34.

267. Ibid., 233–38.

268. Gilbert, *Winston S. Churchill*, 3:572.

3. The Hellish Landscape

1. Gilbert, *Winston S. Churchill*, 3:572.

2. Churchill, *Thoughts and Adventures*, 99; Gilbert, *Churchill: A Life*, 331; Russell, *Winston Churchill, Soldier*, 360.

3. Churchill, *Thoughts and Adventures*, 99.

4. Gerald French, *Some War Diaries*, 229.

5. Cassar, *Tragedy of Sir John French*, 138.

6. Churchill, *Thoughts and Adventures*, 99; Cassar, *Tragedy of Sir John French*, 20, 70–71, 80–83, 138.

7. Churchill, *Thoughts and Adventures*, 99.

8. Ibid.

9. Ibid., 100; Russell, *Winston Churchill, Soldier*, 360.

10. Churchill, *Thoughts and Adventures*, 100; Roberts, *Churchill: Walking with Destiny*, 232.

11. Even Violet Asquith believed that Churchill's actions at Antwerp and his desire to be made a major general were childish and immature. Bonham Carter, *Winston Churchill*, 274; Russell, *Winston Churchill, Soldier*, 350–54.

12. Churchill, *Thoughts and Adventures*, 100.

13. Ibid.; Russell, *Winston Churchill, Soldier*, 360.

14. Roberts, *Churchill: Walking with Destiny*, 232.

15. Frederick Ponsonby, *The Grenadier Guards in the Great War of 1914–1918*, vol. 1. (London: Macmillan, 1920); Russell, *Winston Churchill, Soldier*, 361.

16. D'Este, *Warlord*, 265–68; Ponsonby, *Grenadier Guards*, 1:23–321.

17. Ponsonby, *Grenadier Guards*, 1:322.

18. Churchill, *Thoughts and Adventures*, 100.

19. Ibid.

20. Ibid., 100–101.

21. Ibid., 101.

22. Ibid. For a brutal, self-deprecating, and exaggerated firsthand account of Churchill's struggles with school and headmasters, see Churchill, *My Early Life*, 12–56.

23. Churchill, *Thoughts and Adventures*, 101.

24. Ibid. The official unit history is similarly terse about Churchill's time with the unit, noting, "On the 20th Major the Right Hon. Winston Churchill was attached to the 2nd Battalion Grenadiers for instruction." Ponsonby, *Grenadier Guards*, 1:336. This frustration with having Churchill join the unit appears to have also been widespread. Gilbert, *Winston S. Churchill*, 3:576–78.

25. Churchill, *Thoughts and Adventures*, 101; Russell, *Winston Churchill, Soldier*, 361.

26. Churchill, *Thoughts and Adventures*, 101.

27. Ibid., 102.

28. Ibid.

29. Ibid.

30. Ibid., 103.

31. Ibid.

32. Ibid., 100.

33. Jeffreys and Churchill remained friends and exchanged greetings and political gossip until Jeffreys's death in 1960. For example, see 1932 exchange on India, CHAR 2/189/44-51; 1933 congratulations on Marlborough biography, CHAR 8/326; 1948 discussions of Grenadier Guards dinner, CHAR 2/304; various birthday greetings, CHAR 2/491A-F.

34. Roberts, *Churchill: Walking with Destiny*, 926.

35. Churchill, *Thoughts and Adventures*, 104; Roberts, *Churchill: Walking with Destiny*, 232.

36. Churchill, *Thoughts and Adventures*, 105. This passage is a small part of the Churchill mythos regarding alcohol. Although some accused him of alcoholism, he in fact drank steadily but rarely to excess. He did, however, like to exaggerate and boast about his consumption, as he believed that it would project an image of devil-may-care virility. When viewed in this context, this passage is one of many examples of Churchill seeking to promote himself through his association with the drink.

37. Gilbert, *Winston S. Churchill*, 3:579–80, 588–89.

38. CHAR 2/62/106-108.

39. Edward Grigg, *The Faith of an Englishman* (London: Macmillan, 1936); Grigg, *Britain Looks at Germany* (London: Nicholson and Watson, 1938).
40. Roberts, *Churchill: Walking with Destiny*, 233.
41. Churchill, *Thoughts and Adventures*, 105.
42. Gilbert, *Winston S. Churchill*, 3:588–89.
43. Churchill, *Thoughts and Adventures*, 105. While it would be tempting to conclude that Churchill is exaggerating these conditions for dramatic effect (or for a dig at Indians in the wake of his struggles with Gandhi and the home-rule movement), the official history of the Grenadier Guards describes the environment similarly, noting that the trenches were "all in a very bad condition—communication trenches flooded, and front-line breastworks crumbling and not bullet-proof. There was consequently a great deal of work to be done, which the incessant shelling retarded, while the weather, being cold and raw, with snow at intervals, made things generally unpleasant." Ponsonby, *Grenadier Guards*, 1:336–37.
44. Churchill, *My Early Life*, 57.
45. Churchill, *Thoughts and Adventures*, 105.
46. Russell, *Winston Churchill, Soldier*, 362.
47. Sandys and Henley, *God & Churchill*.
48. Churchill, *Thoughts and Adventures*, 106.
49. Roberts, *Churchill: Walking with Destiny*, 234.
50. Churchill, *Thoughts and Adventures*, 107–8.
51. Ibid., 108.
52. Ibid.
53. Ibid., 108–9.
54. Ibid., 109.
55. On Churchill's lack of punctuality, see Roberts, *Churchill: Walking with Destiny*, 16, 283, 682, 903.
56. Churchill, *Thoughts and Adventures*, 109.
57. Ibid.
58. Ibid., 109–10.
59. Ibid., 110.
60. Ibid.
61. Ibid.
62. Ibid.
63. Ibid.
64. Larry Arnn, *Churchill's Trial: Winston Churchill and the Salvation of Free Government*, (Nashville, TN: Nelson Books, 2015), 56; Sandys and Henley, *God & Churchill*, 56–57.
65. Purnell, *Clementine*, 92.
66. Weidhorn, *Sword and Pen*, 25, 27.
67. Russell, *Winston Churchill, Soldier*, 364.
68. Gilbert, *Churchill: A Life*, 334.

69. Russell, *Winston Churchill, Soldier*, 354.

70. Churchill once scoffed at the forty-three-year-old governor of Uganda, Hesketh Bell, saying that he would be prime minister by that age. Morgan, *Churchill: Young Man in a Hurry*, 210. He also predicted at the tender age of sixteen that he would save England. Sandys and Henley, *God & Churchill*, 3–4.

71. Morgan, *Churchill: Young Man in a Hurry*, 558–59; Shelden, *Young Titan*, 321–22. On the broader theme of Churchill's failures, see James, *Churchill: A Study in Failure*.

72. Roberts, *Churchill: Walking with Destiny*, 232–33; Seely, *Adventure*, 236.

73. Churchill, *World Crisis, 1915*, 500.

74. Ibid.

75. Ibid.

76. Purnell, *Clementine*, 94.

77. CHAR 1/118A/48-49; Purnell, *Clementine*, 92.

78. Diary of Andrew Dewar Gibb, DEP. 217/BOX 18, Diary for 1916, National Library of Scotland. For the importance of sharing food and meals in Churchill's friendships, see von Heyking, *Comprehensive Judgment and Absolute Selflessness*, 12–15; Stelzer, *Dinner with Churchill*, 173.

79. Roberts, *Churchill: Walking with Destiny*, 232.

80. Gilbert, *Churchill: A Life*, 336.

81. Gilbert, *Winston S. Churchill*, 3:573–89, 605–8.

82. French's war diary entry for December 10 is terse but mentions this decision: "The rains have been very heavy. All the rivers are in full flood. The communications trenches are flooded. I have appointed Bridges to command 19th Division (vice Tasker is gone sick) and Winston Churchill to a brigade in that division." Gerald French, *Some War Diaries*, 231–32. See also Russell, *Winston Churchill, Soldier*, 364–65.

83. Seely, *Adventure*, 236.

84. Gilbert, *Churchill Documents*, 7:1322; Russell, *Winston Churchill, Soldier*, 365.

85. Purnell, *Clementine*, 96–98.

86. For an excellent overview of the Royal Navy's shift to a distant blockade and the plan to economically strangle Germany, see Nicholas A. Lambert, *Planning Armageddon: British Economic Warfare and the First World War* (Cambridge, MA: Harvard University Press, 2012).

87. Russell, *Winston Churchill, Soldier*, 364.

88. Gilbert, *Winston S. Churchill*, 3:11, 56, 65–66, 82, 88–89, 91, 172–76, 486.

89. Unfortunately, Churchill appears to have neglected this insight when he ordered the HMS *Prince of Wales* and HMS *Repulse* into the teeth of Japanese torpedo bombers—an action that resulted in their sinking on December 10, 1941. D'Este, *Warlord*, 557–59; Martin Middlebrook and Patrick Mahoney, *Battleship: The Sinking of the* Prince of Wales *and the* Repulse (New York: Charles Scribner's Sons, 1979); Roskill, *Churchill and the Admirals*, 196–204.

90. Bonham Carter, *Winston Churchill*, 365.

91. Lavery, *Churchill*, 243; Roberts, *Churchill: Walking with Destiny*, 236.

92. D'Este, *Warlord*, 281, 288–89.

93. The need to concentrate tanks and wait to reveal them until they were technically mature and sufficiently strong was a continual theme of Churchill's but was repeatedly ignored, much to his dismay. Gilbert, *Winston S. Churchill*, 3:810.

94. Gilbert, *Churchill Documents*, 7:1303–8; Lavery, *Churchill*, 243; Roberts, *Churchill: Walking with Destiny*, 236 (emphasis in the original).

95. Clausewitz, *On War*, 163, 248, 258, 260, 391, 485–89, 595–97, 617–20, 623–24, 633–34.

96. In December 1915, Churchill's divisional commander, Lord Cavan, made extensive comments on a draft of the memo. See CHAR 2/68/63-65.

97. Walter Reid, *Architect of Victory: Douglas Haig* (Edinburgh: Birlinn, 2006), 291.

98. Lavery, *Churchill*, 170–71.

99. Churchill, *Thoughts and Adventures*, 104.

100. Cassar, *Tragedy of Sir John French*, 262–80; Edmonds, *History of the Great War: Battles of Aubers Ridge, Festubert, and Loos*, 378–401.

101. Cassar, *Tragedy of Sir John French*, 273–83.

102. Ibid., 281–86; Roberts, *Churchill: Walking with Destiny*, 237.

103. Aitken, *Politicians and the War*, 75.

104. Gilbert, *Churchill Documents*, 7:1333; Russell, *Winston Churchill, Soldier*, 365.

105. Gilbert, *Winston S. Churchill*, 3:612–26.

106. Reid, *Architect of Victory*, 251.

107. For example, shortly after the Battle of Omdurman, Haig entrusted Churchill, who was traveling by steamer to Cairo, with a personal letter to Sir Evelyn Wood that was very critical of the conduct of Lord Kitchener. While Churchill shared similar views on Kitchener, the potentially explosive contents of this letter indicate that Haig was convinced of the trustworthiness and reliability of the messenger. Reid, *Architect of Victory*, 86.

108. Gilbert, *Churchill: A Life*, 338.

109. Reid, *Architect of Victory*, 251.

110. Russell, *Winston Churchill, Soldier*, 365.

111. Gilbert, *Churchill Documents*, 1333–35; Reid, *Architect of Victory*, 252.

112. Gilbert, *Winston S. Churchill*, 3:616–17, 626–27.

113. Gilbert, *Churchill Documents*, 7:1333. Despite these peevish comments, Churchill paid a visit to Asquith a few days later while in London on Christmas leave. See Roberts, *Churchill: Walking with Destiny*, 237.

114. Gilbert, *Churchill Documents*, 7:1340; Brendon, *Churchill's Menagerie*, 273.

115. Violet acknowledged Churchill's hurt feelings but claimed that her father had her friend's bests interests at heart. Bonham Carter, *Winston Churchill*, 361.

116. Decades later, this was still a sore subject for Churchill's daughter Mary. Soames, *Winston Churchill: His Life as a Painter*, 19.

117. Reid, *Architect of Victory*, 252.

118. Russell, *Winston Churchill, Soldier*, 366; Seely, *Adventure*, 237–38.

119. Aitken, *Politicians and the War*, 76; Russell, *Winston Churchill, Soldier*, 366.

120. During World War II, Churchill suggested a similar path for redemption through military service to a disgraced MP. Roberts, *Churchill: Walking with Destiny*, 231.

121. Seely, *Adventure*, 238.

122. Gilbert, *Winston S. Churchill*, 3:589.

123. De Groot, *Liberal Crusader*, 19.

124. Gilbert, *Churchill Documents*, 7:366.

125. Russell, *Winston Churchill, Soldier*, 366.

126. Purnell, *Clementine*, 99.

127. CHAR 1/118A/1-2; CHAR 1/118B/3.

128. Gilbert, *Churchill: A Life*, 339–40.

129. D'Este, *Warlord*, 293, 327.

130. Russell, *Winston Churchill, Soldier*, 364.

131. Gilbert, *Churchill Documents*, 7:1346–48.

132. Edward Spears, *Assignment to Catastrophe, Part II: The Fall of France* (London: William Heinemann, 1954), 162.

133. Tucker-Jones, *Churchill, Master and Commander*, 81.

134. Spears, *Assignment to Catastrophe, Part II*, 162.

135. Lavery, *Churchill*, 248–49; Russell, *Winston Churchill, Soldier*, 362.

136. Gilbert, *Churchill Documents*, 7:1326–27; Russell, *Winston Churchill, Soldier*, 368.

137. Rene Kraus, *Winston Churchill in the Mirror* (New York: E. P. Dutton, 1944), 63–64. According to biographer William Manchester, "He was probably the only man in London who had more hats than his wife—top hats, Stetsons, seamen's caps, his hussar helmet, a privy counsellor's cocked hat, homburgs, an astrakhan, an Irish 'paddy hat,' a white pith helmet, an Australian bush hat, a fez, the huge beplumed hat he wore as Knight of the Garter, even the full headdress of a North American Indian chieftain. He had closets full of costumes." Manchester, *The Last Lion, Winston Spencer Churchill: Visions of Glory, 1874–1932*, 13.

138. Russell, *Winston Churchill, Soldier*, 366.

139. Winston S. Churchill, *Marlborough: His Life and Times*, vol. 1 (London: Thornton Butterworth, 1933). A particularly interesting interpretation of this book is that Churchill purposely juxtaposed the clearheaded and consistently victorious Marlborough with the plodding failures of World War I generals. See Weidhorn, *Sword and Pen*, 116–17, 222–23.

140. Gilbert, *Churchill: A Life*, 340; Russell, *Winston Churchill, Soldier*, 367.

141. John Buchan, *The History of the Royal Scots Fusiliers (1678–1918)* (London: Thomas Nelson and Sons, 1925), 41–72; Andrew Dewar Gibb, *With Winston Churchill at the Front* (Barnsley: Pen and Sword Books, 2016), 63–65.

142. In fact, Churchill would ultimately lose this "safe" seat as he was increasingly seen as out of touch with the shifting political attitudes of the people. Walker, *Juteopolis*, 440–44, 483.

143. Gilbert, *Churchill Documents*, 7:1353–55; Gibb, *With Winston Churchill at the Front*, 87; Gilbert, *Winston S. Churchill*, 3:629

144. Russell, *Winston Churchill, Soldier*, 367.

145. For the common soldier's reaction to the slaughter at Loos, see Winter, *Death's Men*, 27, 60, 70, 133, 181, 184, 196, 221, 238.

146. Gilbert, *Winston S. Churchill*, 3:628, 631, 633, 637; Roberts, *Churchill: Walking with Destiny*, 238.

147. Adams and Poirier, *Conscription Controversy in Great Britain*, 251; Russell, *Winston Churchill, Soldier*, 368.

148. Gilbert, *Churchill Documents*, 7:1353–55; Gilbert, *Winston S. Churchill*, 3:629.

149. Gibb, *With Winston Churchill at the Front*, 86–87; Lavery, *Churchill*, 245.

150. Russell, *Winston Churchill, Soldier*, 367.

151. Gibb, *With Winston Churchill at the Front*, 158. According to former prime minister Boris Johnson (a man also known for his distinctive appearance and flair for the dramatic), this may have been the only hat that Churchill did *not* like. Johnson, *Churchill Factor*, 138.

152. Gibb, *With Winston Churchill at the Front*, 93.

153. Russell, *Winston Churchill, Soldier*, 367–68.

154. Gilbert, *Winston S. Churchill*, 3:629.

155. Ibid., 599, 615, 619–20, 624–25.

156. Edward Spears, *Liaison 1914: A Narrative of the Great Retreat* (London: William Heinemann, 1930); Spears, *Prelude to Victory* (London: William Heinemann, 1939); Spears, *Assignment to Catastrophe, Part I: Prelude to Dunkirk* (London: William Heinemann, 1954); Spears, *Assignment to Catastrophe, Part II*.

157. CHAR 20/2A/6-7.

158. On Spears's role as liaison to the French government, see Julian Jackson, *The Fall of France: The German Invasion of 1940* (Oxford: Oxford University Press, 2003), 91, 98–100, 103, 134, 138–42, 180, 199, 241.

159. See the debate on unconventional warfare in Giles Milton, *Churchill's Ministry of Ungentlemanly Warfare: The Mavericks Who Plotted Hitler's Defeat* (New York: Picador, 2016), 124–25.

160. Von Heyking, *Comprehensive Judgment and Absolute Selflessness*, 7.

161. Hunter, *Winston and Archie: The Letters of Sir Archibald Sinclair and Winston S. Churchill*, 9.

162. Gilbert, *Winston S. Churchill*, 3:636.

163. Russell, *Winston Churchill, Soldier*, 368.

164. Ibid.

165. Gibb, diary entry from February 25, Diary of Andrew Dewar Gibb, DEP. 217/BOX 18, Diary for 1916, National Library of Scotland; Russell, *Winston Churchill, Soldier*, 368.

4. The Passionate Warrior

1. Gibb, *With Winston Churchill at the Front*, 58–59, 60; Philip Warner, *The Battle of Loos* (London: William Kimber, 1976).

2. Gibb, *With Winston Churchill at the Front*, 61; Gilbert, *Winston S. Churchill*, 3:630.

3. Rev. 6:5–6 (New American Bible, Revised Edition): "When he broke open the third seal, I heard the third living creature cry out, 'Come forward.' I looked, and there was a black horse, and its rider held a scale in his hand. I heard what seemed to be a voice in the midst of the four living creatures. It said, 'A ration of wheat costs a day's pay, and three rations of barley cost a day's pay. But do not damage the olive oil or the wine.'"

4. Gibb, *With Winston Churchill at the Front*, 59.

5. Gilbert, *Winston S. Churchill*, 3:632.

6. Hakewill-Smith, quoted in ibid., 632; Russell, *Winston Churchill, Soldier*, 369.

7. Buchan, *History of the Royal Scots Fusiliers (1678–1918)*, 344–45.

8. Churchill had a lifelong habit of working in bed and in the bathtub as well as a casual attitude toward nudity, habits that were shocking for many of his assistants. D'Este, *Warlord*, 282, 385, 393, 592, 620; Gilbert, *Winston Churchill's War Leadership*, 10–11.

9. Gibb, *With Winston Churchill at the Front*, 155–56.

10. Much to the frustration of his officers, Churchill would continue to insist on bayonet drills over the coming weeks. Gibb, *With Winston Churchill at the Front*, 78.

11. Gilbert, *Winston S. Churchill*, 3:632.

12. John Ellis, *Eye-Deep in Hell: Trench Warfare in World War I* (Baltimore: Johns Hopkins University Press, 1976); John Keegan, *The Face of Battle* (New York: Viking, 1976), 204–84; Winter, *Death's Men*.

13. Gilbert, *Winston S. Churchill*, 3:639.

14. Gibb, *With Winston Churchill at the Front*, 68.

15. Buchan, *History of the Royal Scots Fusiliers (1678–1918)*, 325–29.

16. While Churchill's battle with lice on the western front appears to have been a clear victory, it was by no means the last time he would fight the unwanted pests. On the contrary, during the interwar period a sow at Chartwell was infected with lice, much to his frustration, and during World War II, he attributed a bout of severe itching to lice he contracted on a visit to inspect troops in Egypt. For a detailed description, see Brendon, *Churchill's Menagerie*, 163.

17. Gibb, *With Winston Churchill at the Front*, 68–69.

18. Ibid., 59, 74–75, 77.

19. Bonham Carter, *Winston Churchill*, 362.

20. Russell, *Winston Churchill, Soldier*, 369–70.

21. Gibb, *With Winston Churchill at the Front*, 153.

22. On April 8, for example, Churchill called Asquith a "crafty, supine, pleasure-loving man." Diary of Andrew Dewar Gibb, DEP. 217/BOX 18, Diary for 1916, National Library of Scotland. See also Gibb, *With Winston Churchill at the Front*, 153–55.

23. Gibb, *With Winston Churchill at the Front*, 101. Interestingly, Churchill would become an accomplished amateur bricklayer and would enjoy the vocation so much that he even applied for membership in the bricklayer's union.

24. On the increased tactical importance of grenades in trench warfare, see Ellis, *Eye-Deep in Hell*, 77–78; Gudmundsson, *Stormtroop Tactics*, 35–36, 51, 60–61, 81, 86, 97, 101.

25. Gilbert, *Winston S. Churchill*, 3:629, 634.
26. Gilbert, *Churchill Documents*, 7:1368–70.
27. Russell, *Winston Churchill, Soldier*, 382.
28. Gilbert, *Winston S. Churchill*, 3:641.
29. Prior, *Gallipoli*, 227–36.
30. Tucker-Jones, *Churchill, Master and Commander*, 153.
31. Gilbert, *Winston S. Churchill*, 3:636.
32. Ibid.
33. Even though men were frequently exhausted, soccer and other sports were popular diversions whenever time and battle conditions allowed. Winter, *Death's Men*, 155–57.

34. Gilbert, *Winston S. Churchill*, 3:640.
35. Ibid., 3:640–41.
36. Many of Churchill's early military writings are littered with descriptions of local terrain and explanations of how these geographic features shaped the strategy and tactics of the campaign. See the almost-poetic description of the Nile River and Sudan in Winston S. Churchill, *River War: An Historical Account of the Reconquest of the Soudan*, 1:1–11.

37. Winter, *Death's Men*, 213.
38. Russell, *Winston Churchill, Soldier*, 370.
39. Ibid.
40. Gilbert, *Churchill Documents*, 7:1399. See also Lavery, *Churchill*, 245.
41. Similarly, on December 20, Churchill had written to Clementine that "as one's fortunes are reduced, one's spirit must expand to fill the void." Gilbert, *Churchill Documents*, 7:1339; Roberts, *Churchill: Walking with Destiny*, 965.

42. The classicist Edith Hall claims that one of the secrets to Spartan effectiveness on the battlefield was their sense of humor and their ability to laugh in the face of danger. See Edith Hall, *Introducing the Ancient Greeks: From Bronze Age Seafarers to Navigators of the Western Mind* (New York: W. W. Norton, 2014), 159–79.

43. Bonham Carter, *Winston Churchill*, 365.
44. Gilbert, *Winston S. Churchill*, 3:690.
45. Ibid., 3:692.
46. Gilbert, *Churchill Documents*, 7:1397.
47. Ibid., 7:1421.
48. Gibb, *With Winston Churchill at the Front*, 89.
49. Ibid., 94.
50. Churchill, *My Early Life*, 33–34. See also D'Este, *Warlord*, 5, 11–12; Roberts, *Churchill: Walking with Destiny*, 13.
51. Gibb, *With Winston Churchill at the Front*, 94.
52. Gilbert, *Churchill Documents*, 7:1397.

53. Gibb, *With Winston Churchill at the Front*, 95–96.
54. Gilbert, *Churchill Documents*, 7:1400.
55. Ibid., 7:1386.
56. Russell, *Winston Churchill, Soldier*, 370–71.
57. Gibb, *With Winston Churchill at the Front*, 99.
58. Churchill, *My Early Life*, 57.
59. Gibb, *With Winston Churchill at the Front*, 99.
60. Ibid., 100–101.
61. Gilbert, *Winston S. Churchill*, 3:635. These were not empty words, as McDavid took time from his leave in February 1916 to pay a social call on Clementine and would help schedule a reunion in 1927 when Churchill was visiting Perth, Scotland. CHAR 1/118A/61-62; CHAR 1/194/70-71.
62. Gilbert, *Churchill: A Life*, 340.
63. Roberts, *Churchill: Walking with Destiny*, 240.
64. According to the British 1914 *Manual of Military Law*, section 33: "A sentinel, for example, found asleep or drunk on his post, while on active service, would, if the character and circumstances of the offense were sufficiently grave, be liable to suffer death." War Office, *Manual of Military Law* (London: His Majesty's Stationery Office, 1914), 23. See also Roberts, *Churchill: Walking with Destiny*, 234; Winter, *Death's Men*, 43, 140.
65. Roberts, *Churchill: Walking with Destiny*, 240.
66. Gibb, *With Winston Churchill at the Front*, 141–42.
67. Ibid., 142.
68. Gilbert, *Churchill Documents*, 7:1456.
69. See statement of enlisted man Robert Fox, quoted in Gilbert, *Winston S. Churchill*, 3:637–38.
70. Roberts, *Churchill: Walking with Destiny*, 238.
71. Churchill, *Thoughts and Adventures*, 115.
72. Ibid. While this may strike some readers as creative license, there is significant evidence to support the claims that in quiet sectors of the front, actions such as sniping and artillery barrages were largely tit-for-tat reprisals for the other side initiating action first. Tony Ashworth, *Trench Warfare, 1914–1918: The Live and Let Live System* (New York: Holmes and Meier, 1980); Robert Axelrod, *The Evolution of Cooperation* (New York: Basic Books, 1984), 73–87.
73. Gilbert, *Churchill Documents*, 7:1421.
74. Churchill, *Thoughts and Adventures*, 113.
75. Ibid.
76. This is not unlike the grim statistics faced by World War II bomber crews in the early months of the strategic bombing campaign, where "only" a 2 percent attrition rate made it statistically improbable that a crew would survive their twenty-five-mission tour unharmed. See Mark K. Wells, *Courage and Air Warfare: The Allied Aircrew Experience in the Second World War* (London: Frank Cass, 1995), 103.

77. Gilbert, *Churchill Documents*, 7:1436; Roberts, *Churchill: Walking with Destiny*, 239; Russell, *Winston Churchill, Soldier*, 374.

78. Gibb, *With Winston Churchill at the Front*, 139.

79. Ellis, *Eye-Deep in Hell*, 61–62.

80. Gibb, *With Winston Churchill at the Front*, 140.

81. British infantrymen were particularly suspicious of their own artillery fire as it was often more abundant and was believed to be more dangerous than the German fire. Winter, *Death's Men*.

82. Gilbert, *Churchill: A Life*, 346.

83. Tucker-Jones, *Churchill, Master and Commander*, 82.

84. Gilbert, *Winston S. Churchill*, 3:660n1.

85. Gilbert, *Churchill Documents*, 7:1412.

86. "Orilux Trench Torch," National Trust, Chartwell Collection, https://www.nationaltrust.org.uk/chartwell/features/orilux-trench-torch, accessed April 4, 2024.

87. Tucker-Jones, *Churchill, Master and Commander*, 82.

88. Gilbert, *Churchill Documents*, 7:1419.

89. Churchill, *World Crisis, 1916–1918, Part I*, 411.

90. Stafford, *Oblivion or Glory*, 28, 146, 198.

91. Leeson, *Black and Tans*, 30–37, 45–46, 51, 55, 59–60, 97–101, 125–26, 216–17, 223, 235, 239.

92. Gilbert, *Churchill Documents*, 7:1427; Russell, *Winston Churchill, Soldier*, 372.

93. Churchill, *World Crisis, 1915*, 86–89.

94. Churchill, *Thoughts and Adventures*, 114–15. For the less dramatic version Churchill sent Clementine, see his February 20 letter: Gilbert, *Churchill Documents*, 7:1432–33.

95. Churchill, *Thoughts and Adventures*, 115.

96. Ibid.

97. Perhaps this was maturity talking, or perhaps Churchill was writing to an audience who had recently experienced the horrors of the Great War, but this demonstrates a marked break with many of his earlier writings glorifying war. Ibid., 116.

98. Ibid.

99. Ibid., 116–17.

100. Ibid., 117.

101. Ibid.

102. Ibid., 118.

103. Ibid., 118–19.

104. Ibid., 119.

105. Ibid.

106. Ibid.

107. During World War II, Churchill reproduced this humorous tale under the title "My Secret Tank Plans Were Missing"! Winston S. Churchill, "My Secret Tank Plans Were Missing," *Sunday Dispatch*, January 7, 1940; CHAR 8/665.

108. Churchill, *Thoughts and Adventures*, 120.

109. Gilbert, *Churchill Documents*, 7:1433.
110. Gibb, *With Winston Churchill at the Front*, 117.
111. Soames, *Winston Churchill: His Life as a Painter*, 25.
112. Gilbert, *Churchill: A Life*, 348; Coombs and Churchill, *Sir Winston Churchill's Life through His Paintings*, 16–17.
113. Coombs and Churchill, *Sir Winston Churchill's Life through His Paintings*, 16–17; Tucker-Jones, *Churchill, Master and Commander*, 83.
114. Coombs and Churchill, *Sir Winston Churchill's Life through His Paintings*, 20.
115. Ibid., 17.
116. Soames, *Winston Churchill: His Life as a Painter*, 25, 28. While Churchill was frequently obsessed with the proper colors in his paintings, some such as Field Marshal Harold Alexander would later criticize his painting style as too colorful, noting, "He loved colours, and used far too many. That's why his paintings are so crude. He couldn't resist using all the colours on his palette." Rose, *Literary Churchill*, 140.
117. Gilbert, *Churchill: A Life*, 349.
118. Soames, *Winston Churchill: His Life as a Painter*, 28.
119. Ibid.
120. Coombs and Churchill, *Sir Winston Churchill's Life through His Paintings*, 30; Soames, *Winston Churchill: His Life as a Painter*, 28.
121. Roberts, *Churchill: Walking with Destiny*, 239.
122. Rose, *Literary Churchill*, 140; Thomas Weber, *Hitler's First War: Adolf Hitler, the Men of the List Regiment, and the First World War* (Oxford: Oxford University Press, 2010), 123.
123. Churchill frequently remarked on the beauty of artillery barrages. Rose, *Literary Churchill*, 139.
124. Commentary notes in Gibb, *With Winston Churchill at the Front*, 107. On the importance of patrols and raiding, see Ellis, *Eye-Deep in Hell*, 72–80.
125. Russell, *Winston Churchill, Soldier*, 373–74.
126. Gilbert, *Churchill Documents*, 7:1425.
127. Gilbert, *Winston S. Churchill*, 3:658.
128. Gilbert, *Churchill Documents*, 7:1467; Russell, *Winston Churchill, Soldier*, 374.
129. Bell, *Churchill and the Dardanelles*, 211.
130. While the practice of an active-duty soldier giving a political speech during wartime may strike modern readers as unusual, this was simply a matter of course for Churchill. In fact, he had given his first major political speech on July 26, 1897, while on leave from the Boer War. Now that he was a member of Parliament with much to say about the conduct of the war, he would never allow the opportunity to publicly speak his mind pass. Russell, *Winston Churchill, Soldier*, 156.
131. Gilbert, *Winston S. Churchill*, 3:707–8.
132. Jackie Fisher was born in Sri Lanka and had dark skin and unusual facial features. Because of this, rumors that he was not of English stock but was in fact of Asian

origin followed him for his entire professional life. In the Victorian and Edwardian navy, this was a serious charge. While Churchill would sometimes jokingly refer to him as "the Old Malay," the use of this racist trope to describe his old friend indicates how angry and bent on revenge he truly was. Gough, *Churchill and Fisher*, 3; Massie, *Dreadnought*, 402–3, 428; Morris, *Fisher's Face*, 280.

133. Purnell, *Clementine*, 78–79.
134. Gilbert, *Winston S. Churchill*, 3:187.
135. Gough, *Churchill and Fisher*, 352.
136. Purnell, *Clementine*, 100.
137. Roskill, *Churchill and the Admirals*, 55.
138. Morris, *Fisher's Face*, 224–30.
139. Ibid., 280.
140. Gilbert, *Churchill: A Life*, 351.
141. Morris, *Fisher's Face*, 280.
142. CHAR 2/72/10-15.
143. Bell, *Churchill and the Dardanelles*, 211–13.
144. Gilbert, *Winston S. Churchill*, 3:711–12.
145. CHAR 2/72/45-46.
146. Cassar, *Asquith as War Leader*, 177–78.
147. Gilbert, *Winston S. Churchill*, 3:713.
148. Ibid.
149. Gilbert, *Churchill Documents*, 7:1441–42.
150. Gilbert, *Winston S. Churchill*, 3:715.
151. Ironically, Balfour was the target of both the March 7 speech and his previous speech in opposition. Ibid., 3:716.
152. CHAR 9/53; James, *Winston S. Churchill: His Complete Speeches, 1897–1963*, 3:2405–11; Gilbert, *Winston S. Churchill*, 3:716.
153. Gilbert, *Winston S. Churchill*, 3:716–722.
154. CHAR 9/53; James, *Winston S. Churchill: His Complete Speeches, 1897–1963*, 3:2405–11; Gilbert, *Winston S. Churchill*, 3:718.
155. Gilbert, *Winston S. Churchill*, 3:718–719.
156. Ibid., 719.
157. Ibid., 725.
158. CHAR 9/53; James, *Winston S. Churchill: His Complete Speeches, 1897–1963*, 3:2405–11; Gilbert, *Winston S. Churchill*, 3:721–22.
159. Marder, *From Dreadnought to Scapa Flow*, 2:398–99.
160. Penn, *Fisher, Churchill, and the Dardanelles*, 230.
161. Gilbert, *Winston S. Churchill*, 3:709, 713, 718, 721–23, 731–33.
162. Bonham Carter, *Winston Churchill*, 368.
163. Ibid.
164. Margot Asquith was a remarkable lady with an incredible wit and political instincts. In many ways, she was responsible for making her husband a national figure who would ultimately become prime minister. Massie, *Dreadnought*, 569–80.

165. Penn, *Fisher, Churchill, and the Dardanelles*, 231.
166. Gilbert, *Winston S. Churchill*, 3:726.
167. Ibid., 3:727–28.
168. Bell, *Churchill and the Dardanelles*, 214–15; Marder, *From Dreadnought to Scapa Flow*, 2:400–401.
169. Bell, *Churchill and the Dardanelles*, 216.
170. CHAR 2/72/16-27; CHAR 2/72/52-54.
171. This was not the first time that Churchill had considered leaving the army. In fact, he had first been broached by Max Aitken in December 1915. Gilbert, *Churchill: A Life*, 339.
172. While Churchill and Violet were extremely close friends, it is notable that he spent private time with her but very little with his wife, Clementine, during this disastrous trip home. Purnell, *Clementine*, 111. In one of the very few examples of the couple discussing the physical side of their relationship in the written record, Clementine requested to see Churchill "alone" the next time he was in town. Roberts, *Churchill: Walking with Destiny*, 243.
173. Bonham Carter, *Winston Churchill*, 372.
174. Ibid.
175. Ibid.
176. Ibid., 372–73.
177. Cassar, *Asquith as War Leader*, 179.
178. Bonham Carter, *Winston Churchill*, 373; Cassar, *Asquith as War Leader*, 179.
179. Much has been made about the relationship (or lack thereof) between Winston and Randolph. Clearly, Winston idolized his father, as evidenced by his emulation of his style and his biography, which bordered on hagiography. Winston S. Churchill, *Lord Randolph Churchill*, 2 vols. (London: Macmillan, 1906).
180. Bell, *Churchill and the Dardanelles*, 216.
181. Cassar, *Asquith as War Leader*, 179.
182. Ibid., 179–80.
183. Bonham Carter, *Winston Churchill*, 373.
184. Word of Churchill's disastrous speech reached the front quickly, as Gibb's March 10 diary entry noted his speech to the House of Commons and claimed that he was making himself "rather unpopular." Diary of Andrew Dewar Gibb, DEP. 217/BOX 18, Diary for 1916, National Library of Scotland (emphasis in the original).
185. Gilbert, *Churchill: A Life*, 355.
186. CHAR 2/71/34.
187. Gilbert, *Churchill: A Life*, 357.
188. Gilbert, *Churchill Documents*, 7:1453.
189. Gibb's diary entry of March 13 notes that Churchill was "very dispirited" but that he warmed up some at dinner. Diary of Andrew Dewar Gibb, DEP. 217/BOX 18, Diary for 1916, National Library of Scotland.
190. Russell, *Winston Churchill, Soldier*, 375.

191. CHAR 1/118A/107; De Groot, *Liberal Crusader*, 22.
192. De Groot, *Liberal Crusader*, 23.
193. Gilbert, *Churchill Documents*, 7:1460.
194. CHAR 1/118A/108-119; CHAR 1/118A/125-126; CHAR 1/118A/133-138.
195. Purnell, *Clementine*, 93.
196. Gilbert, *Churchill: A Life*, 359; Russell, *Winston Churchill, Soldier*, 376.
197. CHAR 1/124/17; CHAR1/124/18-21. See also Gibb, April 19 diary entry, Diary of Andrew Dewar Gibb, DEP. 217/BOX 18, Diary for 1916, National Library of Scotland.
198. Buchan, *History of the Royal Scots Fusiliers (1678–1918)*, 346.
199. Russell, *Winston Churchill, Soldier*, 376.
200. Gibb, *With Winston Churchill at the Front*, 173.
201. Churchill, *World Crisis, 1916–1918, Part I*, 241.
202. Roberts, *Churchill: Walking with Destiny*, 244.
203. CHAR 1/124/28-30; CHAR 1/124/33.
204. Russell, *Winston Churchill, Soldier*, 376.
205. See Gibb, April 30 diary entry, Diary of Andrew Dewar Gibb, DEP. 217/BOX 18, Diary for 1916, National Library of Scotland; Buchan, *History of the Royal Scots Fusiliers (1678–1918)*, 345–46.
206. David Torrance, *The Scottish Secretaries* (Edinburgh: Birlinn, 2006), 121.
207. De Groot, *Liberal Crusader*, 43.
208. Torrance, *Scottish Secretaries*, 121.
209. Ibid., 121–24.
210. Ibid., 121–25.
211. While there is no reason to doubt the factual accuracy of Gibb's account, it is worth nothing that he chose to highlight Churchill's admiration for Scotland and his Scottish soldiers. By the time Gibb published his book in 1924, he was a committed Scottish nationalist who would go on to be a key leader in the Scottish Nationalist Party. Gibb, *With Winston Churchill at the Front*, 175.
212. Ibid., 176–77.
213. In his diary, Gibb noted that "the C.O. was in magnificently good form" during his speech and farewell. Diary of Andrew Dewar Gibb, DEP. 217/BOX 18, Diary for 1916, National Library of Scotland.
214. Gibb, *With Winston Churchill at the Front*, 174.
215. Manchester, *Last Lion, Winston Spencer Churchill: Visions of Glory, 1874–1932*, 13.
216. CHAR 1/124/43.
217. Russell, *Winston Churchill, Soldier*, 378–79.
218. Bonham Carter, *Winston Churchill*, 373.
219. Ibid., 372; D'Este, *Warlord*, 285–86.
220. For an excellent account of the Somme that relies heavily on firsthand accounts, see Peter Hart, *The Somme: The Darkest Hour on the Western Front* (New York: Pegasus Books, 2008).

221. Martin Gilbert, *The Somme: Heroism and Horror in the First World War* (New York: Henry Holt, 2006).
222. Gilbert, *Churchill Documents*, 7:1502.
223. Russell, *Winston Churchill, Soldier*, 379.
224. Ibid., 378.
225. Churchill would return to Plugstreet in January 1918 while on official business as minister of munitions. He visited the old trenches and wrote to Clementine expressing regret about how they had changed. Gilbert, *Churchill: A Life*, 382; Roberts, *Churchill: Walking with Destiny*, 256–57.

5. The Uncertain Future

1. Manchester, *Last Lion, Winston Spencer Churchill: Visions of Glory, 1874–1932*, 397.
2. Gilbert, *Churchill Documents*, 7:1498; Soames, *Winston Churchill: His Life as a Painter*, 29.
3. In addition to coordinating with Churchill, Hamilton also worked closely with the disgraced generals William Birdwood and Alexander Godly, who served under his command during the Gallipoli Campaign. Travers, *Gallipoli 1915*, 210–13.
4. By 1920, Lady Hamilton's view of her friend's painting had soured, as she noted in her diary: "Winston painted dull pictures all day [of the orangery] . . . and was quite happy." Coombs and Churchill, *Sir Winston Churchill's Life through His Paintings*, 30, 33. However, this private peevishness did not keep her from accepting a gift of a painting from Churchill in 1921. CHAR 1/138/102.
5. CHAR 1/117/95.
6. Coombs and Churchill, *Sir Winston Churchill's Life through His Paintings*, 27.
7. Ibid., 30.
8. Roberts, *Churchill: Walking with Destiny*, 244.
9. Russell, *Winston Churchill, Soldier*, 379.
10. Gilbert, *Winston S. Churchill*, 3:762.
11. Despite being at the front, Churchill paid close attention to the conscription debate thanks in no small part to the efforts of Clementine, who provided gossip and newspaper clippings. CHAR 1/118A/6-21.
12. Bew, *Churchill and Ireland*, 87–88, 134.
13. Tim Pat Coogan, *1916: The Easter Rising* (London: Weidenfeld and Nicolson, 2002).
14. While Churchill's views on Ireland have been criticized as inconsistent and self-serving, a theme ran throughout his policies concerning the Emerald Isle: he always thought pragmatically about the best interest of Great Britain and the empire. Bromage, *Churchill and Ireland*, xi, 24, 60–61.
15. The Irish Division suffered significant losses at Gallipoli in the failed attempt to outflank the Ottomans at Suvla Bay. It is therefore possible that this heckle was

intended to evoke the sacrifice of these Irish volunteers and was not completely unrelated. Bew, *Churchill and Ireland*, 85.

16. Gilbert, *Churchill: A Life*, 361.
17. Ibid.
18. Johnson, *Churchill*, 57, 109.
19. D'Este, *Warlord*, 215, 232, 292–93.
20. James, *Winston S. Churchill: His Complete Speeches, 1897–1963*, 3:2429–41.
21. Gilbert, *Winston S. Churchill*, 3:762–63, 769.
22. Gilbert, *Churchill: A Life*, 362; Russell, *Winston Churchill, Soldier*, 380.
23. Lavery, *Churchill*, 251–52, 322–24.
24. Gilbert, *Winston S. Churchill*, 3:776; Gilbert, *Churchill: A Life*, 363; Lavery, *Churchill*, 253.
25. Gilbert, *Churchill: A Life*, 362.
26. Addison, *Churchill on the Home Front*, 19–69.
27. Gilbert, *Churchill: A Life*, 364–65; Russell, *Winston Churchill, Soldier*, 380.
28. Winter, *Death's Men*, 189–91.
29. James, *Winston S. Churchill: His Complete Speeches, 1897–1963*, 3:2439; Russell, *Winston Churchill, Soldier*, 380.
30. Following the advice of Fisher, Churchill had worked on behalf of enlisted sailors as First Lord of the Admiralty. Massie, *Dreadnought*, 776–77.
31. Gilbert, *Churchill: A Life*, 365–66; Churchill, *World Crisis, 1915*, 89–90.
32. Churchill, *World Crisis, 1915*, 89–90.
33. Roskill, *Churchill and the Admirals*, 58.
34. CHAR 8/33-34; Lough, *No More Champagne*, 114.
35. Lough, *No More Champagne*, 114.
36. In a July 15 letter to his brother, Jack, Winston incorrectly boasts that the paper had a circulation of 448,000—an impressive number to be sure, but notable because it was less than half the true number, and it was one of the few times that Churchill understated the reach of his words or publicity. Gilbert, *Winston S. Churchill*, 3:790.
37. Gilbert, *Churchill: A Life*, 364.
38. Gilbert, *Somme*; Roberts, *Churchill: Walking with Destiny*, 246.
39. Bell, *Churchill and Sea Power*, 76.
40. Ibid.
41. Churchill had a long history of understanding the futility of frontal assaults. He first witnessed the firepower of modern weapons in Cuba and along the Afghan border, and perhaps his most poignant description of the horrors of modern war was that of the Dervish dead at Omdurman. Before World War I, he witnessed German military maneuvers, and he would later remark that the Germans adapted their tactics, moving from grand displays and massed charges fit for a parade to more dispersed formations that were less vulnerable to fire from modern weaponry. Churchill, *Thoughts and Adventures*, 78–83.

42. Churchill's criticism of the British generals would become considerably more mainstream during his Wilderness Years of the 1930s, but he was out of office and unable to exploit the change in public opinion. Bell, *Churchill and the Dardanelles*, 332–34.

43. Russell, *Winston Churchill, Soldier*, 380.

44. CHAR 2/97/9-12.

45. Cassar, *Asquith as War Leader*, 200–201.

46. Reynolds, *In Command of History*, 26, 33.

47. Gilbert, *Winston S. Churchill*, 3:790–91, 798, 802–8.

48. Travers, *Gallipoli 1915*, 211.

49. In his postwar memoirs, Hamilton repeatedly claimed that administrative failures were the result of the War Office and generally spared Kitchener. While he focused on the ground campaign, he mentioned Churchill on multiple occasions, praising his energy and efficiency. Hamilton, *Gallipoli Diary*, vols. 1 and 2.

50. Winter, *Death's Men*, 23–36.

51. Bell, *Churchill and the Dardanelles*, 219–20.

52. Travers, *Gallipoli 1915*, 210.

53. C. Brad Faught, *Kitchener: Hero and Anti-hero* (London: I. B. Tauris, 2016), 245; Gilbert, *Winston S. Churchill*, 3:780; Royle, *Kitchener Enigma*, 381.

54. Gilbert, *Churchill: A Life*, 363.

55. Faught, *Kitchener: Hero and Anti-hero*, 246–47.

56. Hunter, *Winston and Archie: The Letters of Sir Archibald Sinclair and Winston S. Churchill*, 39.

57. Bell, *Churchill and the Dardanelles*, 236–38.

58. Gilbert, *Winston S. Churchill*, 3:809.

59. CHAR 2/83/1; Gilbert, *Churchill Documents*, 7:1562–63. See also Bell, *Churchill and the Dardanelles*, 236.

60. Gilbert, *Winston S. Churchill*, 3:809.

61. Bell, *Churchill and the Dardanelles*, 239.

62. Ibid., 239–41.

63. Ibid., 245; Moorehead, *Gallipoli*, 51.

64. Great Britain Parliament, *Dardanelles Commission First Report and Supplement* (London: His Majesty's Stationery Office, 1917); Great Britain Parliament, *Dardanelles Commission Final Report, Conduct of Operations* (London: His Majesty's Stationery Office, 1919).

65. CHAR 2/101; Parliament, *Dardanelles Commission First Report and Supplement*, 6–13, 43; Trumbull Higgins, *Winston Churchill and the Dardanelles: A Dialogue in Ends and Means* (New York: Macmillan, 1963), 67.

66. This view has been generally supported by professional historians ever since. Prior, *Gallipoli*, 71.

67. Parliament, *Dardanelles Commission First Report and Supplement*, 21; Higgins, *Winston Churchill and the Dardanelles*, 83.

68. Churchill expanded on this tactic in *The World Crisis*. Here, he simultaneously takes credit for the conception of the operation and implies that others were to blame for its failure. Prior, *Churchill's "World Crisis" as History*.
69. Travers, *Gallipoli 1915*, 219.
70. Bell, *Churchill and the Dardanelles*, 4.
71. Ibid., 281–90.
72. Ibid., 280.
73. Ibid., 274–80.
74. Churchill and Hamilton had hoped that the Mitchell Report would be released before the Dardanelles Commission Report. CHAR 2/106/32-33; Bell, *Churchill and the Dardanelles*, 293–94. *Report of the Committee Appointed to Investigate the Attacks Delivered on and the Enemy Defences of the Dardanelles Straits*, National Archives, ADM 186/601.
75. Despite the title and informal style, *Gallipoli Diary* was not a contemporary diary but rather a post hoc memoir. Bell, *Churchill and the Dardanelles*, 305–7; Travers, *Gallipoli 1915*, 216.
76. For a discussion of Churchill's criticism of Haig in *The World Crisis*, see Denis Winter, *Haig's Command: A Reassessment* (New York: Viking, 1991), 238, 248, 252, 256.
77. One critic noted, "*The World-Crisis* is a brilliantly written and powerfully reasoned work, but it is the work of a man specifically trained in public speaking, wise in every artifice to rivet public attention and to arouse sympathy for his own cause. It is a work of a man specifically trained in sifting and arranging evidence; in learning speeches by heart and in practicing every gesture before a looking glass. . . . Churchill the writer is the specialist successful in his own sphere; Churchill the military leader, is an amateur who blundered." Germains, *Tragedy of Winston Churchill*, 47.
78. Manchester, *Last Lion, Winston Spencer Churchill: Visions of Glory, 1874–1932*, 768. For critical but flawed contemporary responses, see George Clarke, Reginald Bacon, Frederick Maurice, W. D. Bird, and Charles Oman, *"The World Crisis" by Winston Churchill: A Criticism* (London: Hutchinson, 1927); Frederick Maurice, "Mr. Churchill as a Military Historian," *Foreign Affairs* 5 (July 1927): 663–74.
79. A. J. P. Taylor, *Beaverbrook* (New York: Simon and Schuster, 1972), 119.
80. Russell, *Winston Churchill, Soldier*, 380–81.
81. Churchill was perpetually late. He frequently missed trains, was late for military formations and parades, kept important guests waiting, and almost missed proposing marriage to Clementine because he overslept. On Churchill's tardiness, see Manchester, *Last Lion, Winston Spencer Churchill: Visions of Glory, 1874–1932*, 193, 231.
82. Bonham Carter, *Winston Churchill*, 381.
83. Ibid.
84. Ibid., 382.
85. Ibid.
86. Ibid., 382–83.
87. Ibid., 383.

Conclusion

1. Churchill, *Painting as a Pastime*, 16; Roberts, *Churchill: Walking with Destiny*, 219.
2. Gilbert, *Churchill: A Life*, 440; Stafford, *Oblivion or Glory*, 195–96.
3. During the early days of World War II, Franklin D. Roosevelt wrote to advise Churchill that he was essential for the war effort and recommend that he take additional days of rest, saying, "I wish you would lay a few bricks or paint another picture." Winston S. Churchill, *The Hinge of Fate* (Boston: Houghton Mifflin, 1950), 201.
4. Lough, *No More Champagne*, 238–39.
5. Rose, *Literary Churchill*, 411; Moran, *Churchill*, 321.
6. Tucker-Jones, *Churchill, Master and Commander*, 328.
7. Reynolds, *In Command of History*, 10.
8. Soames, *Winston Churchill: His Life as a Painter*, 131.
9. As the official meetings of the Casablanca Conference were ending, Churchill used his eye for beauty to lure Roosevelt into spending additional time with him. He insisted that Roosevelt should stay two days longer than planned, asserting, "You cannot go all the way to North Africa without seeing Marrakech. Let us spend two days there. I must be with you when you see the sunset on the snows of the Atlas Mountains." After a five-hour drive, "I took the President up the tower of the villa. He was carried in a chair, and sat enjoying a wonderful sunset on the snows of the Atlas. We had a very jolly dinner . . . we all sang songs. I sang, and the President joined in the choruses, and at one moment he was about to try a solo. However, someone interrupted and I never heard this." After seeing the president off the next day, Churchill "returned to the Villa Taylor, where [he] spent another two days in correspondence with the War Cabinet about [his] future movements, and painting from the tower the only picture [he] ever attempted during the war." Churchill, *Hinge of Fate*, 694–95; Roberts, *Churchill: Walking with Destiny*, 753, 768. According to Inspector Walter Thompson's unpublished notes, Churchill painted two additional paintings in Marrakech in 1943 while recovering from severe illness. Further details about these potential canvases are unknown. Hickman, *Churchill's Bodyguard*, 293n12.
10. During World War II, Churchill used his eye for color to alter the British military maps. He chose less vivid colors to prevent eye strain after a long day of studying the movements of convoys and armies. Roberts, *Churchill: Walking with Destiny*, 465.
11. Von Heyking, *Comprehensive Judgment and Absolute Selflessness*.
12. During this period, Sinclair introduced Churchill to several prominent members of the British intelligence services, including Desmond Morton and Stewart Menzies. Stafford, *Oblivion or Glory*, 44–45.
13. While Sinclair had many friends in politics, he was more liberal than nearly all of them. Despite this, he never lost a friendship over political differences. De Groot, *Liberal Crusader*, 40.

14. Addison, *Churchill on the Home Front*, 320; Torrance, *Scottish Secretaries*, 120–25.

15. Brendon, *Churchill's Menagerie*, 16–17, 212.

16. Hunter, *Winston and Archie: The Letters of Sir Archibald Sinclair and Winston S. Churchill*, 173–213; De Groot, *Liberal Crusader*, 132–50.

17. Addison, *Churchill on the Home Front*, 330.

18. Richard Overy is less charitable, calling Sinclair a "gifted amateur" but noting that Churchill trusted him, and he was an effective communicator and dedicated public servant. Richard Overy, *The Battle of Britain: The Myth and the Reality* (New York: W. W. Norton, 2001), 31.

19. Winston S. Churchill, *Their Finest Hour* (Boston: Houghton Mifflin, 1949), 12–17.

20. See Richard Hough and Denis Richards, *The Battle of Britain: The Greatest Air Battle of World War II* (New York: W. W. Norton, 1989), 320–21; Hunter, *Winston and Archie: The Letters of Sir Archibald Sinclair and Winston S. Churchill*, 215–422. While Churchill's confidant John "Jock" Colville would later assert that Churchill bullied Sinclair during the war, these claims are probably exaggerated. In fact, according to Gerald De Groot, there is no evidence to support this accusation, and the very fact that Sinclair served loyally for five years during the war is a testament to their friendship and mutual respect. De Groot, *Liberal Crusader*, 157–58.

21. Much to Churchill's dismay, Sinclair frequently clashed with another close friend, the minister of aircraft production, William "Max" Aitken, the 1st Lord Beaverbrook. The prime minister had to mediate these clashes, but both men would eventually defer to Churchill's pleas to think about the best interests of the country. De Groot, *Liberal Crusader*, 165, 169–70; Taylor, *Beaverbrook*, 416, 419–21.

22. Gilbert, *Churchill: A Life*, 657.

23. Tucker-Jones, *Churchill, Master and Commander*, 155–56.

24. Hough and Richards, *Battle of Britain*, 85–87, 98–100. On the desperate condition of the Royal Air Force, see Overy, *Battle of Britain*.

25. See the February 2, 1942, letter from Sinclair to Churchill, where he told his friend, "I am currently not satisfied with anything less than 100% support for the Government from the Liberal Party." Hunter, *Winston and Archie: The Letters of Sir Archibald Sinclair and Winston S. Churchill*, 339.

26. Kelly, *Never Surrender*, 247.

27. De Groot, *Liberal Crusader*, 220.

28. Archibald Sinclair to Winston Churchill, September 15, 1940, in Hunter, *Winston and Archie: The Letters of Sir Archibald Sinclair and Winston S. Churchill*, 253–54.

29. His 1930 work, *Scotland in Eclipse*, was particularly shrill, alleging centuries of persecution of the Scottish people by the English. Despite some dubious historical claims, the book established Gibb as one of the leading voices in the Scottish Nationalist movement. Andrew Dewar Gibb, *Scotland in Eclipse* (London: Humphrey

Toulmin, 1930). Hints of Gibb's Scottish nationalism can be seen in his earlier work: Gibb, *With Winston Churchill at the Front*, 173.

30. Churchill quickly discovered that Gibb was the author and wrote him a letter expressing his belief that the book had been well received by Max Aitken and others. CHAR 2/134/6.

31. The trial of Field Marshal Albert Kesselring was extremely politically charged, yet Hakewill-Smith did his best to faithfully discharge his duties. Kerstin von Lingen, *Kesselring's Last Battle: War Crimes Trails and Cold War Politics, 1945–1960*, trans. Alexandra Klemm (Lawrence: University Press of Kansas, 2009).

32. CHAR 2/367.

33. In the words of Churchill's daughter Mary, they had a "warm and lasting friendship." Soames, *Winston Churchill: His Life as a Painter*, 23.

34. Stafford, *Oblivion or Glory*, 74, 133, 193.

35. Churchill's other reliable source for the pulse of the common man was his long-time bodyguard, Inspector Walter Thompson. Hickman, *Churchill's Bodyguard*, 240.

36. Purnell, *Clementine*, 91.

37. Gilbert, *Churchill: A Life*, 146; Rose, *Literary Churchill*, 99.

38. Gilbert, *Churchill: A Life*, 337; Russell, *Winston Churchill, Soldier*, 362.

39. Gilbert, *Churchill Documents*, 7:1399.

40. Bonham Carter, *Winston Churchill*, 365.

41. Martin Gilbert, *Winston Churchill's War Leadership*, 48.

42. Lukacs, *Blood, Toil, Tears, and Sweat*, 48.

43. Erik Larson, *The Splendid and the Vile: A Saga of Churchill, Family, and Defiance during the Blitz* (New York: Crown, 2020), 223, 421, 483.

44. Churchill's friend J. E. B. Seely had also resigned his cabinet position in disgrace and chosen to serve in the front. His service was considerably longer and more adventurous than Churchill's; he rose to the temporary rank of major general and commanded what has been described by some as the last cavalry charge in British history in 1918. Like Churchill, Seely kept his seat as a Liberal MP and returned to take an active role in politics as one of Churchill's deputies at the Ministry of Munitions. See Seely, *Adventure*, 173–312.

45. Bell, *Churchill and the Dardanelles*, 208.

46. D'Este, *Warlord*, 26, 29, 42, 45, 70–71, 74, 91, 96, 101–4, 148, 163, 166, 209, 214–15, 234, 236, 238, 251, 279–80, 292, 388–89, 507, 682, 696.

47. Churchill, *My Early Life*, 34.

48. Callahan, *Churchill and His Generals*, 7.

49. Byron Farwell, *Queen Victoria's Little Wars* (New York: Harper and Row, 1972).

50. Byron Farwell, *Mr. Kipling's Army* (New York: W. W. Norton, 1981).

51. Gilbert, *Winston S. Churchill*, 3:578.

52. James, *Churchill: A Study in Failure*; Rose, *Literary Churchill*.

53. One example of Churchill's romanticism and new appreciation for modern weapons was his use of animalistic metaphors to describe modern war. He talked frequently of the war of rats and noted how flying shrapnel could easily be mistaken as a flock of birds to an untrained observer. Brendon, *Churchill's Menagerie*, 47.

54. Winston S. Churchill, *The Grand Alliance* (Boston: Houghton Mifflin, 1950), 200.

55. Of particular note was his discussion with his fellow officers on the night of December 7, 1915, where he proposed that torpedo-carrying aircraft could destroy a fleet at anchor, a prediction that would come true twenty-six years to the day later at Pearl Harbor. Before Pearl Harbor, Churchill was a driving force behind the conception of the British attack on the Italian fleet at Taranto in November 1940. Thomas P. Lowry and John W. G. Wellham, *The Attack on Taranto: Blueprint for Pearl Harbor* (Mechanicsburg, PA: Stackpole Books, 2000).

56. On January 17, 1916, Churchill said that this would not be an issue if he was still at the Admiralty. Gilbert, *Churchill: A Life*, 343–44.

57. Ibid., 293–94, 299.

58. D'Este, *Warlord*, 214, 550; Weidhorn, *Sword and Pen*, 71–75.

59. Russell, *Winston Churchill, Soldier*, 382.

60. Ashley, *Churchill as Historian*, 89.

61. Callahan, *Churchill and His Generals*, 8; Russell, *Winston Churchill, Soldier*, 387.

62. Bryant, *Turn of the Tide*; Bryant, *Triumph in the West*.

63. While Churchill was a proponent of airpower, he was by no means omniscient. In fact, he failed to properly understand the vulnerability of ships to air attack, overestimated the survivability and utility of fighters with turrets, and learned mixed lessons from the German and Italian air campaigns during the Spanish Civil War. James, *Churchill: A Study in Failure*, 263.

64. For example, in a 1938 article, "How Wars of the Future Will Be Waged," he famously predicted that war would be largely static and that positional struggle would be waged inside fortresses. In this article, he also overestimated the ability of the French Army and the Maginot Line to withstand a German attack. James, *Churchill: A Study in Failure*, 262.

65. Lavery, *Churchill*, 507; Lukacs, *Five Days in London: May 1940*, 217–19; Lukacs, *Blood, Toil, Tears, and Sweat*, 129; Allan R. Millett and Williamson Murray, eds., *Military Effectiveness*, vol. 3, *The Second World War* (Cambridge: Cambridge University Press, 2010), 90–135.

66. Winston S. Churchill, *The Grand Alliance* (Boston: Houghton Mifflin, 1950), 511–12. See the November 6, 1941, memo detailing the need for increased conscription and increased reliance on women. Although Churchill was generally on the right side of rearmament during the interwar period, he altered his memoirs to make himself seem more supportive of conscription than he was at the time. See Reynolds, *In Command of History*, 99.

67. Gilbert, *Churchill: A Life*, 349.

68. Prior, *Gallipoli*, 34; Reynolds, *In Command of History*, 181.

69. Robert Rhodes James, ed., *Winston S. Churchill: His Complete Speeches, 1897–1963*, vol. 6, *1935–1942* (New York: Chelsea House, 1974), 6231–35.

Index

Page numbers in italics refer to illustrations.

Abdication Crisis, 1, 193
Admiralty, 51, 166, 185; and dazzle-painting camouflage schemes, 67–68; dismissal of Churchill from, 4–5, 9, 17–18, 30, 38, 41–44, 221n173; and plan for Dardanelles Campaign, 13–18, 31, 187; resignation of Fisher, 5, 26, 29, 30–40, 220n133; work schedules of Churchill and Fisher, 31
Agamemnon, 22
Air Ministry, 74, 195–96
airpower, 140–41, 178, 205–7, 257n55
Aitken, William "Max," 248n171, 255n21, 256n30
Alexander, Harold, 246n116
Alexandra of Denmark, 38
Amethyst, 20–21
ANZAC Cove, 24
armored vehicles, 89, 115, 116, 206, 207, 233n220
art, 60, 65–66. *See also* painting
Ashley, Maurice, 207
Asquith, H. H., 9, 11, 15, 25, 46–47, 49, 55, 58, 80, 91, 136, 166, 176, 177, 180, 181, 187, 203, 206; appointment of new War Committee, 90; coalition government, 26, 29, 38, 41, 42–43, 97; coalition government, Churchill's plan to collapse, 155–60; coalition government, collapse of, 30, 188; and conscription issue, 84, 85, 86; creation of chemical forces, 83; denial of brigade command to Churchill, 118, 120; and dismissal of Churchill from Admiralty, 4, 5, 38, 42, 43, 44, 221n173; dissolution of Dardanelles Committee, 87, 88; and fact-finding mission to Gallipoli, 76, 78; and farewell to Churchill, 96, 97; Fisher's demands to, 39–40; and inspection trip of Kitchener to Dardanelles, 89; Liberal government, collapse of, 7, 26, 30, 40–44; meetings with Churchill (March 1916), 167–68; and resignation of Churchill, 88, 90, 91, 92–93; and resignation of Fisher, 34, 35, 36, 40; and resignation of French, 117, 118; rivals, political strategy of, 26–27, 28; and Shell Crisis, 26, 28–29, 30; and Stanley, 26, 42; and Tory demands for coalition government, 41, 42
Asquith, Margot, 97, 98, 160–61, 165, 247n164
Asquith, Violet. *See* Bonham Carter, Violet
Attlee, Clement, 197

Baldwin, Stanley, 6
Balfour, Arthur, 48, 54, 74, 81, 87, 88, 90, 157, 162, 165, 166, 188, 223n209
Baron Moran, 1st (Charles Wilson), 71, 72–73, 193
Battle of Festubert (1915), 27–28
Battle of Loos (1915), 81, 116, 117, 126, 131, 137, 144, 206
Battle of Neuve Chapelle (1915), 27, 123

Battle of Omdurman (1898), 45, 205
Battle of Sarıkamış (1914–1915), 12–13
Battle of Tannenberg (1914), 10
Battle of the Somme (1916), 173–74, 178–79, 182
Beatty, David, 17, 38
Bell, Christopher, 221n173
Bell, Hesketh, 238n70
Beresford, Charles, 68
Birdwood, William, 250n3
Black and Tans, 148
Black Sea raid (1914), 10
Blenheim Palace, 175–76
Blunt, Wilfrid, 70–71, 228n109
Bonar Law. *See* Law, Andrew Bonar
Bonham Carter, Maurice, 74, 166, 201, 226n70
Bonham Carter, Violet, 4, 34, 35, 38, 40, 43, 72, 78, 91, 93–94, 96, 97, 120, 130*b*, 134–35, 165, 166–67, 189–90, 221n170, 222n178, 222n193, 222n196, 235n11, 239n115, 248n172
Borkum, 10
Bouvet, 22
Breslau, 10
Brett, Reginald. *See* Esher, 2nd Viscount of
Brutinel, Raymond, 229n120
Burns, Robert, 127
Bush, George W., 228–29n110
"business as usual" policy, 26

Caldwell, Charles, 232n193
Carden, Sackville, 21
Cassel, Ernest, 96–97
Caucasus campaign, 10–11
Cavan, 10th Earl of (Rudolph Lambart), 102–4, 119, 239n96
Chamberlain, Neville, 2, 6–7, 84, 195, 196
chemical weapons, 82–83, 231n177, 232n183
Churchill, Clementine (wife of WC), 5, 9, 43, 51, 61, 67, 70, 71, 76, 77–78, 95, 97, 98, 104, 111, 114, 125, 155, 170, 175, 199, 213n24, 248n172, 250n11, 250n225; and Churchill's painting, 62, 65; Churchill's frontline communications with, 110, 112–14, 119, 120, 122–24, 127, 137, 138, 140, 141, 142, 147, 152, 153, 155, 168, 169–70, 199, 243n41; and Fisher, 156–57; portrait of, 153–54; sending packages to Churchill, 112, 113, 199
Churchill, Diana (daughter of WC), 60
Churchill, Gwendeline "Goonie" (sister-in-law of WC), 60, 99, 169, 225n38
Churchill, Jack (brother of WC), 58, 59, 60, 73, 76, 137, 181, 204, 232n207, 251n36
Churchill, Jennie (mother of WC), 46, 98, 193, 235n262
Churchill, John (ancestor of WC). *See* Marlborough, 1st Duke of
Churchill, John (nephew of WC), 60
Churchill, Marigold (daughter of WC), 193
Churchill, Peregrine (nephew of WC), 60
Churchill, Randolph (father of WC), 4, 49, 60, 111, 167, 179, 248n179
Churchill, Randolph (son of WC), 60, 77
Churchill, Sarah (daughter of WC), 5, 60, 67, 222n180, 227n88, 229n122
Churchill, Winston (WC), 1, 50; accolades in United States, 189; as advocate for needs of the common soldier, 178–79, 201; and Anglo-Egyptian conquest of Sudan, 205; application of trench experience in politics, 180; argument against renewed offensives on western front, 74–75; and art, 65–66; attempt to become governor-general of British East Africa, 89–90; belief in destiny, 108–10, 146, 147; in Blenheim Palace, 175–76; and Bonar Law, 41–42, 89; as chancellor of the Duchy of Lancaster, 5, 46–48, 49, 51, 52–53, 59, 87, 88, 223–24n3, 223n200; confidence of, 111; and conscription, 84–87, 177–78, 203, 250n11, 257n66; critical year of (May 1915–May 1916), 3–7; and Dardanelles Campaign, 5–7, 9–12, 13, 14, 15, 16–19, 21, 23, 25, 31–32, 35, 37, 51, 52, 53, 54, 56–57, 58, 81, 82, 91–92, 93, 94, 203, 218n94; and Dardanelles Commission, 18, 31, 176, 182–88; on Dardanelles Committee, 47,

50–51, 53, 54, 87–88, 223n2; defection from Tory party, 4, 41, 78; depression of, 5, 43, 51, 71–73, 193–94; dismissal from Admiralty, 4–5, 9, 17–18, 30, 38, 41, 42, 43–44, 221n173; and dissolution of Dardanelles Committee, 87; electoral defeat (1945), 193; empathy for working-class people, 200, 201; and fact-finding mission to Gallipoli, 76–79; false hope on reentry into politics, 155–62; farewell to (1915), 96–100; financial crisis of, 47, 59, 96, 181, 223n200; financial preparations before frontline service, 96–97, 235n263; firearms of, 98, 124, 234–35n260, 234n258; and Fisher, 15, 16, 30–31, 32, 33, 34–38, 43, 93, 135–36, 156–57; Fisher's attempts to oust, 38–39; Fisher's letters to, 37–38, 158–59, 160, 161–62, 166; focus on airpower, 140–41, 178, 205–6, 207, 257n55; French helmet of, 124–25, 141; friendships of, 7, 52, 54–56, 66–67, 68–69, 105–6, 113, 128–29, 135–36, 156, 166–67, 169, 171–72, 189–90, 194–99, 218n89; Gardiner on, 213n22; at Hoe Farm, 59–60, 62–63, 70, 71, 198; humor of, 1, 124, 201; on improving conditions for frontline troops, 178–79; and Kitchener, 75, 84, 87–88, 136, 173, 184; lack of consultation with Fisher, 31, 32, 34, 220n124; leadership of, 106, 108, 125, 127, 131, 142–45, 146, 200, 202, 207; letters to Fisher, 35–36, 37, 178; London trip (December 1915), 123; London trip (March 1916), 155–56; luggage and equipment for frontline service, 98, 103, 112–13, 132; marginalization of, 9, 18, 49, 52, 53, 58, 74–76, 120, 180; meeting with French in France (November 1915), 101–2; meeting with George VI (1940), 1–2; meeting with Kitchener, 45–46; meeting with Hazel Lavery, 63–64, 198; meetings with Asquith, March 1916, 167–68; military qualifications of, 3, 211–12n8, 212n10; as minister of munitions, 141, 147, 171, 188–89, 206, 232n182; naval estimates debate speech (March 7, 1916), 156, 162–66; painting of, 7, 59–65, 66–74, 152–54, 175, 176–77, 189–90, 191–94, 198–99, 226n66, 226n70, 227n85, 228n99, 228n102, 229n115, 229n120, 229n122, 246n116, 250n4, 254n9; personal growth of, 7, 111, 199–202; perspectives on modern war, 7, 115, 203–7, 251n41; plan for offensive attack on High Seas Fleet, 114–15; political irrelevance of, 7, 202–3; political qualifications of, 3; as prime minister, 172; resignation of (1915), 88, 90–91; and resignation of Fisher, 32–33, 34–38; resignation speech of, 91–96; return to politics, 175–90; romantic notions of war, 110, 203–4, 256n53; at Sandhurst, 61, 107, 204; on sea power, 13, 182; and Seeley, 99; self-doubt of, 49, 72; sense of justice, 142; and Shell Crisis, 29, 30; strategic frustrations of, 56–59; "This was their finest hour" speech (1940), 208; thoughts of frontline military service, 52, 95; transfer to Territorial Force Reserve, 173; trip to Antwerp, 43, 204, 222n180, 233n219; trip with Spears to Neuve Chapelle and Vimy Ridge (December 1915), 123–24; "Variants of the Offensive" memo, 115–16, 148–49; visit from Blunt, 70–71; as war correspondent, 61, 77; war strategy of, 52–54, 114–16; Wilderness Years, 72, 141, 193, 194, 199, 252n42; work schedule of, 31; writing of, 180–82, 187–88. *See also* 6th Battalion of the Royal Scots Fusiliers, Churchill in; Grenadier Guards, Churchill in

Clark, Kenneth, 65
Collins, Michael, 63, 226n65
Colville, John "Jock," 255n20
conscription, 75, 84–87, 170, 177–78, 203, 232n193, 250n11, 257n66
Cornwallis, 20
Craig, James, 226n65
Crewe Commission, 85
Crewe-Milnes, Robert, 85

Cromer, Earl of, 185
Cuba, 61
Curzon, George, 78, 84, 86, 90

Daily Mail, 29–30
Dalziel, Henry, 159
Dardanelles Campaign, 5–7, 9–12, 51, 74, 81, 90, 91–92, 93, 175, 203, 213n26, 216n53, 250–51n15; Allied attacks, 20, 22–23, 24–25; assumptions and misinformation, 12–13, 14; battle of March 18, 22–23; blame of Churchill, 17–18, 25, 39, 51, 183; and Carden, 21; Churchill as scapegoat for, 5, 17, 25; Churchill's attempts to clear his name, 51; Churchill's proposal to deploy poison gas, 82–83, 231n177; classified documents, 51, 77, 94, 183, 187; evacuation, 82, 137; fact-finding mission to Gallipoli, 76–79, 83–84; failure of the Allied landings on April 25, 24–25; and Fisher, 15–16, 18, 24; ground troops, 23–24, 80; initial bombardment of fortifications, 19; inspection trip of Kitchener, 89, 90; and Kitchener, 12, 18, 23, 25, 80, 215n18, 217n73, 252n49; long-range artillery fire, 20; minesweeping, 20–21; naval mines, 20–22, 217n64, 217n73; plan for, 13–14, 15, 16–17, 18–19, 21, 23, 31, 218n94; reconnaissance flights, 22; reinforcement by Ottomans, 19–20; reinforcement by Allies, 32, 52, 53, 54, 56, 57; relationship between Churchill and Fisher, 31–32; replacement of Hamilton with Monro, 81; and resignation of Fisher, 32, 34–37; Shell Crisis, 26–30; strengthening of Ottoman defenses, 15, 21, 24, 230n136; Suvla Bay offensive, 80
Dardanelles Commission, 16, 18, 31, 176, 182–88. *See also* Dardanelles Committee
Dardanelles Committee, 47, 50–51, 53, 54, 87–88, 223n2. *See also* Dardanelles Commission
dazzle-painting camouflage, 67–68

Deakin, William, 211n5
Defense of the Realm Act (1914), 29
de Gaulle, Charles, 128
Derby, 17th Lord of (Edward Stanley), 86
de Robeck, John, 21, 22–23, 217n64
Dowding, Hugh, 196
dumdum bullets, 232n181

East Africa, 89–90
Edward VIII, 1
Enchantress, 106
Esher, 2nd Viscount of (Reginald Brett), 117

Fergusson, Charles, 174
56th Brigade (19th Division), 114
Fisher, John "Jackie," 25, 34, 246–47n132; and Churchill, 15, 16, 30–31, 32, 33, 34–38, 43, 93, 135–36, 156–57; Churchill's lack of consultation with, 31, 32, 34, 220n124; Churchill's letters to, 35–36, 37, 178; and Churchill's plan to collapse coalition government, 157–60, 161; contradictory advice of, 31; and Dardanelles Campaign, 15–16, 18, 24, 31–32, 36–37, 185, 186; demands to Asquith, 39–40; letters to Churchill, 37–38, 158–59, 160, 161–62, 166; letters to Law, 38–39; resignation of, 5, 26, 29, 30–40, 220n133; return, Churchill's demand for, 164–65, 166, 176, 188; work schedule of, 31
France, 1, 19, 53, 74–75, 96–97, 100, 123–24, 137, 168, 193, 196
French, John, 75–76, 82–83, 111, 120, 156, 184, 206, 230n131, 238n82; and Battle of Neuve Chapelle, 27; and Churchill's thoughts of frontline military service, 52; meeting with Churchill in France (November 1915), 101–2; promise of brigade command to Churchill, 113–14; resignation of, 117–18; and Shell Crisis, 28, 29; and "Variants of the Offensive" memo, 116, 148
Furse, William T., 126

Gallipoli. *See* Dardanelles Campaign
Gallipoli Diary (Hamilton), 187
Gardiner, A. G., 213n22
Gascoyne-Cecil, James. *See* Salisbury, 4th Marquess of
Gaulois, 22
George VI, 1–2
Germany, 10, 12, 34, 75, 142; airpower of, 140, 141, 178, 205; artillery fire of, 107, 109, 145, 146–47, 148; and Dardanelles Campaign, 15, 19, 24; High Seas Fleet, 10, 114–15; Nazi Germany, 106, 196; Second Battle of Ypres, 82; on western front, 53
Gibb, Andrew Dewar, 130, *130f*, 131, 132, 134, 135, 136, 141, 142, 143, 150, 152, 171, 172–73, 197–98, 248n184, 248n189, 249n211, 256n30; *Scotland in Eclipse*, 255n29; *With Winston Churchill at the Front*, 197
Glengarry cap, 127, 128
Godly, Alexander, 250n3
Goeben, 10, 14, 215n26
Gombrich, Ernst, 229n115
grenade training, 136–37
Grenadier Guards, Churchill in, 103–8, 237n43, 238n82; communication with Clementine, 110, 112, 113, 114, 119, 120; denial of brigade command, 118, 119–21; as deputy commander, 106; and Grigg, 106; growth as a leader, 111–13; life on the front lines, 105–7, 111–112; near miss incident, 108–10; offer of battalion command, 118–19; promise of brigade command, 113–14; transfer, 125; trench warfare, 104, 107–8
Grey, Edward, 96, 117
Grigg, Edward, 106, 107
Guest, Freddie, 96

Haig, Douglas, 116, 117, 118–19, 122, 128, 148, 187, 206, 239n107
Hakewill-Smith, Edmund, 129, 130, *130f*, 132–33, 136, 153, 154, 171, 197, 198, 256n31
Haking, Richard, 108

Haldane, Richard, 41, 42
Halifax, 1st Earl of (Edward Wood), 1, 196
Hall, Edith, 243n42
Hamilton, Ian, 23–24, 53, 54, 80, 81, 175–76, 184, 217n73, 218n89, 250n3, 252n49
Hamilton, Jean, 175, 250n4
Hanbury-Williams, John, 11
Hankey, Maurice, 34, 74, 78
High Seas Fleet (Germany), 10, 114–15
Hitler, Adolf, 154, 172, 193, 195, 196
Hobhouse, Charles, 47
Holland, 16
Holland, Arthur, 137
Hopwood, Francis, 156
Hozier, Nellie, 70

Indefatigable, 19
Indomitable, 19
Inflexible, 22
Ireland, 99, 147–48, 177, 226n65, 250n14
Irresistible, 22–23, *130b*, 218n81

James, Robert Rhodes, 212n12
Jed, 218n81
Jeffreys, George, 104, 105–6, 111–12, 236n33
Jellicoe, John, 38
Jolie, Angelina, 70

Kay-Shuttleworth, Charles, 47
Kemp, Laurence, 148
Kerr, John Graham, 67–68, 227–28n91
Kesselring, Albert, 198, 256n31
Kitchener, Horatio, 11, 40, 48, 57, 76, 223n2, 239n107; and Anglo-Egyptian conquest of Sudan, 45; and chemical weapons, 83; and Churchill, 75, 84, 87–88, 136, 173, 184; and conscription, 84, 85, 86, 232n193; and Dardanelles Campaign, 12, 18, 23, 25, 80, 215n18, 217n73, 252n49; and Dardanelles Commission, 184, 186; on Dardanelles Committee, 53; death of, 184; inspection trip to Dardanelles, 89, 90; meeting with Churchill, 45–46; and Shell Crisis, 28

Lambart, Rudolph. *See* Cavan, 10th Earl of
Lavery, Hazel, 63, 198–99, 226n65, 228n98
Lavery, John, 63, 68–69, 152, 176, 198–99, 226n65, 228n98
Law, Andrew Bonar, 26, 82, 90, 117, 188, 221n170; and Churchill, 41–42, 78, 89, 93; deal with Asquith for coalition government, 41, 42; Fisher's letters to, 38–39
leadership, of Churchill, 106, 108, 125, 127, 131, 142–45, 146, 200, 202, 207
Lloyd George, David, 29, 33, 81, 87, 89, 90, 117, 140, 159, 164, 172; and Churchill, 41, 74, 82, 96, 120, 187, 188, 203; and conscription issue, 85, 86; as prime minister, 188
London Magazine, 181
Long, Walter, 117
Louis of Battenberg, 15, 164

Majestic, 22
Manchester, William, 240n137
Markham, Arthur, 159
Marlborough, 1st Duke of (John Churchill), 103, 126
Marlborough, 8th Duke of (George Spencer-Churchill), 126
Marlborough, 9th Duke of (Charles "Sunny" Spencer-Churchill), 47
Marsh, Eddie, 62, 97, 98, 165
Masurian Lakes, first battle of (1914), 10
Maze, Paul, 67, 193, 227n85
McDavid, Jock, 143, 147, 244n61
McKenna, Reginald, 90
military reforms, 179, 201
Military Service Act, 177
modern war, perspectives on, 7, 115, 203–7, 251n41
Mond, Alfred, 159
Monro, Charles, 81, 82, 83–84
Montag, Charles, 65, 66
Montagu, Edwin, 42, 47
Morocco, 70, 254n9

Morris, Jan, 220n132
Mussolini, Benito, 193, 196

National Gallery, 65
naval mines, 20–22, 217n64, 217n73
near miss incidents, 108–10, 146–47, 148–51, 152, 155
Nicholas (Grand Duke), 11, 215n23
Nicholson, William, 67, 227n88
Northcliffe press, 28–30

Ocean, 23, 218n81
Olsson, Julius, 67
Orpen, William, 176
Ottoman Empire, 10–11, 12–13, 14, 15, 19–20, 215n17. *See also* Dardanelles Campaign
Overy, Richard, 255n18

painting, of Churchill, 7, 59–64, 175, 176–77, 189–90, 191–94, 198–99, 229n115, 229n120, 229n122, 254n9; exhibitions of, 69, 228n102; on front lines, 152–54; meeting with Hazel Lavery, 63–64; obsession with colors, 246n116, 250n4; scenery of North Africa, 69–70; as soulcraft, 71–74; studying and interacting with great artists, 66–70, 193, 226n66; as substitute for war, 64–65; training in, 60–61
Palmer, William Waldegrave. *See* Selborne, 2nd Earl of
Pershing, John, 189
Phoenix Assurance Society, 76–77, 96
Ploegsteert, Belgium, 138–39, 145–52, 168
poison gas, 82–83, 231n177
Ponsonby, Arthur, 80
Prince of Wales, 238n89

Queen's Own Oxfordshire Hussars, 101, 173

Race to the Sea (1914), 11
Repington, Charles à Court, 28–29
Repulse, 238n89
Richardson, John, 176

Riddell, George, 51, 164
Roberts, Andrew, 211n5
Robertson, William, 117
Roosevelt, Franklin D., 70, 254n3, 254n9
Rothenstein, John, 72
Rowntree, B. Seebohm, 200
Royal Irish Constabulary, 148
Royal Naval Air Service, 115, 140
Royal Navy, 9–10, 12, 14, 19, 30, 49, 114–15, 162, 165, 204. *See also* Dardanelles Campaign
Royal Scots Fusiliers. *See* 6th Battalion of the Royal Scots Fusiliers, Churchill in
Russia, 10, 75, 214n15; Ottoman attacks on, 10; plea for assistance from Britain, 10–11, 12; reversal of Ottoman advance, 13

Salisbury, 4th Marquess of (James Gascoyne-Cecil), 28
Sanderson, F. R., 181
sanitation, 133–34
Scotland in Eclipse (Gibb), 255n29
Scott, C. P., 159, 161
Scott, F. G., 131
Second Battle of Ypres, 82
Seely, J. E. B., 55, 99, 111–12, 114, 120–21, 138, 256n44
Selborne, 2nd Earl of (William Waldegrave Palmer), 84
Shell Crisis, 5, 26–30, 97
Sickert, Walter, 67, 226n66
Sinclair, Archibald, 58, 73, 99, 152–53, 155, 169, 184, 254n12, 254n13, 255n18, 255n20, 255n21; and Churchill, 54–56, 79–80, 94–95, 194–97; life after World War I, 172; military service of, 171–72; in 6th Battalion of the Royal Scots Fusiliers, 122, 128–29, 131–32, 138, 148, 150
6th Battalion of the Royal Scots Fusiliers, Churchill in, 126–29, 131, 200; arrival at front lines, 141–42; bonding with enlisted rank, 143–44; casualty rate of, 146; communication with Clementine, 137, 138, 140, 141, 142, 147, 152, 153, 155, 168, 169–70, 243n41; consolidation with 7th Battalion, 170–71; disciplinary actions, 144; fascination with airpower, 140–41; fighting condition of troops, 126–27; final meeting, 172–73; first impression, 131–33; hoping for brigade command, 169; leadership, 127, 131, 142–45, 146; lice issue, 133–34; lines at Ploegsteert, 145–52; near misses, 146–47, 148–51, 152, 155; night patrols, 154; painting, 152–54; preparation for battle, 129–30; preparation for moving to the front, 138–40; routine of Churchill, 143; staff selection, 128–29; training, 136–37, 139; uniform, 127–28; winning the officers, 134–36; winning the rank and file, 136–38
Smith, F. E., 157
Smuts, Jan, 90, 233n220
Soames, Mary (daughter of WC), 64–65, 71, 95, 226n65
Spears, Edward, 114, 122, 123–24, 128
Spencer-Churchill, Charles "Sunny." *See* Marlborough, 9th Duke of
Spencer-Churchill, Frances "Fanny" (grandmother of WC), 61
Spencer-Churchill, George. *See* Marlborough, 8th Duke of
Stanley, Edward. *See* Derby, 17th Lord of
Stanley, Venetia, 26, 42
Strand, 181
Suffren, 19, 22
Sunday Pictorial, 181
Swiftsure, 22
Swinton, Ernest, 116

tanks, 115, 116, 180, 205, 206, 207, 239n93
Tennant, Harold, 140
Territorial Force Reserve, 173
Thompson, Walter, 211n6, 254n9, 256n35
Times, 29
trench warfare, 11–12, 27, 102, 104, 107–8, 112, 125, 128, 136, 139, 143, 147, 155, 204–5, 237n43
Tudor, Henry H., 147–48
Turner, J. M. W., 66

US War Department, 189

Vengeance, 20
Vérité, 19
von Sanders, Otto Liman, 24, 57, 230n136

War of Spanish Succession, 103, 126
war supplies, shortage of, 27–30
Wear, 23
Wilderness Years, 72, 141, 193, 194, 199, 252n42
Wilkinson, Norman, 228n91
Wilson, Arthur, 18, 38

Wilson, Charles. *See* Baron Moran, 1st
With Winston Churchill at the Front (Gibb), 197
Wood, Edward. *See* Halifax, 1st Earl of
World Crisis, The (Churchill), 6, 17, 32, 48, 170, 183, 187–88, 207, 220n122, 253n77
World War II, 3, 68, 70, 71, 106, 108, 130, 142, 152, 193, 194, 195, 196–97, 202, 205, 207, 212n10, 233n207, 238n89, 244n76
writings of Churchill, 180–82, 187–88